Lloyd J. Ogilvie General Editor

THE
PREACHER'S
COMMENTARY

LUKE

Bruce Larson

THOMAS NELSON PUBLISHERS
Nashville

Grateful acknowledgment is made to the author and publisher for permission
to reprint on p. 206 "The Joggers' Prayer" from IN OUR TIME by Tom Wolfe.
Copyright © 1961, 1963, 1964, 1965, 1968, 1971, 1972, 1973, 1975, 1976,
1977, 1978, 1979, 1980 by Tom Wolfe. Reprinted by permission of Farrar,
Straus and Giroux, Inc.

Library of Congress Cataloging in Publication Data

The preacher's commentary (formerly The communicator's commentary).

Includes bibliographical references.
Contents: v. 26. Luke/Bruce Larson
1. Bible. N.T.—Commentaries—Collected works.
I. Ogilvie, Lloyd John II. Larson, Bruce.

BS2341.2.C65   225.7'7   81–71764
ISBN 0-7852-4801-3   AACR2

1 2 3 4 5 6 7 – 07 06 05 04 03

Printed in the United States of America

CONTENTS

EDITOR'S PREFACE

God has called all of His people to be communicators. Everyone who is in Christ is called into ministry. As ministers of "the manifold grace of God," all of us—clergy and laity—are commissioned with the challenge to communicate our faith to individuals and groups, classes and congregations.

The Bible, God's Word, is the objective basis of the truth of His love and power that we seek to communicate. In response to the urgent, expressed needs of pastors, teachers, Bible study leaders, church school teachers, small group enablers, and individual Christians, the Preacher's Commentary is offered as a penetrating search of the Scriptures of the New Testament to enable vital personal and practical communication of the abundant life.

Many current commentaries and Bible study guides provide only some aspects of a communicator's needs. Some offer in-depth scholarship but no application to daily life. Others are so popular in approach that biblical roots are left unexplained. Few offer impelling illustrations that open windows for the reader to see the exciting application for today's struggles. And most of all, seldom have the expositors given the valuable outlines of passages so needed to help the preacher or teacher in his or her busy life to prepare for communicating the Word to congregations or classes.

This Preacher's Commentary series brings all of these elements together. The authors are scholar-preachers and teachers outstanding in their ability to make the Scriptures come alive for individuals and groups. They are noted for bringing together excellence in biblical scholarship, knowledge of the original Greek and Hebrew, sensitivity to people's needs, vivid illustrative material from biblical, classical, and contemporary sources, and lucid communication by the use of clear outlines of thought. Each has been selected to contribute to this series because of his Spirit-empowered ability to help people live in the skins of biblical characters and provide a "you-are-there" intensity to the drama of events of the Bible which have so much to say about our relationships and responsibilities today.

The design for the Preacher's Commentary gives the reader an overall outline of each book of the New Testament. Following the introduction, which reveals the author's approach and salient background on the book, each chapter of the commentary provides the Scripture to be exposited. The New King James Bible has been chosen for the Preacher's Commentary because it combines with integrity the beauty of language, underlying Greek textual basis, and thought-flow of the 1611 King James Version, while replacing obsolete verb forms and other archaisms with their everyday contemporary counterparts for greater readability. Reverence for God is preserved in the capitalization of all pronouns referring to the Father, Son, or Holy Spirit. Readers who are more comfortable with another translation can readily find the parallel passage by means of the chapter and verse reference at the end of each passage being exposited. The paragraphs of exposition combine fresh insights to the Scripture, application, rich illustrative material, and innovative ways of utilizing the vibrant truth for his or her own life and for the challenge of communicating it with vigor and vitality.

It has been gratifying to me as Editor of this series to receive enthusiastic progress reports from each contributor. As they worked, all were gripped with new truths from the Scripture—God-given insights into passages, previously not written in the literature of biblical explanation. A prime objective of this series is for each user to find the same awareness: that God speaks with newness through the Scriptures when we approach them with a ready mind and a willingness to communicate what He has given; that God delights to give communicators of His Word "I-never-saw-that-in-that-verse-before" intellectual insights so that our listeners and readers can have "I-never-realized-all-that-was-in-that-verse" spiritual experiences.

The thrust of the commentary series unequivocally affirms that God speaks through the Scriptures today to engender faith, enable adventuresome living of the abundant life, and establish the basis of obedient discipleship. The Bible, the unique Word of God, is unlimited in its resource for Christians in communicating our hope to others. It is our weapon in the battle for truth, the guide for ministry, and the irresistible force for introducing others to God. In the New Testament we meet the divine Lord and Savior whom we seek to communicate to others. What He said and did as God with us has been faithfully recorded under the inspiration of the Spirit of God. The cosmic implications of the Gospels are lived out in Acts and spelled out in the Epistles. They have stood the test of time because the eternal Communicator, God Himself, communicates through them to those who would be communicators of grace. His essential nature is exposed, the plan of salvation is explained, and the gospel for all of life, now and for eternity, is proclaimed.

A biblically rooted communication of the gospel holds in unity and oneness what divergent movements have wrought asunder. This commentary series courageously presents personal faith, caring for individuals, and social responsibility as essential, inseparable dimensions of biblical Christianity. It seeks to present the quadrilateral Gospel in its fullness which calls us to unreserved commitment to Christ, unrestricted self-esteem in His grace, unqualified love for others in personal evangelism, and undying efforts to work for justice and righteousness in a sick and suffering world.

A growing renaissance in the church today is being led by clergy and laity who are biblically rooted, Christ-centered, and Holy Spirit-empowered. They have dared to listen to people's most urgent questions and deepest needs and then to God as He speaks through the Bible. Biblical preaching is the secret of growing churches. Bible study classes and small groups are equipping the laity for ministry in the world. Dynamic Christians are finding that daily study of God's Word allows the Spirit to do in them what He wishes to communicate through them to others. These days are the most exciting time since Pentecost. The Preacher's Commentary is offered to be a primary resource of new life for this renaissance.

This volume, Luke, was written by one of the truly original thinkers of our time. Bruce Larson is the originator of vision and concepts that have become strong strands of the fabric of the contemporary renaissance in the church today. He is one of the most often quoted and emulated spiritual leaders in America. As the founder of relational theology, he has proclaimed Christ's message of the kingdom of right relationships—with God, ourselves, others, and the world. His thinking is solidly rooted in the Bible. In his expository preaching and incisive writing of fifteen best-sellers and in his own personal devotions, his commitment to in-depth study and interpretation of God's Word shines through with gripping application for life.

Bruce Larson's extensive academic training in both biblical theology and psychology has been utilized to make him an insightful expositor and profound analyst of human nature. Throughout the years, he has been deeply involved in research and analysis of the dynamics of spiritual, physical, and emotional wholeness. A few years ago, he spent a prolonged period of time on a special research project, evaluating the discoveries of modern medicine and psychology in an effort to communicate more effectively in response to people's longing to add life to their years and years to their life.

His vibrant love for God and people enables him to speak and write with sensitivity and empathy. He is a master parabolizer, seeing illustrations in life, the human drama, and our struggle to live to the maximum with all stops out. An avid and extensive reader, he digs out applicable quotes and illustrations from contemporary literature, research, and magazines other communicators often miss. Because he lives his faith with verve and intensity, he is able to illustrate from his own adventure in Christ a quality of discipleship that is both impelling and contagious. Hundreds of thousands of people are living the abundant life and will live forever because they met Christ through knowing Bruce Larson personally, listening to his messages, or reading his many books.

I know that first hand. Bruce Larson introduced me to Christ when we were students in college. Over the past thirty-five years, he has been one of my best friends. We have shared the joys and challenges of life in Christ together. I have learned much about authentic communication from him. That's why, when the vision of this commentary series was born, he was the first person with whom I shared the dream. With his customary insight and enthusiasm, he helped immensely in developing its direction. It followed naturally that he should be asked to contribute one of the key volumes.

At that time, Bruce Larson was just beginning his now widely acclaimed ministry at University Presbyterian Church in Seattle, Washington. Since he had planned to preach the Gospel of Luke in a subsequent year, he elected to do this volume, utilizing in it his research and preparation for that year. That has made this volume one of the most helpful and useful expositions in the series, for in it we are able to observe a skilled craftsman at work. Not only does it provide fresh insight into Luke's Gospel, but it also shows us how to get a grasp on the deeper meaning of each passage and communicate it with contemporary, personal, and real-life illustrations.

Here is evangelical, biblical theology that throbs with life. There is rich scholarship, but we never lose touch with what that means personally to the author, nor what it can mean to us. Because of his ability to probe the deeper levels of both human behavior and potential, he helps us to live in a Scripture passage, and we emerge from our experience much more free to risk in our own adventure in Christ.

We are living in a time when biblical preachers and teachers are struggling to find new ways of communicating the Scriptures to a complex, contemporary society. We need models and mentors of methods that work. Bruce Larson shows us how to be innovative without gimmicks, and profound without jargon.

The author of this volume is a deeply committed churchman. All through his ministry, even when he was the leader of a parachurch renewal movement, he has been dedicated to enabling church leaders and congregations to live at full potential. This has made him a popular speaker at clergy conferences and church renewal retreats. Now as Senior Pastor of a pivotal church, he speaks and writes out of the reservoir of his experience of the exciting, new life springing forth in his own local congregation. I have been there to observe the renewal that has resulted from his preaching, teaching, and new forms of ministry. His treatment of Luke's Gospel exemplifies the quality of communication of the faith that has made this kind of renewal possible.

My gratitude for Bruce Larson's writing is coupled with my admiration for his wife Hazel, who plays a crucial role in preparing his manuscripts for publication. Her skilled editing and insightful contributions to this volume have heightened its excellence.

My prayer now is that you will be as enriched as I have been by Bruce Larson's exposition, illustration, and application of Luke for your study and communication. A great communicator of the gospel shows us how to do it with depth and power.

—LLOYD J. OGILVIE

INTRODUCTION—ABOUT THIS BOOK

Do you remember how you felt as a child on Christmas Eve? Most of us simply couldn't wait until Christmas morning to see what was under the tree. I feel like that when I consider the treasures that God has for us in this particular book of the Bible. The Gospel of Luke has been called the most beautiful book in the world and I agree. I seem to appreciate it more with each reading. I may be like the man who had written many books and was confessing to a friend that he felt his latest was not up to his usual standards. His friend protested, "Oh, I think it's up to your standards. It's just that your taste is improving." Whether or not my taste is improving, I am moved afresh with each reading of this "most beautiful book in the world."

Luke was also the author of the Book of Acts, which means he is responsible for one-quarter of the New Testament. In sheer volume, he has contributed more to the New Testament than even the apostle Paul, the other major writer. Scholars are still debating the exact date of this Gospel. Of the three possible dates suggested, A.D. 63, A.D. 75–85, and early second century, the weight of evidence seems to favor the earliest date. It seems logical to assume the Gospel is earlier than its sequel, the Book of Acts, and Acts records no date after A.D. 62.

1. Luke's is the Gospel of stories. Luke shows us who Jesus is through story after story, vignette after vignette. That's particularly interesting just now when the newest fad in theology in that rarified and academic atmosphere of the seminary is that truth is basically story, not concept. The idea was not new to Luke. In the Old Testament and much of the new, God's interaction with His people is conveyed not by means of theology or philosophy, but through stories. The Bible is a collection of stories about individuals and events and nations.

In a close brush with death, we are told, you may have the experience of seeing your whole life flash before your eyes, and I imagine when that happens you see your life as a series of stories. You remember certain times and events, and one event may seem to sum up five years of living. One picture or one story can crystallize a particular vacation or relationship. That's how we think. Your life and mine right now are stories. We are involved in something sad or happy, painful or pleasing. Years from now all these interwoven feelings will be summed up in a series of pictures or stories.

2. *The Gospel of Luke is a Gospel of joy.* Pierre Teilhard de Chardin, the great Roman Catholic philosopher and theologian, said, "Joy is the surest sign of the presence of God." There are no sad saints. Joy does not depend on circumstances. No matter how bad the circumstances of your life may be, if you know the Source and Giver of life, and He has loved and forgiven you, how can you not have joy? This is the joy Luke communicates in his Gospel.

3. *Luke's Gospel is universal*—the most universal of the four Gospels. Matthew's Gospel is written to the Jews and gives all sorts of background and details that have particular meaning for a Jewish audience. Mark is written for the Romans, the pragmatists, lovers of power. Mark's Gospel is full of fast-moving events written with brief and pithy language to communicate the mighty acts of God to people who understand power. John wrote for the church. His Gospel is a deeply spiritual book for the believer. In Luke's account it is as if he were saying, "This is good news for the whole world, not just for some Jewish sect, not just for some isolated spiritual group, and not just for the powerful decision-makers."

While Matthew's Gospel traces Jesus' earthly genealogy back to Abraham to make his point, Luke takes that genealogy all the way back to Adam, our universal ancestor. His Gospel makes frequent mention of the Samaritans, underscoring again that Jesus was the Redeemer of non-Jews as well as Jews. Luke wants to demonstrate that Jesus is not simply a new Jewish prophet. Christianity is a world faith applicable to both the religious and secular world. Luke portrays Jesus as the hope of the world. *But he is not a universalist.* He does not say that everyone *will* be saved. He says everyone *can* be saved—old, young, slave, free, rich, poor, Jew, Samaritan. Whatever and whoever you are, Jesus died for you.

4. *The Gospel of Luke is for the poor, the lost, and the broken.* The message of the Old and New Testaments is that God cares about the

poor and His people must care for the poor. There are grave warnings here for the wealthy, which most of us are in America and Europe. Even the poorest person in the West is richer than most of the rest of the world. Luke's Gospel speaks to our affluence and our responsibility to the poor.

5. Luke is the Gospel for women. How timely. Luke, written over nineteen centuries ago, introduces us to all sorts of interesting, fascinating women whom we would not know, apart from him. He gives us a picture of women who are co-laborers in the gospel.

6. Luke writes about home life. He gives us the only scene from Jesus' boyhood and explains just a little of his relationship with Mary and Joseph. He introduces us to John the Baptist's parents and tells in detail the circumstances of his birth. Through Luke, we have a glimpse of the home where Jesus loved to stay, where Mary, Martha, and Lazarus lived. He predates another physician, Sigmund Freud, who also emphasized the shaping influence of home life and family and who further suggested that we are still those children who interacted with our parents and siblings.

7. Luke's Gospel is deeply spiritual. It mentions angels, prayer, and the Holy Spirit more than any of the other Gospels. Luke gives us seven more prayers of Jesus than the other writers. He describes the Holy Spirit as the motivator and source of life and stresses that the Spirit is the key to understanding Emmanuel—God with us—which Jesus was and is.

About the Writer

Luke, called by Paul "The Beloved Physician," reports what he does because of who he is. As we see the great events of God through Luke's eyes, we come to know Luke himself. Who you are determines what you see. Your own faith and hope influence your view of the world and determine whether you believe these are the last days, or the first days of a new order. No one perceives life quite the way you do.

My wife and her sister often reminisce about the "old days." They are just a few years apart in age and slept in the same bed all through their growing-up years. One says, "Those were such wonderful days. I wish we could go back to them." The other says, "I'm just glad they're over. I can't think of them without pain." Two sisters, in the same home with the same siblings and parents, saw that chapter of their lives very differently.

Your genes, your training, your education, your environment, your disappointments and pains give you a unique position from which to interpret what is happening. In the same way, Luke interprets the world of his time in a way that only he can. We find the same kind of bias in the Gospel of Luke. Luke was a missionary and the apostle Paul's frequent traveling companion. He was a Greek. It's fairly certain he came from Antioch. He wrote in the popular, nonliterary Greek style, the world language of his time. Had he lived a thousand years later, he would have written in Latin. Were Luke alive today, he'd write in English. Difficult and unpredictable as it is, our language happens to be the present world language.

Luke, physician and scientist, was a clinical observer of life who communicated, as we said earlier, through stories. He painted life with words as a painter covers a canvas with paints. He pioneers a great tradition. Some of our most brilliant novelists, writers, and poets have been and are physicians: Lloyd Douglas, Somerset Maugham, A. J. Cronyn, John Keats, Robert Browning, Anton Chekhov, Sir Arthur Conan Doyle, and one of my favorite contemporary writers, Walker Percy. So Luke is especially equipped to record some aspects of this life of our Lord as none of the other Gospel writers were. Because of his personality and his training, he records and emphasizes details of Jesus' life and ministry that Matthew, Mark, and John weren't equipped to see.

A Personal Note

One final word about how this commentary came to be. About three years ago my old friend, Lloyd Ogilvie, told me about his dream for a "Preacher's Commentary" on the New Testament. I am delighted that he included me among the authors. I chose my favorite New Testament book, the Gospel of Luke.

About the same time I accepted a call to be pastor of the University Presbyterian Church in Seattle. It seemed like one of God's happy coincidences. Since this was to be a "Preacher's Commentary," why not preach through the entire book? I spent the next year doing just that, and I am grateful to my patient, wonderful church family in Seattle for being partners in dialogue and for holding me accountable for the implications and applications of truth in God's Word that we discovered together.

But forty-nine sermons are not a book. The real architect and coauthor of this commentary is my beloved wife and best friend,

Hazel. She has labored long and faithfully, and her editorial hand is on every page.

Typing the original sermons from tapes fell to my friend, Hal Jaenson. He is a marvel of speed and accuracy. But working with Hazel on the many revisions on weekends and in the wee hours of the morning was my beloved colleague, Gretha Osterberg. She not only made excellent suggestions as she typed, retyped, and proofread, she supplied affirmation and encouragement at every step.

Finally, I am indebted to my old friend, Floyd Thatcher, editor-in-chief at Word, and his colleague and my friend, Pat Wienandt, for final editing and for many helpful insights.

AN OUTLINE OF LUKE

CHAPTER ONE—COMMUNICATING ONE TO ONE

LUKE 1:1–4

1:1 Inasmuch as many have taken in hand to set in order a narrative of those things which have been fulfilled among us, [2] just as those who from the beginning were eyewitnesses and ministers of the word delivered them to us, [3] it seemed good to me also, having had perfect understanding of all things from the very first, to write to you an orderly account, most excellent Theophilus, [4] that you may know the certainty of those things in which you were instructed.

—Luke 1:1–4

Luke is the only one of the Gospel writers who did not know the physical Jesus. He was not present during our Lord's three-year ministry and did not witness His death and Resurrection. His sources for this Gospel are eyewitnesses of these events. He visited the people who actually saw the physical Jesus: His family, His disciples, His friends. These are the sources of his information.

The second verse of the first chapter of the story tells us that Luke is reporting these events *"just as those who from the beginning were eyewitnesses and* ministers *of the word delivered them to us.* He is not concerned about eyewitnesses who aren't ministers. By ministers he does not refer to clergy, but to those people who are ministering and doing the will of God. We Protestants believe strongly in the doctrine of "the priesthood of all believers"—that every Christian is a minister, serving Jesus Christ wherever he or she happens to be, in laboratories, schools, offices, shops, or neighborhoods. Ministers like this were Luke's sources.

The story is told about a man who was so intrigued by a Christian friend at work that he came to him one day and asked how he could find God. His friend said, "You need a theologian. You'd better talk to my pastor." When he talked to the pastor he was told, "I'm not a theologian, I'm just a poor preacher who learned some things in seminary. I suggest you see my seminary professor." Undaunted, the man made an appointment to see the seminary professor. At the start of the visit, he asked, "Are you a theologian?" "No, no," was the reply. "I am just a teacher. I get my material from all these theology books in my library. You'd better go and see some of the authors of these books." When he finally arranged an interview with one of the important authors, his first question again was, "Are you a theologian?" "No, no," answered the author. "I'm just a scientist who observes life and who writes about what I see. If you want a theologian, talk to somebody who is living out the faith day by day." I think this points up what Luke is implying. He got his story from the authentic theologians of his time. Beyond being eyewitnesses, they were living out their faith day by day.

Perhaps the genius of Luke's Gospel is that it is written to one person, to Theophilus. I am convinced that Luke is the most universal of the four Gospels because he is the most personal. The personal is universal; the general is vague. Some time ago I was in downtown Seattle shopping and I observed a man standing in front of one of our large department stores talking about Jesus. He was shouting at all those passing by. He was ranting about salvation to the world and nobody was listening. Though he was shouting loudly about the Good News, no one stopped and no one heeded. His message was so general it was meaningless.

In contrast, the secret of genuinely effective communication is caught by one of the television commercials advertising a brokerage firm. When somebody whispers the firm's name in a crowd, all conversation stops. When someone says, "Listen, this is not for the world, this is just for you," the whole world—waiters, cab drivers, passersby—stops. We all want to eavesdrop on intimate conversation.

Luke's Gospel, written just for Theophilus, had this quality. He is saying, "This is good news just for you, Theophilus." And the whole world has been reading ever since Luke's words to Theophilus. Whenever I am asked about speaking or writing effectively, I say, "Try to imagine one person sitting across the desk from you, and write your book or sermon to that one person. If your writing is for groups of people or for the world, it's going to be vague. The more personally aimed your speaking or writing is, the more universal it is."

This personal Gospel was written to a fellow Greek of high rank. Luke writes, *"Most excellent Theophilus."* Theophilus was either a believer or an active seeker. His name means "Friend of God," which may have been a nickname, or his actual name. The first verses tell us why this account was written. Luke says, *"That you may know the certainty of those things in which you were instructed."* Theophilus has been instructed in certain things, but Luke wants him to *know*. There's the difference between great and ordinary teaching. Do we enable others to *know*, or do we just pass on some body of content?

God is a person, not a concept. We can be instructed in a concept; we can only know a person. We can't teach specific rules to govern relationships. We may try. We may tell our six-year-old, "Aunt Florence is coming to visit and here's how you should behave. This is what to say, and what not to say." Trying to teach people how to behave in a relationship just doesn't work. Luke is saying, "This is not a new teaching about the concept of God. I want you to know the truth of God in the person of Jesus."

A certain medieval monk announced he would be preaching the next Sunday evening on "The Love of God." As the shadows fell and light ceased to come through the great cathedral windows, the congregation gathered. In the darkness of the altar, the monk lighted a candle and carried it to the crucifix. First of all, he illumined the crown of thorns; next, the two wounded hands; then the marks of the spear wound. In the hush that fell, he blew out the candle and left the chancel. There was nothing else to say. The love of God is Jesus' life given for us.

Luke goes on to say he writes *"an orderly account."* That sounds very Presbyterian, as this is the group which strives above all to do things decently and in order. Luke planned to address these important matters in a leisurely fashion. He is saying, "I will not rush through this, Theophilus. I want you to have an orderly account, and we've got plenty of time."

Luke wants Theophilus to know some things with certainty. Lloyd Douglas tells about a man who on a visit to his old violin teacher, asked, "What's new?" "I'll tell you what's new," said the teacher. He grabbed his tuning fork and banged it. The "A" came out loud and clear. "Do you hear that? That's an 'A'," he proclaimed. "Now, upstairs a soprano rehearses endlessly and she's always off key. Next door I have a cello player who plays his instrument very poorly. There is an out-of-tune piano on the other side of me. I'm surrounded by terrible noise, night and day." Plunking the "A" again, he continued, "Do you hear that? That's an 'A' yesterday, that's an 'A' today, that will be an 'A' tomorrow. It will never change." Luke is insisting on the same kind of certainty: "Jesus Christ, the same yesterday, today, and forever."

CHAPTER TWO—TOO GOOD TO BE TRUE
LUKE 1:5–25

Scripture Outline

AN UNUSUAL COUPLE

5 There was in the days of Herod, the king of Judea, a certain priest named Zacharias, of the division of Abijah. His wife was of the daughters of Aaron, and her name was Elizabeth. 6 And they were both righteous before God, walking in all the commandments and ordinances of the Lord blameless. 7 But they had no child, because Elizabeth was barren, and they were both well advanced in years.

—Luke 1:5–7

If you're like me, you sometimes wake up at 2:00 A.M. and cannot get back to sleep. Let's suppose that the next time that happens, you go out to the kitchen, turn on the light, and find an angel standing there. He might call you by name. I say *he* because the Bible indicates angels are masculine. What would you say? And what do you think he would say?

Luke's story begins with a situation like this. An angel appears and speaks to Zacharias, a priest. Zacharias and his wife, Elizabeth, were both from priestly stock, a fact that had a great deal of weight with the Jews. Verse 6 says that they were *"both"* righteous before God. Just think what that means. Most of us are playing our lives to someone. We may be trying to be righteous and Christian for the benefit and esteem of our neighbors, friends, and family. That's not all bad. But how much better to be righteous before the One who sees us in secret, who knows our thoughts and actions when we are alone. Zacharias and Elizabeth were righteous but not sinless. Sinlessness is not an option for any of us. The desire of their hearts was to belong to God and to serve Him. They were playing their lives to God. We might say these were very unusual people.

These two unusual people were suffering. Most Jews did not believe in eternal life. Immortality came through their children and heirs; it was through them that one lived on forever. So although righteous, Zacharias and Elizabeth had no children, and were thus suffering the ultimate disappointment and humiliation. If you think life is fair, the Bible does not encourage you in that view.

Zacharias and Elizabeth, like so many Old Testament characters, have meaningful names. Zacharias means "The Lord Remembers." Elizabeth is "My God Is an Absolutely Faithful One," or, "My God Is an Oath." These two, whose very names were affirmations of faith, married. I have spoken and written a good deal about the power of a name and of how much we Christians need new names with positive and spiritual connotations. The Jews gave their children names with profound meaning. Later, Elizabeth and Zacharias were to name their son John, which means "Gift of God."

AN UNPLANNED INTERRUPTION

8 So it was, that while he was serving as priest before God in the order of his division, 9 according to the custom of the priesthood, his lot fell to burn incense when he went into the temple of the Lord. 10 And the whole multitude of the people was praying outside at the hour of incense.

11 Then an angel of the Lord appeared to him, standing on the right side of the altar of incense. 12 And when Zacharias saw him, he was troubled, and fear fell upon him.

13 But the angel said to him, "Do not be afraid, Zacharias, for your prayer is heard; and your wife Elizabeth will bear you a son, and you shall call his name John."

—*Luke 1:8–13*

There were twenty-four divisions of priests in Israel at that time, far more priests than needed. Each division took a turn yearly to serve for a week. Only one priest at a time had the honor of burning the incense at the altar, an important task since this was the symbolic representation of the rising up to God of the prayers and longings of the people. There were so many priests that this special honor might come just once in a lifetime or perhaps not at all.

On this occasion Zacharias was chosen by lot as the one to burn incense before God. During this, his great moment, the angel appeared. Zacharias's reaction was fear. You might think that this man, born of a priestly tribe and righteous before God, would have been delighted about seeing an angel. But when God intervened in his life personally, he was afraid and troubled. Perhaps it's not surprising. If a preacher were to announce that everybody who came to church next Sunday would hear the Lord speak to them by name directly, do you think there would be an overflow crowd? If God really were there personally or through an angel to give us a direct message, we might react just as Zacharias did. We might say, "Oh, that's my Sunday to wash the car or visit the sick. I'm not sure I can be there."

The angel said to Zacharias, *"Your prayer is heard."* Zacharias didn't believe it. He had been praying without conviction. He did not really believe God would answer his fervent prayers. Even a righteous man can pray with no sense of expectation. The angel says, *"Do not be afraid,"* the same assurance the angels gave to Mary and the shepherds in the fields of Bethlehem later in this same Gospel.

ANGELIC PROPHECY

14 And you will have joy and gladness, and many will rejoice at his birth. 15 For he will be great in the sight of the Lord, and shall drink neither wine nor strong drink. He will also be filled with the Holy Spirit, even from his mother's womb. 16 And he will turn many of the children of Israel to the Lord their God. 17 "He will also go before Him in the spirit and power of Elijah, *'to turn the hearts of the fathers to the children,'* and the disobedient to the wisdom of the just, to make ready a people prepared for the Lord."

—Luke 1:14–17

The angel promised Zacharias that he personally would have joy and gladness and that many would rejoice at the birth of his son. But not all. Eventually this baby grew to manhood and was beheaded for speaking out against the sins of the king. Nevertheless, according to the angel, *many* were to rejoice at the birth of John the Baptist.

Did many (or any) rejoice at your birth? If nobody rejoiced at or about your birth, then you've missed your inheritance. Certainly

John was special, but remember what Jesus said about his cousin, John: "Among those born of women there is not a greater prophet than John the Baptist, but he who is least in the kingdom of God is greater than he" (Luke 7:28). If you are in the kingdom of God then you are meant to be a greater source of blessing than John.

A farmer once told me that a watermelon seed is able to reproduce itself two hundred thousand times. That tiny seed draws power from the earth to become a great, green watermelon. In the same sense, God can use a single life—John's or yours, or mine—to reproduce blessings for countless others.

The angel says John will be filled with the Holy Spirit from birth on. This is a whole new concept of the Holy Spirit. Throughout the Old Testament God anointed special people, prophets and kings, with His Spirit. The Spirit was given for specific tasks at particular times. Gideon was filled with the Spirit to lead the Israelites in battle. Moses was filled with the Spirit to carry out the Exodus from Egypt. John is the first person who from his birth was to be filled with the Holy Spirit. At Pentecost, the apostle Peter, quoting the prophet Joel, said, "I will pour out of My Spirit on all flesh" (Acts 2:17). Henceforth, it would be possible for all believers to live in the Spirit. John was a forerunner of that Pentecost experience.

The angel tells Zacharias that John is going to turn many of the children of Israel to the Lord their God. The wording indicates that there were many Israelites who did not know God. By birth they belonged to God's chosen race, but through John they would find the center of their faith. That is still an important dimension of evangelism. Many birthright Christians, brought by believing parents for baptism into the covenant, do not find God until much later, if at all. My father was seventy-six when it happened to him, although he had been baptized as an infant into the family of God. John's call was to help those who were by birthright God's special people to know Him. And that's a valid evangelistic thrust for us today.

The angel says that others will know that John is of God because he will *"turn the hearts of the fathers to the children."* In other words, there will be family reconciliation. I consider that a good test of the presence of the Spirit in any age. If you want to know whether or not you are filled with the Holy Spirit, examine the emotional climate of your family. Authentic love between family members is one sign of God's presence. The bad news is that the real you is the person you are at home with your family.

You may perform well at church and on the job, but the real test comes in how you treat the people you live with every day. That's somewhat frightening. But when God's Spirit is at work, the parents are reconciled to their children, according to the angel's promise. Reality, love, openness, and acceptance within the family structure are the proof of an authentic work of the Spirit. The angel promises that through John's ministry there will be revival and renewal in the home.

I met a new friend for lunch one day and asked him what he did in his spare time and if he had any hobbies. It turned out he is a Little League coach and a Boy Scout leader. He is involved in all sorts of activities with his young family. My wife reminds me that when our children were young, I was on the road as an evangelist three weeks out of every month. I think my children have forgiven me, but I have some real regrets about those years. Apart from any ministry to the world, we are called, like John, to bring love and reconciliation to our families.

ANSWERED PRAYER

18 And Zacharias said to the angel, "How shall I know this? For I am an old man, and my wife is well advanced in years."

19 And the angel answered and said to him, "I am Gabriel, who stands in the presence of God, and was sent to speak to you and bring you these glad tidings. 20 But behold, you will be mute and not able to speak until the day these things take place, because you did not believe my words which will be fulfilled in their own time."

21 And the people waited for Zacharias, and marveled that he lingered so long in the temple. 22 But when he came out, he could not speak to them; and they perceived that he had seen a vision in the temple, for he beckoned to them and remained speechless.

23 So it was, as soon as the days of his service were completed, that he departed to his own house.

—Luke 1:18–23

John the Baptist is the morning star that announces the dawn. You see that first star while the sky is still dark and you have the certainty that it will soon be light. John appears as a harbinger proclaiming that "great days are coming." Zacharias could not have known that. His reaction to all that the angel had predicted was disbelief. It was all too good to be true. He was like Thomas, the disciple who doubted the Resurrection and said, "Unless I see in His hands the print of the nails, and put my finger into the print of the nails, and put my hand into His side, I will not believe" (John 20:25). He was given proof and he believed.

Think of the dialogue: The angel tells Zacharias that he and Elizabeth are going to have a son. Zacharias argues that he is an old man. The angel pulls rank. He says, *"I am Gabriel, who stands in the presence of God."* In other words, "God sent me. How dare you argue with me?" Zacharias could not believe the good news, chiefly because of his age. I love the story of the man in his nineties who went to his doctor with knee trouble. The doctor said, "At your age, what do you expect?" "I expect you to fix this knee," was the reply; "my other knee's the same age, and it works fine." Our age can be a barrier, whatever age we are, and we can believe we are restricted because of it. Zacharias's age was not a factor in his ability to carry out God's purposes.

If an angel said to you, "Your prayer is heard," what would it mean for you? What is the "too good to be true" news in your life? You may have given up believing God can bring it about. You may think you're too old to start something new and exciting. Remember that people in their nineties have written plays and governed nations. Perhaps you have been praying about your loneliness. You are single and well past the age of expecting to marry. I had a wedding invitation recently from somebody well past the accepted age. It said, "Celebrate with me. I have found my true love." And that message gladdened my heart. Whatever it is that might seem too good to be true for you, remember Zacharias.

Sometimes we tire of waiting for God's answer, and we take things into our own hands. God told Abraham he would be the father of a great nation. He and Sarah were old and Sarah was barren. Abraham waited what seemed a reasonable length of time. He finally decided to help matters along and had a son by Hagar, Sarah's maid. From that union came Ishmael. In his impatience, Abraham decided to help God out and, in the vernacular, he blew it. In the same way, Zacharias could not believe that God had an answer for him. We've all been guilty of that at some time. It may be that we enter into an affair because we can't trust God with our loneliness. We may in desperation take the wrong job, not trusting that the right one will turn up. In our hopelessness, suicide may seem the only answer. We can't believe God can untangle the mess we are in. We pay a price for our unbelief, just as Zacharias did.

It was apparent when Zacharias came out of the temple that something awesome had happened. An authentic experience with God is discernible. Zacharias couldn't pass on God's blessing because he was mute. This was not the usual priest coming out to give the routine blessing. Something strange had happened to him, and the crowd perceived it.

First of all, he was late, off schedule. Would that we had the freedom to be off schedule occasionally in worship. If we come to church to have authentic dialogue with God, we can't always do it in one neat and precise hour with the sermon taking just twenty minutes and no more. Real dialogue may take time. We can't always follow the printed bulletin. Sometimes God wants to scrap the schedule. He may have something special to say to us as He did to Zacharias, and we may run overtime. Try as we might, we can't organize God and put Him on our timetable.

> 24 Now after those days his wife Elizabeth conceived; and she hid herself five months, saying, 25 "Thus the Lord has dealt with me, in the days when He looked on *me,* to take away my reproach among people."
>
> —*Luke 1:24–25*

I think the thing God wants for us is not too unlike what He wanted for Zacharias and Elizabeth in verse 25—to take away our reproach among men and women. He wants to restore that which robs us of dignity. He wants to give us the desires of our hearts. He wants to give us something too good to be true.

CHAPTER THREE—GOD OF THE IMPOSSIBLE

Scripture Outline

Favored by God (1:26–38)

Sharing Good News (1:39–45)

A Call to Revolutions (1:46–56)

FAVORED BY GOD

26 Now in the sixth month the angel Gabriel was sent by God to a city of Galilee named Nazareth, 27 to a virgin betrothed to a man whose name was Joseph, of the house of David. The virgin's name was Mary. 28 And having come in, the angel said to her, "Rejoice, highly favored one, the Lord is with you; blessed are you among women!"

29 But when she saw him, she was troubled at his saying, and considered what manner of greeting this was. 30 Then the angel said to her, "Do not be afraid, Mary, for you have found favor with God. 31 And behold, you will conceive in your womb and bring forth a Son, and shall call His name JESUS. 32 He will be great, and will be called the Son of the Highest; and the Lord God will give Him the throne of His father David. 33 And He will reign over the house of Jacob forever, and of His kingdom there will be no end."

34 Then Mary said to the angel, "How can this be, since I do not know a man?"

35 And the angel answered and said to her, "The Holy Spirit will come upon you, and the power of the Highest will overshadow you; therefore, also, that Holy One who is to be born will be called the Son of God. 36 Now indeed, Elizabeth your relative has also conceived a son in her old age; and this is now the sixth month for her who was called barren. 37 For with God nothing will be impossible."

³⁸ Then Mary said, "Behold the maidservant of the Lord! Let it be to me according to your word." And the angel departed from her.

—Luke 1:26–38

In the dialogue that took place between Mary and the angel Gabriel, the angel told her first of all that she was "highly favored with God." Mary was troubled. Perhaps because of her humility, she may have been thinking, "Why me? I'm too insignificant to find favor with God." On the other hand, perhaps she had the innate wisdom to comprehend something at the very heart of the mystery of life and the mystery of God: that those highly favored by God do not have a life of unbroken happiness.

Remember that Mary was a Jew, and the Jews were the chosen people, a people who found favor with God. Jews are still the chosen people. For three thousand years those chosen people have suffered perhaps as no other people. The Auschwitzes and the Dachaus are only the latest in a whole line of indignities and obscenities endured by the chosen people. And I would like to believe that Mary understood at some level that there is a tremendous price to be paid by those who are highly favored by God.

She was wise. In the 1960s and '70s we had whole generations of young people who thought that to find God was to find perfect peace and that being favored by Him resulted in a laid-back life of contemplating one's navel and thinking great thoughts. The Bible discourages us of that notion. The chosen, the highly favored of God, should be prepared for pain and suffering. I think that somehow Mary understood that.

We cannot talk about these Scripture verses without discussing the fact of the Virgin Birth. Luke, the physician, would of all people be the most skeptical about such a birth. He must have had an understanding of the birth process as only doctors have. And yet he is the one who records in detail the angel's message to Mary, that she, a virgin, was to be mysteriously impregnated by God's Holy Spirit and that no earthly father was to be involved. For two thousand years the church has not made belief in the Virgin Birth a requirement for membership but has accommodated those who believe that Jesus had a natural father. On the other hand, essential to Christianity is the belief in the Incarnation. You must, if you are a believer who is in the mainstream of orthodox Christianity, believe that God was in Jesus as in no other human being.

In terms of fact, I feel the evidence strongly supports the doctrine of the Virgin Birth. All four Gospels record the events of Jesus' earthly life. Two of them say nothing about the manner of His birth. The two accounts that give us details concur that He was born of a virgin. Luke tells us from the beginning that he has set down these accounts painstakingly and in great detail. It's logical to assume that Luke had many visits with Mary and talked about all of these events. Mary outlived her son for an indeterminate number of years—how long we don't know, but there is evidence that she lived with John in his exile on Patmos. Luke, in doing this chronicle, must have talked often to Mary, and we can imagine him saying, "Let's go over the facts one more time. What really happened?"

The Old Testament prophecy was that Jesus would be of David's lineage, that David would be His spiritual forebear. Now, while Joseph was of the house of David, Luke again was careful to record that Mary was the kinswoman of Elizabeth, who was of the house of Aaron, and therefore Mary also was of the house of David. Through Mary, the prophecy was also fulfilled.

Some devout Christians have never been able intellectually to accept the idea of the Virgin Birth. But if you believe it's impossible, then I would question your view of God. You are limiting God. In the words of J. B. Phillips's great book of thirty years ago, *Your God Is Too Small.* We Christians believe in a God who is big enough to deal with our most pressing personal problems. He is big enough to deal with our most pressing national problems and the problems of our world. Our Creator and Redeemer is the God of the impossible.

I believe Mary was chosen to bear God's own Son because she was one of that faithful remnant in Israel who understood that with God nothing is impossible. She was chosen when the more worthy or high-born or well-positioned were bypassed. Why does God choose certain people for unusual assignments? For example, why did He choose Billy Graham? God seems to have entrusted Billy Graham with the privileged position of being Protestantism's number one spokesman to the twentieth-century world. He himself has said that his gifts are not all that unusual.

Mary had a choice. She responded as though she had made a decision: *"Let it be to me according to your word."* God never forces His love or His will on anyone. The implication here is that the angel was announcing God's plan and purpose to Mary and it would not be carried out without her consent. When this little teen-aged girl, Mary, chose to serve God, it was not as Joan of Arc, marching out clad in her armor to lead armies. A figure like Joan of Arc is glamourous, even though in the end she suffered death. Mary suffered the ridicule and contempt of being pregnant and unmarried in a small town full of gossips. Knowing all this, she said, *"Let it be to me according to your word."* It is surely one of the most courageous statements ever recorded.

SHARING GOOD NEWS

> 39 Now Mary arose in those days and went into the hill country with haste, to a city of Judah, 40 and entered the house of Zacharias and greeted Elizabeth. 41 And it happened, when Elizabeth heard the greeting of Mary, that the babe leaped in her womb; and Elizabeth was filled with the Holy Spirit. 42 Then she spoke out with a loud voice and said, "Blessed are you among women, and blessed is the fruit of your womb! 43 But why is this granted to me, that the mother of my Lord should come to me? 44 For indeed, as soon as the voice of your greeting sounded in my ears, the babe leaped in my womb for joy. 45 Blessed is she who believed, for there will be a fulfillment of those things which were told her from the Lord."
>
> *—Luke 1:39–45*

Notice how Luke puts the divine encounter and a very human one side by side. Mary had just had the most earth-shaking experience in the world. Nothing will ever surpass it. And what did she do? She immediately ran off to tell someone, in this case her cousin, Elizabeth. She couldn't wait to share what had happened to her. You can just imagine Elizabeth's response, "Tell me all about it. What happened? Then what did Gabriel say? And what did you say?" How much we need other human beings to share the watershed moments of our lives. To be a Christian is to believe in a God who is the God of the impossible and to belong to a family of brothers and sisters who are there when you need them most. Because you belong to this family of faith, you have someone to go to who will listen to you when great joy or sorrow overwhelm you.

The person with whom Mary wanted to share this overwhelming news had certain qualities. First of all, she was not jealous. Elizabeth had also had a visit from the angel Gabriel and she herself was bearing a miraculous child. But when she heard the good news, she acknowledged that the child Mary was carrying was even greater, and she rejoiced. How blessed we are to have even a few friends like that. When you receive a great honor, I trust you have some friends who can enjoy your success and that joy may leap inside of them, as the baby leaped in Elizabeth's womb.

Elizabeth was also able to affirm Mary's experience and encourage her. She was not in the least skeptical. She said, *"Blessed is she who believed . . . those things which were told her from the Lord"* (v. 45). When God has spoken to us we need a friend who will say, "I believe that was authentic. I believe God is speaking to you."

We have the power to affirm and bless each other as Elizabeth did. We need a few people in our lives upon whom we are free to call at any hour, even two o'clock in the morning, if we are in trouble, though they may be less than cheerful at that hour. I heard about a man who came to work with a broken nose, and his friend asked him what happened. "Well," he said, "I called someone at 2:00 A.M. and said, 'Guess who?' He guessed correctly, and the next day he came by and did this to me." I don't suggest you say, "Guess who?" at 2:00 A.M. Just say, "I am calling you because I need you and I want to share my pain or my joy."

Mary stayed at Elizabeth's home for three months, until John was born. What else would a kinswoman and a friend do in that society but stay until the delivery day? I like to speculate on what they talked about during those three months. I'm sure they covered everything—angels and babies and God and Israel and the world. They shared life.

Captain Kangaroo, Bob Keeshan, has said, "Attention is like a daily bouquet of love." You and I need to have love expressed in attention when something earthshaking, good or bad, has happened. We are blessed by someone who will sit down and say, "And then what? And then what?" and hear us through without interruption.

A CALL TO REVOLUTION

46 And Mary said:
"My soul magnifies the Lord,
47And my spirit has rejoiced in God my Savior.
48For He has regarded the lowly state of His maidservant;
For behold, henceforth all generations will call me
blessed.
49For He who is mighty has done great things for me,
And holy is His name.
50And His mercy is on those who fear Him
From generation to generation.

⁵¹He has shown strength with His arm;
He has scattered the proud in the imagination of their
hearts.
⁵²He has put down the mighty from their thrones,
And exalted the lowly.
⁵³He has filled the hungry with good things,
And the rich He has sent away empty.
⁵⁴He has helped His servant Israel,
In remembrance of His mercy,
⁵⁵As He spoke to our fathers,
To Abraham and to his seed forever."
⁵⁶ And Mary remained with her about three months, and
returned to her house.

—Luke 1:46–56

Mary's hymn of response to the angel is the famous Magnificat,
so named by the Roman church for the key word in the Latin
translation of the first line of this prayer of praise offered by Mary.
Mary, in her naturalness, unself-consciousness and humility, was
now able to sing about how proud she was that God had chosen
her. In her true humility, she praised God that she was especially
blessed.

There is a danger in trying to spiritualize the Magnificat. These
are the most revolutionary words ever spoken. Through the
Messiah, the mighty will be brought low; the humble, the lowly,
will be exalted. William Temple, Archbishop of Canterbury,
warned his missionaries to India never to read the Magnificat in
public. Christians were already suspect in that country and they
were cautioned against reading verses so inflammatory. Jesus, the
ultimate revolutionary, completely reverses all human values.
What Mary was prophesying about her unborn son is terrifying to
the establishment, whoever and wherever they are. They cannot
hear these words gladly. We may attempt instead to spiritualize
these verses, but deep down we all know that Jesus has come to
instigate the kind of revolution we need.

Henry James, great novelist of the past, said in *Ivan Turgenieff,*
"Life is, in fact, a battle. Evil is insolent and strong; beauty
enchanting but rare; goodness very apt to be weak; folly very apt
to be defiant; wickedness to carry the day; imbeciles to be in great
places; people of sense in small (a comforting thought); and
mankind generally unhappy, but the world as it stands is no illusion, no fanaticism, no evil dream of the night; we wake up to it

again forever and ever; we can neither forget it nor deny it nor dispense with it; that's what the world is."

José Ortega y Gasset, one of the greatest of all Spanish writers, said, "Before long there will be heard throughout the planet a formidable cry rising like the howling of innumerable dogs to the stars asking for someone or something to take command." And that's why Jesus has come—to take command to lead the revolution, an incredible revolution, unlike Mao's or Marx's or Castro's; a revolution of love.

I was interviewed once by a reporter who had covered Mother Teresa's visit to Boys Town. I asked him about that visit and her reactions. He said, "They showed her all over the grounds of Boys Town, the dormitories, the classrooms, the gymnasium, the dining hall. At the end of the tour, she turned to the head priest and said, 'You have all this, but do you really love them?' Jesus loves us. This is the strategy of this ultimate social revolutionary. And God of the impossible is leading His people in this revolution.

CHAPTER FOUR—THE ULTIMATE QUESTION
LUKE 1:57–80

Scripture Outline

Naming the Baby (1:57–66)

A New Covenant (1:67–72)

Preparing for the Dayspring (1:73–80)

NAMING THE BABY

57 Now Elizabeth's full time came for her to be delivered, and she brought forth a son. 58 When her neighbors and relatives heard how the Lord had shown great mercy to her, they rejoiced with her.

59 So it was, on the eighth day, that they came to circumcise the child; and they would have called him by the name of his father, Zacharias. 60 His mother answered and said, "No; he shall be called John."

61 But they said to her, "There is no one among your relatives who is called by this name." 62 So they made signs to his father—what he would have him called.

63 And he asked for a writing tablet, and wrote, saying, "His name is John." So they all marveled. 64 Immediately his mouth was opened and his tongue loosed, and he spoke, praising God. 65 Then fear came on all who dwelt around them; and all these sayings were discussed throughout all the hill country of Judea. 66 And all those who heard them kept them in their hearts, saying, "What kind of child will this be?" And the hand of the Lord was with him.

—Luke 1:57–66

At John's birth friends and neighbors wondered, *"What kind of child will this be?"* (v. 66). It's an appropriate question at the birth of any child. Thoreau says, "What a man thinks of himself determines his fate." But we receive our opinions about ourself from those very people who are asking the question, "What kind of child will this be?" Rabbi Zusya said years ago, "In the world to come I will not be asked, 'Why were you not Moses?' I will be asked, 'Why were you not Zusya?' The problem, as Zusya says, is how to be the person we were meant to be.

In the last chapter we dealt with one of the two great questions of life: Who is your God? Is He the God of the impossible or have we made Him something less? The second great question is: Who are you? If you believe the Word of God, you are His child, made in His image, potentially the most marvelous and perverse creature in all of His creation.

The birth of John the Baptist prepared the way for the birth of our Lord. Later on his ministry prepared the way for Jesus' own ministry. Jesus said of John that among those born of women, none was greater than John the Baptist. Let's see if we can find some answers to who we are as we examine who John was and why he was so great.

First of all, his birth was unusual and totally unexpected. His birth delighted his mother and his father who, because of their age, had given up all hope of having a baby. John's birth was met with joy and thanksgiving. The message given to him at that early age, both verbally and nonverbally, was that people delighted in him. His parents were thrilled and the neighbors were in awe, saying, *"What kind of child will this be?"* Certainly that must have been an important influence in this boy's having become a very special man. Sigmund Freud, father of psychoanalysis, has said that the details of your birth and early life are powerful determining factors in the person you become.

I was reminded of his words when I visited with two different families recently, each of which was expecting a new baby. The reaction of one family was, "Oh, isn't this awful! Pregnant again." The second couple couldn't wait to tell me the good news, "We are expecting. We can't believe our good fortune." Already, two little lives were being influenced by parental attitudes, one set positive and one negative. The mystery of who you are is tied up in whether you were wanted or unwanted, whether or not one or both parents died early on or abandoned you. Perhaps you were reminded all your growing-up years of the enormous physical price your mother paid to give birth to you. Some of us have had the pain of childbirth reviewed again and again for us with the implication that it was a mighty big price, and she's not sure you were worth it. We can't imagine Elizabeth saying that. I'm sure

John realized early on how much he was wanted by his parents and held in awe by his neighbors.

Some years ago we were doing a renewal conference in a great Gothic cathedral-like Presbyterian church in Omaha. As people came in they were given a balloon filled with helium. They were told to release it at some point in the service where they felt like expressing the joy in their hearts—during the anthem, the hymns, the prayers, or the sermon. Since they were Presbyterians, they were not free to say "Hallelujah" or "Praise the Lord." Letting go of the balloon would represent praise going up to God. So all through the service, brightly colored balloons were rising up to bounce off the ceiling, visual signs of praise to the Lord. But oddly enough, when the service was over, about a third of those balloons were still unreleased. Those Presbyterians either felt no joy or, feeling it, could not bring themselves to express it. You may have had parents who have hung onto their balloons all their lives. They can't rejoice at your birth if they are unable to rejoice at all. At John's birth, parents and neighbors alike released their balloons.

John, at birth, was given a second gift—his own identity. When his mother said, *"He shall be called John"* (v. 60), family and friends were disapproving. There was no other John in the family. They expected the father to overrule Elizabeth in this strange notion. But remembering what the angel told him nine months earlier, Zacharias wrote on the tablet, *"His name is John"* (v. 63). John was given a name that was uniquely his. Our names themselves influence how others regard us. A recent test was done in which a number of girls in a beauty contest were given fictitious names. Though equally pretty, girls they had named Gertrude or Agnes for the purpose of the test invariably lost out to those with names more popular in this generation, for example, Debbie or Cindy.

My name was changed just after I was born. My mother had given me my father's Swedish name—Bror, meaning brother. When my father came to the hospital he vehemently vetoed this idea. He was convinced that Bror was too difficult a name for a kid growing up in America. And so I was called Bruce. Who would I have been had my name been Bror, or Benjamin, or Bert? John's name, meaning, as we said, Gift of God, was a means of blessing and power.

A friend of mine grew up deeply ashamed of her family's lowly origins. She tells me that as a little girl she used to pretend the gypsies had left her at the door; that she didn't belong there at all. But the good news is that no matter how positive or negative our home situation, we all belong to somebody else. We are God's children and He gives us worth and importance.

When Zacharias wrote, *"His name is John,"* his tongue was immediately loosed. Struck dumb because he doubted, he suddenly spoke after nine months of silence. As soon as he obeyed God's instructions in the naming of the child, he was healed. With that, he burst into his marvelous hymn of praise to the Messiah, whose coming would be announced by his son John.

Healings like Zacharias's are still happening. They ought to be a normal part of worship. I believe there are people in every congregation who are healed by the power of God when they decide to be obedient in some area. That response triggers something frozen inside or some hidden repression or denial, and God deals with it. It's one of the reasons for worship. We meet the One who is the Giver of life, the Source of joy, and He still has power to heal. Spiritual healing should not surprise us. When we say to God, "I'm tired of resenting this person. This morning I choose to forgive him/her," healing forces are released. You may go home from church with your long-term illness cured. Worship is the time when we are doing business with God who wants to make us whole.

A NEW COVENANT

67 Now his father Zacharias was filled with the Holy
Spirit, and prophesied, saying:
68"Blessed is the Lord God of Israel,
For He has visited and redeemed His people,
69And has raised up a horn of salvation for us
In the house of His servant David,
70As He spoke by the mouth of His holy prophets,
Who have been since the world began,
71That we should be saved from our enemies
And from the hand of all who hate us,
72To perform the mercy promised to our fathers
And to remember His holy covenant,
—*Luke 1:67–72*

We read that Zacharias uttered these amazing words of prophecy because of the infilling of the Holy Spirit. He spoke of the horn of salvation. The horn is the point of strength of an animal. It is the focus of power for a cow, a moose, or a rhinoceros. Jesus is to be that horn of salvation where all the power of God is focused. Zacharias spoke of remembering the holy covenant, the promise God made with Israel that they would be the chosen people. You and I are the new Israel, members of a new covenant God has made in Jesus Christ. In baptism, we affirm for our children the covenant God has made with us through Jesus Christ.

I love the story of Martin Luther who, on those dark and discouraging days we all have, would say to himself over and over, "I am baptized. I am baptized." He affirmed that whatever was happening to him at the moment, he was a child of the covenant God had made with His people. Try that on one of your bad days. You might get surprising results.

PREPARING FOR THE DAYSPRING

73The oath which He swore to our father Abraham:
74To grant us that we,
Being delivered from the hand of our enemies,
Might serve Him without fear,
75In holiness and righteousness before Him all the days of
our life.
76"And you, child, will be called the prophet of the
Highest;
For you will go before the face of the Lord to prepare His
ways,
77To give knowledge of salvation to His people
By the remission of their sins,
78Through the tender mercy of our God,
With which the Dayspring from on high has visited us;
79To give light to those who sit in darkness and the
shadow of death,
To guide our feet into the way of peace."
80 So the child grew and became strong in spirit, and was
in the deserts till the day of his manifestation to Israel.
—*Luke 1:73–80*

The Israelites equated salvation with political deliverance, and John was to give them a new understanding of salvation—that the enemy is within, not without. John was to prepare the way for the One who would deliver us all from the enemy within. Zacharias compared the Messiah to the dayspring and to the light. But the light itself doesn't do the delivering. We are given the picture of a band of people moving into the wilderness. When darkness falls upon them, they must halt. Suddenly, they discover the dayspring is coming. It will be morning. When the light comes they are free to proceed and to save themselves. In the same way, Christ brings the light and shows us the way, but you and I must respond to the light and walk toward it. Zacharias's hymn was not some religious incantation. He was talking about life and light and deliverance.

The final verses tell us that John spent years in the desert before he began his ministry. Many of us have been in the desert figuratively. Those are bleak times. Nobody chooses the desert. But in terms of preparing us for life and ministry, the desert is better than a university. All the great prophets have come out of the wilderness or the desert. When life is bleak and stark we begin to see what the real issues are.

Viktor Frankl, the Viennese psychiatrist and father of logotherapy, says to us, "Project yourself onto your death bed, and think back. What, from that point of view, do you wish you had done with your life?" How do we do that? By entering again into the mystery of birth by rebirth and finding those who can celebrate that event with us.

As Jesus said, "Among those born of women there is none greater than John." And no wonder. His parents rejoiced in his coming. His birth was celebrated by family and friends. He had great genes from his righteous mother and father. He had no identity crisis. He was filled with the Holy Spirit. But for those of us in the new covenant there is a good word. Jesus gives us a new identity, a new set of spiritual genes, a new family, your mothers and fathers and sisters and brothers in the Spirit who say at the time of your *new* birth, "What wonderful things this child will be and do." The good news is that you and I can be born again with all the joy and promise that attended the birth of John the Baptist.

CHAPTER FIVE—CALLED TO BE PEACEMAKERS

LUKE 2:1–20

Scripture Outline

Miracle in Bethlehem (2:1–7)

A Threefold Peace (2:8–20)

MIRACLE IN BETHLEHEM

2:1 And it came to pass in those days *that* a decree went out from Caesar Augustus that all the world should be registered. ² This census first took place while Quirinius was governing Syria. ³ So all went to be registered, everyone to his own city.

⁴ Joseph also went up from Galilee, out of the city of Nazareth, into Judea, to the city of David, which is called Bethlehem, because he was of the house and lineage of David, ⁵ to be registered with Mary, his betrothed wife, who was with child. ⁶ So it was, that while they were there, the days were completed for her to be delivered. ⁷ And she brought forth her firstborn Son, and wrapped Him in swaddling cloths, and laid Him in a manger, because there was no room for them in the inn.

—Luke 2:1–7

John Lennon once said of the Beatles, the phenomenal group of musicians of the sixties and seventies of which he was a part, that they were more popular than Jesus. That may have been so, but they were not and are not better-known. Hundreds of millions of people, even those in non-Christian lands, know the events and details of Jesus' life and death and Resurrection. The details are universal.

Luke begins this Christmas story with the mention of Caesar Augustus, nephew of Julius Caesar and one of the most powerful of the Caesars. It was said of him that he came to a Rome made of brick and left it a city of marble. He transformed not just Rome but the entire known world with his roads and his armies. At his funeral, his mourners comforted themselves with the belief that he was a god and therefore immortal. The man believed to be a god intercepted in time and space the God who became a man. And this mightiest man of his time decreed that a census was to be taken, which forced Joseph and Mary to travel to Bethlehem.

You might ask, "Who determines history—the Caesars, the kings, and the presidents?" In faith we believe that God is not only the Ruler of all things, but even the Ruler of human history and that many unwittingly serve Him. Bethlehem is a Hebrew word meaning "house of bread." Micah predicted that the Savior who said to us, "I am the bread of life, and he that eats of Me shall never die," would be born in Bethlehem, the House of Bread. Most of us have seen countless Sunday school pageants portraying these events of Jesus' birth, and invariably the innkeeper is cast as something of a villain. But let's not be hard on the innkeeper. He represents most of us. He is not a bad man, but a busy man.

We can identify with that. In the season when we celebrate this birth we get so busy with Christmas cards and presents, with year-end internal revenue matters, with shopping and cooking, that there is no room in our lives for the most important guest of all. Like the innkeeper, we are not villains; we're just preoccupied and harried.

Have you ever looked for lodging in some strange city and found only "no vacancy" signs? A few years ago my wife and I went to Atlanta for a conference, and the hotel in which we thought we were registered wouldn't take us. They told us repeatedly, "Sorry, we're filled." We were with a friend who overheard all this and offered to help. Approaching the desk clerk, he said that he was with a certain well-known firm and that he wanted a room for some friends. Somehow, one was found. Our friend explained, "There's always room if you belong to the right company." Well, Mary and Joseph did not have any right connections. There was no room. The innkeeper was unaware that these were very special people and that the most earthshaking event in history was to take place on his property. And so Mary gave birth to her son Jesus in the stable of the inn.

A birth is an all-time great adventure, whoever it is—the Messiah's birth, your birth, the birth of one of your children, a birth you're expecting even now as you feel life stirring inside of you. Life is the great mystery and God alone is the Giver of that life.

A THREEFOLD PEACE

8 Now there were in the same country shepherds living out in the fields, keeping watch over their flock by night. 9 And behold, an angel of the Lord stood before them, and the glory of the Lord shone around them, and they were greatly afraid. 10 Then the angel said to them, "Do not be afraid, for behold, I bring you good tidings of great joy which will be to all people. 11 For there is born to you this day in the city of David a Savior, who is Christ the Lord. 12 And this will be the sign to you: You will find a Babe wrapped in swaddling cloths, lying in a manger."

13 And suddenly there was with the angel a multitude of the heavenly host praising God and saying:

14"Glory to God in the highest,
And on earth peace, goodwill toward men!"

15 So it was, when the angels had gone away from them into heaven, that the shepherds said to one another, "Let us now go to Bethlehem and see this thing that has come to pass, which the Lord has made known to us." 16 And they came with haste and found Mary and Joseph, and the Babe lying in a manger. 17 Now when they had seen Him, they made widely known the saying which was told them concerning this Child. 18 And all those who heard it marveled at those things which were told them by the shepherds. 19 But Mary kept all these things and pondered them in her heart. 20 Then the shepherds returned, glorifying and praising God for all the things that they had heard and seen, as it was told them.

—Luke 2:8–20

Through the angel, God tells the shepherds the meaning of this most significant event in cosmic history. The meaning is peace; Jesus' birth is to bring peace, *shalom,* blessedness, fullness. This is the message from the angels to the shepherds and through them to us. Christ's coming means peace. Not the abolition of war necessarily, but a different kind of peace. Jews in Israel still greet each other by saying *"Shalom"* ("peace"). You can wish nothing better for anyone than *shalom,* blessedness, fullness.

However, this peace the angels speak of is not for everyone. The Greek word used here for "all people" is *laos,* from which comes the word "laity." The laity are not second-class Christians (with clergy being first-class). The *laos* are all the people of God. *Laos* was the word used to describe the Israelites, God's special people. We who are the new Israel are the *laos*. The best translation the Greek scholars have come up with for this message of peace is: "Peace among men [and certainly women as well] who are the recipients of God's good pleasure." If you are able to receive what God wants to give, the message of peace is for you. Would that it were for all. It is available for all, and when and if we receive what God wants to give us, we have peace.

The angel told the shepherds this peace was to come by a Savior who is Christ the Lord. The Babe they found was to be named Jesus, a common name in that time meaning "The Lord Is Salvation." (Jesus is a very common name even today in Latin American countries.) The angel used three names to identify the one who would bring this peace. First was "Savior," a Hebrew word meaning rescuer; then "Christ," a Greek word for "the anointed one, the chosen one." The third was a word used by Greek-speaking Hebrews to refer to God Himself. So Jesus was to be the Rescuer, the Anointed One, God Himself, and the Bearer of this peace.

The angels predicted this peace will come when we give glory to God in the highest. The peace does not come when the arms race ends. Peace will not come with arms limitations treaties. Peace does not come when a general glow of good will wells up and we all feel magnanimous about our neighbors. The angels give us the precondition for peace—that we give glory to God in the highest. That has nothing to do with whether or not we win the arms race.

The tragedy is that we have made war glorious and peace dull and uninteresting. I can remember watching TV on July 4, 1976, our nation's two-hundredth birthday. Arthur Fiedler conducted the Boston Pops Orchestra in a stirring program of patriotic songs and marches climaxed with a fireworks finale. When John Philip Sousa's "Stars and Stripes Forever" was played, didn't you want to march off into battle someplace? War is so exciting. Even as a child in Sunday school, my favorite hymn was "Onward, Christian Soldiers." Fortunately, we don't often sing that hymn any more. But we have glamorized war and all its pursuits and have missed the excitement of the ultimate cause which is peace. It is a gift only God can give us, and it is the one thing for which our hearts yearn.

How surprising that this profound message of peace was entrusted to shepherds. They were a despised class of people, outcasts from all respectable society. Their honesty and integrity was so questionable that they were not even allowed to testify in a court of law in those days. Now these particular shepherds were probably pious Jews, but they were a part of an outcast class through whom God chose to reveal the meaning of Christ's birth.

There is an old saying that "war is too important to be left to the generals." I suggest peace is too important to be left to the diplomats. The professionals have messed it up again and again. In giving this message to the shepherds God bypassed the professional peacemakers. He gave the message and its interpretation to amateurs. We need amateur peacemakers. The great diplomats and ambassadors of two thousand years ago, the councils that met and the peace treaties that were signed are mostly forgotten. But the world still reverberates with the peacemaking message of a group of amateur preachers and peacemakers like the apostle Paul and Luke himself.

I counseled a young woman recently who was in training to go and live in Russia. Her goal is to become a peacemaker in that nation. I confess that at first I thought that was a pretty far-fetched idea. But God has used a lot of people with crazy ideas over the centuries. A retired florist and his wife from our congregation on a holiday in Africa met a tribe of Masai, ancient nomadic warriors of Africa. God gave Denny and Jeanne Grindall in that one meeting such a concern for those Africans that they have spent six months a year for the last twelve years living with them, teaching them to grow crops, to fish, and to settle down peacefully in a village. These two lay people are a force for peace in one village in Africa.

Jesus is called the Reconciler. In reconciliation, that which is broken comes together. The devil is the father of division. I heard about two little first-grade girls who left Sunday school one Sunday morning discussing theological matters. "Do you believe that business about the devil?" asked one. "Of course not," said her friend. "I think it's like Santa Claus. It's really your father." Whether or not you believe in a personal devil, there is an evil force at work in the world dividing families, neighbors, nations.

The lesson God has for us here is that we need to make peace, first of all, with God. That's where peace begins. We may be running because we are afraid of God. "Fear not," the angel says. We need only stand still and let Him catch us. Francis Thompson's wonderful poem portrays Him as the Hound of Heaven. We may simply be caught up in our own busyness as the innkeeper was.

God has dealt with our sin and His grace is sufficient. We can come home. We belong to Him. Whatever we have done, we can come home and be reconciled.

The next step is to make peace with our neighbor. We need reconciliation between the haves and the have-nots in our cities and in our land. America is a nation of haves like no other nation. How do we begin to be peacemakers with all the have-not nations? We are called to reconciliation in families, between husbands and wives, between parents and children. We are called to effect political reconciliation between right and left, radical and conservative, the minority and the majority, between pacifists and those who defend the arms race.

Finally, we need to find the inner peace that comes from being in harmony with ourselves. No longer are we like the demoniac who said, "My name is Legion," because so many different selves possessed him. Jesus brought integration to a man who was described as "beside himself," and that man became one person. One dimension of peace is that head and heart and all our conflicting emotions come together.

That last verse of our Scripture says that after the shepherds had seen such wondrous things they went back to the commonplace. That's true for us each year at Christmas as we celebrate these events. Where will we be when the excitement and fun are over? How do these events change the lives we lead back at our jobs, our homes, our schools? If we believe the message of the angels we go back to the ordinary as peacemakers. We begin to bear the message out and become peacemakers.

Joseph Bayly has written a wonderful poem about the meaning of Christmas.

> Praise God for Christmas.
> Praise him for the Incarnation, for the Word
>   made Flesh.
> I will not sing of shepherds watching flocks on
>   frosty nights, or angel choristers
> I will not sing of a stable bare in Bethlehem, or
>   lowing oxen, wise men trailing star with
>   gold, frankincense and myrrh.
> Tonight I will sing praise to the Father who
>   stood on heaven's threshold and said
>   farewell to his Son as he stepped across the
>   stars to Bethlehem and Jerusalem.

And I will sing praise to the infinite, eternal
    Son, who became most finite, a baby who
    would one day be executed for my crime.
Praise him in the heavens, praise him in the
    stable, praise him in my heart.*

* Used by kind permission of the author.

21 And when eight days were completed for the circumcision of the Child, His name was called JESUS, the name given by the angel before He was conceived in the womb.

22 Now when the days of her purification according to the law of Moses were completed, they brought Him to Jerusalem to present Him to the Lord 23 (as it is written in the law of the Lord, *"Every male who opens the womb shall be called holy to the LORD"*), 24 and to offer a sacrifice according to what is said in the law of the Lord, *"A pair of turtledoves or two young pigeons."*

25 And behold, there was a man in Jerusalem whose name was Simeon, and this man was just and devout, waiting for the Consolation of Israel, and the Holy Spirit was upon him. 26 And it had been revealed to him by the Holy Spirit that he would not see death before he had seen the Lord's Christ. 27 So he came by the Spirit into the temple. And when the parents brought in the Child Jesus, to do for Him according to the custom of the law, 28 he took Him up in his arms and blessed God and said:

29"Lord, now You are letting Your servant depart in peace,
According to Your word;
30For my eyes have seen Your salvation
31Which You have prepared before the face of all peoples,
32A light to bring revelation to the Gentiles,
And the glory of Your people Israel."

33 And Joseph and His mother marveled at those things which were spoken of Him. 34 Then Simeon blessed them, and said to Mary His mother, "Behold, this Child is destined for the fall and rising of many in Israel, and for a sign which will be spoken against 35 (yes, a sword will pierce through your own soul also), that the thoughts of many hearts may be revealed."

36 Now there was one, Anna, a prophetess, the daughter of Phanuel, of the tribe of Asher. She was of a great age, and had lived with a husband seven years from her virginity; 37 and this woman was a widow of about eighty-four years,

who did not depart from the temple, but served God with fastings and prayers night and day. [38] And coming in that instant she gave thanks to the Lord, and spoke of Him to all those who looked for redemption in Jerusalem.

—Luke 2:21–38

As we move on from the Christmas story, the shepherds have gone back to their sheep and Joseph and Mary back to Nazareth. We can imagine Joseph putting up with irate customers in the carpenter shop while Mary was washing diapers. The glamour is gone and life is back to normal. We pick up Luke's narrative with Mary and Joseph going through the ritual activities, taking their baby to the temple in Jerusalem to offer a sacrifice. Mary and Joseph were proceeding with all the usual Jewish customs in connection with this most unusual infant.

In the temple they met two Jewish prophets, Simeon and Anna. The Holy Spirit was upon Simeon, and he recognized this baby and His importance for both Israel and the Gentiles. No angels appeared this time as they did to Zacharias, to Mary, and to the shepherds. This revelation came through a faithful believer, just and devout, who was a prophet through the power of the Holy Spirit.

Actually, what Simeon said was not exactly a prophecy. In the Greek, his words give the image of a servant who has been instructed by his master to stay at his post until a certain visitor arrives. Simeon had been watching all night and was sleepy. When the visitor finally came in the early hours of the morning, he said, "Master, it's happened. I have announced the coming of the one you're waiting for. Now I can go to sleep." Having seen the consolation of Israel, Simeon was telling God that he was ready to die in peace.

I'm sure this encounter astounded Mary and Joseph, but they had a further sign from God in the person of Anna. By any estimate, she was at least a hundred and three years old. At that time, thirteen was the minimal age to marry, and when we add all the other figures given us by Luke, we find that Anna must have been a very old lady indeed. This old woman was in the temple night and day. She probably lived in a little house nearby or even on the premises. Whenever the church opened for worship, she was there. Do you know anyone like that? We probably consider such people fanatics. If you've visited the great cathedrals of Europe, you've seen any number of women in the tradition of Anna—

nondescript, dressed in black, kneeling devoutly and murmuring endless prayers. The message Luke gives us is that we had best not dismiss such people lightly. They may have a special understanding of God's plan and purpose. We assume from Luke's account that Anna's testimony about the baby Jesus was honored. At one hundred and three she was an effective witness.

Part of Simeon's prophecy must have been a great shock to Mary and Joseph. For thousands of years, the Jews had expected a Messiah who would deliver Israel. No one expected the Messiah to be for all people. Simeon said that this light, this salvation, was not just for the Jews. It is for all. Then, paradoxically, he added that *not* all will be blessed but many in Israel will fall because of Jesus. Simeon was a true and accurate prophet, and I think we have a hard time knowing what to make of prophets then or now. There have always been false prophets, as well as true ones.

I read about the arrest of three sisters in Lansing, Michigan. These young women had removed their clothes, smeared themselves with mustard and were riding around in a stolen van. The police tried to determine the motive for this bizarre crime. It seems they were reading the Bible when the Holy Spirit seemed to speak to them. They discarded their clothes, having read that in the Garden of Eden Adam and Eve were naked. They read elsewhere the passage that likens faith to a grain of mustard seed, and so they lathered on mustard. The stolen van seems to have had no biblical explanation. They claimed they were under the compulsion of the Holy Spirit. We all know people around us who claim that the Holy Spirit is directing them. There are many warnings in the Bible about testing the spirits.

Simeon and Anna were true prophets. They were not prophets in the sense of future telling or fortune telling. Prophecy is forthtelling. You speak forth for God to a person or a nation about that person's or that nation's unrighteousness and about those things they might do to be faithful and obedient. The true prophet speaks to us of our sins, our false values and our unloving behavior. A friend of mine sent me the following poem written by an anonymous prophet:

> I was hungry and you formed a humanities club and discussed
>   my hunger,
> Thank you.
> I was imprisoned and you crept off quietly to your chapel in
>   the cellar and prayed for my release.

I was naked and in your mind you debated the morality of
my appearance.
I was sick and you knelt and thanked God for your health.
I was homeless and you preached to me of a spiritual shelter
of the love of God.
I was lonely and you left me alone to pray for me.
You seemed so holy, so close to God, but I'm still very hun-
gry and lonely and cold.

The prophets usually have had hard words for us, words we prefer to think are meant for someone else. I heard about a boy celebrating his birthday. Among his presents was the gift of a dollar
bill. He immediately began to make plans to invest in an ice cream
sundae with all the trimmings. The party guests were a somewhat
pious group, and someone suggested that he give part of the dollar to the poor. "I thought of that," admitted the birthday boy,
"but I think I'll give it to the ice cream man instead and let him
give it to the poor." A lot of us are like that. We are trusting someone else to follow the admonitions of the prophets.

I think one of the most important lessons in this particular
Scripture is that we must live in hope. Simeon and Anna lived in
hope. Actually, all of us are living in hope, although it may be a false
hope. On the national scene, both the arms race group and the pacifists may have false hopes for peace. One group believes that peace
will come if we are strong enough to police the whole world. Others
are convinced we will have peace only when we seriously pursue
disarmament. I consider both of those hopes false.

As a nation, our false hopes have misled us at many crucial
times. Those of us who lived through World War II recall all the
attempts to appease Hitler. As a result, his power grew and millions
died on the battlefields and in concentration camps. Pacifism
doesn't work in the face of evil and aggression. If we are hoping in
the might of our arms, we need only look at the events in Iran in
1979 for an important lesson. Iran was one of the strongest nations
in the world militarily, but the Shah's mighty regime was ousted
through a religious revolution.

If we think that we as a nation are trusting in God, the *Ladies'
Home Journal* has unsettling news for us. The September 1981
issue of the magazine conducted a poll in which they asked readers to answer the question, "In whom do you trust?" The winner,
with 40 percent of the vote, was Walter Cronkite. Pope John Paul

came in third with 26 percent of the vote. Billy Graham got 6 percent, 3 percent more than God.

Simeon prophesied suffering for Mary. To begin with, we learn how poor she and Joseph were because they have brought two turtle doves to sacrifice for the ritual of cleansing, whereas the usual sacrifice was a lamb. The mother of the Lamb of God who takes away the sin of the world could not afford a lamb. And while she and Joseph were sacrificing their turtle doves, Simeon addressed her directly, warning her that a sword would pierce her soul. I wonder if she remembered at that moment the angel's greeting, "Blessed are you among women." She was to suffer poverty and pain and yet she was most blessed among women. Poverty is a relative thing. Mary and Joseph had nothing, but they had everything. They had great joy along with pain and sorrow, and this is what life is for most of us. The angel spoke only of joy, but life for all of us is bittersweet. Mary was to have a great deal of pain, just as Simeon predicted.

Joseph was an old man when he and Mary were married, and he did not live long enough to endure the suffering. He had only blessings. But Mary was to see Joseph die, her son crucified, and many of his disciples persecuted and martyred.

Viktor Frankl tells about a patient, a medical doctor, who was inconsolable because of his wife's death. He could not stop grieving. After many sessions, Frankl had the wisdom to say, "Doctor, what if you had died and your wife had lived?" "Oh," he said, "she would have been decimated. She was entirely dependent on me." "Then, don't you see," explained Frankl, "your grief is the price you must pay for sparing her such suffering." His patient found meaning in his suffering. Those of us who live long and love deeply ultimately will suffer, whether we find meaning in it or not. If you love the world enough it will break your heart.

Simeon, the prophet, discerned the present. Standing in the midst of the temple, the most splendid building imaginable, resplendent with gold and marble and alabaster, Simeon predicted that this baby would divide the people who built and loved that very temple. He saw the ultimate rift between Jesus and the religious Jews, because Jesus did and does come to divide. He comes to do a new thing in our lives, and the traditionalists, those who support the past, who insist on maintaining business as usual, understand why this troublemaker must be done away with.

True prophets, then and now, are the hope of the world. You and I need to be prophets like Simeon and Anna, not consumed with the ordinary and temporal, but caught up in the ultimate issues. I confess I hope for the glory of Israel, just as Simeon did. The glory of the new Israel is one church, solely committed to Jesus Christ, serving the world in all of its needs. I live in the hope that I will, in my lifetime, see the glory of Israel in and through the church.

Years ago in England, I saw a tombstone of an old Cavalier soldier who had lost his life and property in the battle for the royalist cause. The epitaph was:

> He served King Charles with a constant, dangerous and expensive loyalty.

You and I are called to serve the Prince of Peace with this same constant, dangerous, and expensive loyalty.

CHAPTER SEVEN—TRIANGULAR LIVING
LUKE 2:39–52

³⁹ So when they had performed all things according to the law of the Lord, they returned to Galilee, to their *own* city, Nazareth. ⁴⁰ And the Child grew and became strong in spirit, filled with wisdom; and the grace of God was upon Him.

⁴¹ His parents went to Jerusalem every year at the Feast of the Passover. ⁴² And when He was twelve years old, they went up to Jerusalem according to the custom of the feast. ⁴³ When they had finished the days, as they returned, the Boy Jesus lingered behind in Jerusalem. And Joseph and His mother did not know *it;* ⁴⁴ but supposing Him to have been in the company, they went a day's journey, and sought Him among *their* relatives and acquaintances. ⁴⁵ So when they did not find Him, they returned to Jerusalem, seeking Him. ⁴⁶ Now so it was *that* after three days they found Him in the temple, sitting in the midst of the teachers, both listening to them and asking them questions. ⁴⁷ And all who heard Him were astonished at His understanding and answers. ⁴⁸ So when they saw Him, they were amazed; and His mother said to Him, "Son, why have You done this to us? Look, Your father and I have sought You anxiously."

⁴⁹ And He said to them, "Why did you seek Me? Did you not know that I must be about My Father's business?" ⁵⁰ But they did not understand the statement which He spoke to them.

⁵¹ Then He went down with them and came to Nazareth, and was subject to them, but His mother kept all these things in her heart. ⁵² And Jesus increased in wisdom and stature, and in favor with God and men.

—Luke 2:39–52

On our first Christmas in Seattle our three children, plus Virginia, our new daughter-in-law, came from Florida to be with us. It was interesting to see how Virginia seemed to hang on every word as we regaled her with stories about her bridegroom's boyhood. She was learning the legends of his youth. Perhaps you have had that experience. You brought your mate home and your parents couldn't wait to relate all the cute things you did and said from babyhood on.

Of the Gospel writers, only Luke gives us any report of Jesus' childhood. We are fortunate that, as a clinician and observer of life, he has a sense of the importance of such stories. Someone has said that Jesus' childhood is like a walled garden, the inside of which no one has seen. Luke has plucked one flower from inside that garden and that's what we have here.

Out of all the things Luke must have heard from Mary, he has chosen this one incident, perhaps because it reveals so much about the boy Jesus. After the experience in the temple in Jerusalem, Mary and Joseph returned to Nazareth with the baby. We have no details of the next twelve years in Nazareth. Incidentally, Nazarenes are not to be confused with Nazarites. John the Baptist belonged to the Nazarite sect, a very pious, ascetic group who had strict dietary rules and did not cut their hair. Jesus was a Nazarene, not a Nazarite. He lived in Nazareth, a very inauspicious place to live. It's an area we might refer to as "across the tracks." Palestine itself was a despised place and the Son of God came from a lowly village in this despised area. Years later, Nathanael, when asked to meet Jesus, was to make the disparaging remark, "Can any good thing come out of Nazareth?" (John 1:46).

The law required every male Jew to attend three annual festivals in Jerusalem each year. With Jews scattered in many far places throughout the Roman Empire, most went only once a year. The women were not required to go, but they often did. The Feast of the Passover, the occasion of this particular trip, is a seven-day event celebrating the deliverance from Egypt. It seems natural that whole families would share this week-long festivity. Jesus was twelve years old. It was the year before His bar mitzvah. Somehow we never think of Jesus as having a bar mitzvah, but He must have had one. In a year He was to become an adult Jewish male, responsible for Himself and for all of Israel.

I think for those of us who travel in little nuclear families, four or five in a single car, it's hard to understand how Joseph and Mary could lose their son. But the Jews of that time lived in extended families, and whole caravans of relatives and friends traveled together. The danger from robbers was lessened and fellowship was heightened. Mary and Joseph would be in the Nazarene or Galilean caravan. They may have joined caravans from neighboring towns to form a great company moving across the hills and deserts to and from Jerusalem.

Just as in covenant theology, the children belonged to every-body. When a child is baptized in the reformed tradition, all the church members take the vows. They are the godparents. Every child who is baptized within the congregation belongs not just to his or her blood parents but to the family of God. In Nazareth, families lived out this belief in their everyday lives.

Usually the women and young children traveled at the front of the caravan and the men and boys in the rear. We can imagine Joseph saying on that return trip, "Jesus must be with His mother," while His mother assumed He was back with the men. It was probably not until they made camp at night that they realized He was missing. The text gives us the impression that they searched for Him for three days. Actually, it seems more logical to assume it took one day for the journey out from Jerusalem, one day to go back, and one day to look for the boy in the city.

After all this searching and anxiety, Jesus' parents eventually found Him in the temple with the teachers. You may remember see-ing the Hoffman picture of the boy Jesus in the temple—a boy in white expounding to all these wise, old rabbis. That's not what the Scripture says. Jesus was not some precocious quiz-kid straightening out His elders. Luke tells us He was listening and asking questions. How appropriate. God is love and love is listening.

When Mary and Joseph found Him Mary rebuked Him, and said in effect, "Why have you done this? Your father and I have been frantic, looking for you everywhere." In Jesus' marvelous answer He made a clear distinction between His heavenly and earthly father:

"Did you not know that I must be about My Father's business?" (v. 49). We might assume Jesus talked about two fathers because He had been told the odd circumstances of His birth; that Joseph wasn't really His father. I don't think that's the case. I'm sure that Jesus loved and honored Joseph, this man who gave Him His name and raised Him. He introduced here the concept of another Father who had an agenda for Him that might not always coincide with that of Joseph. "Did you not know that I must be about My *Father's* business?"

At age twelve we find Jesus for the first time introducing us to the concept of God as a father who is present, someone you can call "Abba," which means father or daddy. This was not the awe-some God of the rabbis and theologians, the Yahweh whom the Jews worshiped, served, and feared. Jesus was saying, God is like a daddy. If that's so, then we can talk to Him about anything. We can begin to relate to Him and He can give us direction. Jesus modeled for us here and throughout His ministry a new dimension of living.

I think there are only three dimensions in which it is possible for any of us to live our lives. There is, first of all, one-dimensional living: that is, self-centered living, where you are the center of things wherever you go. All kinds of people around us are living one-dimensionally. They are both good and bad, boring and charming. We need make no value judgement except to say that they are always center stage. Wherever they go, in the classroom, at home, on the job, they are the sun and the rest of us are seen as a kind of solar system revolving around them.

I'm sure you know at least a few people like this. They direct and organize the lives of their families and friends. They come in to a party and take over; they tell the jokes and suggest the games. They relate their latest exploits and, depending on their degree of charisma, are either tedious or delightful. It was said of Teddy Roosevelt that he had to be the bride at every wedding and the corpse at every funeral. I am sure he was a good man, but wherever he went—that bully man—he was the hero, and the surrounding company held the spears while he sang. He was the star of the opera.

Kurt Vonnegut, a contemporary science fiction writer whom I happen to enjoy greatly, talks in one of his books about Mythotherapy. It's the condition I've been describing, where you see yourself as the center of every event. Someone asks for details of a wedding you attended. You say, "Well, I sat about a third of the way back and I was in a draft. The service was long and the minister somewhat boring. The organist played one of my favorite numbers and the refreshments were really good." There is no sense that the bride might have been at the center of the wedding. These one-dimensional types tell you about their grand tour of Europe in the same way. You hear about all the faulty plumbing, the meals they ate and how much they cost. I've had people like that tell me all about World War II. It was terrible. They couldn't get butter or sugar or tires for the car. As one who spent part of the war in a foxhole, I find this description interesting, to say the least.

The great disasters are seen in terms of personal inconvenience. An earthquake with three thousand dead is translated into "I had to move out of my hotel and I had no hot meals." In one-dimensional living, the people and events around you are so much window-dressing. I heard about a young man who went into a greeting card store and asked for a very sentimental and special valentine. The salesgirl, after much looking, found a lovely one that said, "To the only girl I have ever loved." "That's wonderful," said the customer. "I'll take four." He had at least four planets revolving around his sun.

Next we move up to a much more realistic view of life—two-dimensional living. You are aware of the people around you. They motivate you and you motivate them. Two-dimensional living is political living. A politician is a man who says he agrees with you in principle. Those who agree with you in principle are trying to break it to you gently that you are wrong. Two-dimensional living is a trade-off. It's the unspoken covenant between parent and child, husband and wife, employee and boss. The "I will if you will" of life. You are doing your part and the other had better do his or her part. I laugh at your joke and you are obliged to laugh at mine. Two-dimensional marriage has a lot of built-in peril. Perhaps one party is perceived as not doing his or her part. Perhaps he/she doesn't even understand what that part is.

A lot of us who are parents tend to live two-dimensional lives with our children. We patronize them. We expect certain behavior and withhold our approval if we don't get it. We know what is best. "Wear your sweater today; it's cold." "Put your rubbers on, it's raining." I heard a definition of a parent a while back that applies here. "A parent is a person who has to give a lecture on nutritional values to a kid who has reached six-foot-six by eating potato chips." After our kids reach a certain age they know as much about nutrition and rubbers and sweaters and driving carefully as we do. If they're uninformed, it's because they choose to be.

But we make political deals with our children. We say, "You won't get your allowance this week because you failed us." I think this is a little like what Jesus' parents did in this instance. Mary was shaming her son for causing them concern, and the unspoken message we could add is, "—after all we've done for you."

But now we come to three-dimensional living, the kind that Jesus introduced here in this scene in the temple with His parents. He is not self-centered and He is beyond living politically. He submitted to his parents and their wishes and he returned home with them. He was a dutiful son. But in this case he said, "There is a third person in the relationship." Jesus exemplifies three-dimensional living, or we might call it triangular living.

Imagine that you and every person you meet are both on the rim of a circle and the hub of that circle is God Himself. Every relationship, then, is three-dimensional when we are aware that God is at the hub of every relationship. We go beyond two-dimensional or political living to affirming that God as our father is a part of every encounter and situation. That third person is God Himself. In the relationship we no longer need to take responsibility for the other person's behavior or performance. Instead we trust that situation to the third person in the triangle. We say, "Father, here's my boss, or my friend, my child, or my parent." When we are aware of God at work in the other person's life, we can stop trying to manipulate and coerce him or her. Like the gal who was asked by her coworker, "Did you wake up grouchy this morning?" "No," she said, "I just let him sleep in." She no longer had to run her husband's life. If he wanted to sleep in, let him. If she's living triangularly she can ask God to wake that guy up at the right time and she can breeze off to the office.

You may be in a touchy situation at work, perhaps with your boss. Somebody sent me a cartoon a while ago picturing two men in an office. The one sitting behind a huge desk smoking a big cigar is saying to the other, "In His mysterious way God has given each of us different talents, Ridgeway. It just so happens that mine is intimidating people." Perhaps you work with someone like that. The third person in the triangle can give you a sense of freedom and a strategy for dealing with that kind of a problem. If you feel betrayed by someone (and we've all been both betrayers and betrayed), even the people who seem out to get you can somehow serve God's ends when you move into triangular living.

I heard a wonderful story from a member of our congregation about living three-dimensionally in the midst of disaster. When Ruth was seven years old, she lived in a small town in North Dakota. She went to a one-room schoolhouse and one winter's day a typical North Dakota blizzard hit. It was forty degrees below zero. One by one, parents arrived to escort their children home safely in this blinding storm. Soon only she and the teacher remained. It looked as if they were to be stranded all night.

The teacher, though obviously worried, tried to reassure her young charge. "Ruth, I have one bucket of coal and one sandwich. I hope it will get us through the night." Ruth answered firmly, "Don't worry. My father will come for us." Since so many hours had elapsed, the teacher was skeptical. "How do you know your father will come for us?" she asked. Pointing upward, Ruth explained, "My Father up there will tell my other father about us and he will come. My mother taught me that. When I'm in trouble, I can ask my heavenly Father for help and He will send it." The teacher was unconvinced, but sure enough, as darkness fell, Ruth's father arrived to rescue them. He tied the two of them behind him with ropes, and they started off through the blizzard, faces wrapped against the deadly cold. Eventually they reached the safety of home. Ruth had an unforgettable lesson in triangular living.

Our Father up above cares about us in all the situations of life. To be a new being in Christ means we begin to live triangularly in more and more situations.

In the last verse in our Scripture, we have the bottom line in all of this: *"And Jesus increased in wisdom and in stature, and in favor with God and men."* In the new life in Christ you and I find favor with God and man. If you find favor only with God or only with man, you miss something. The new being in Christ lives in a new dimension. All of life is triangular.

CHAPTER EIGHT—HOLY HORTICULTURE: ROOTS OR FRUITS

LUKE 3:1–20

3:1 Now in the fifteenth year of the reign of Tiberius Caesar, Pontius Pilate being governor of Judea, Herod being tetrarch of Galilee, his brother Philip tetrarch of Iturea and the region of Trachonitis, and Lysanias tetrarch of Abilene, 2 while Annas and Caiaphas were high priests, the word of God came to John the son of Zacharias in the wilderness. 3 And he went into all the region around the Jordan, preaching a baptism of repentance for the remission of sins, 4 as it is written in the book of the words of Isaiah the prophet, saying:
"The voice of one crying in the wilderness:
'Prepare the way of the LORD;
Make His paths straight.
5*Every valley shall be filled*
And every mountain and hill brought low;
The crooked places shall be made straight
And the rough ways smooth;
6*And* all flesh shall see the salvation of God.'"
7 Then he said to the multitudes that came out to be baptized by him, "Brood of vipers! Who warned you to flee from the wrath to come? 8 Therefore bear fruits worthy of repentance, and do not begin to say to yourselves, 'We have Abraham as our father.' For I say to you that God is able to raise up children to Abraham from these stones. 9 And even now the ax is laid to the root of the trees. Therefore every tree which does not bear good fruit is cut down and thrown into the fire."
10 So the people asked him, saying, "What shall we do then?"
11 He answered and said to them, "He who has two tunics, let him give to him who has none; and he who has food, let him do likewise."
12 Then tax collectors also came to be baptized, and said to him, "Teacher, what shall we do?"

13 And he said to them, "Collect no more than what is appointed for you."

14 Likewise the soldiers asked him, saying, "And what shall we do?"

So he said to them, "Do not intimidate anyone or accuse falsely, and be content with your wages."

15 Now as the people were in expectation, and all reasoned in their hearts about John, whether he was the Christ or not, 16 John answered, saying to all, "I indeed baptize you with water; but One mightier than I is coming, whose sandal strap I am not worthy to loose. He will baptize you with the Holy Spirit and fire. 17 His winnowing fan is in His hand, and He will thoroughly clean out His threshing floor, and gather the wheat into His barn; but the chaff He will burn with unquenchable fire."

18 And with many other exhortations he preached to the people. 19 But Herod the tetrarch, being rebuked by him concerning Herodias, his brother Philip's wife, and for all the evils which Herod had done, 20 also added this, above all, that he shut John up in prison.

—Luke 3:1–20

How do you handle your mail? On those days when you are overwhelmed by sheer quantity, I'm sure you occasionally take all the fourth-class junk mail and drop it right in the wastebasket. But I find that very hard to do. How would I ever know if I'd won the *Reader's Digest* Sweepstakes? And then we've all gotten those letters that say, "We have checked you out and you qualify as part of a very select group who will be receiving this letter." We feel flattered until we examine the envelope and find it marked "Occupant."

But how do we know when we have truly received something special and just for us in terms of spiritual messages? In this passage of Luke, John the Baptist's message does not sound unlike the one we hear on the street corners in every large city in the land. "This is the Word of the Lord. Repent and believe." How do you sort out your spiritual mail—the fourth class from the registered first-class air mail? How do you know which message is from God and has your name on it? Most of us ignore those people we hear from time to time on the street corners of great cities, while John the Baptist catches our attention. John is different, perhaps because in the words of the philosopher Marshall McLuhan, "The medium is the message." The message is not what is said. The message is wrapped in the personality delivering the message.

John was the message. John had such authority and authenticity that crowds came out to listen. That kind of popular appeal is a rare occurrence in any time and in any nation. Henry David Thoreau once said, cynically, "Nations have great men only in spite of themselves, like families. They direct all their efforts to not having them. And thus the great man must have in order to exist a force of attack greater than the force of resistance developed by millions of individuals." Society would seem to encourage mediocrity rather than greatness. Those who excel must be very gifted innately or else be special instruments of God.

I think John was an unusual attraction for several reasons. First of all, there had been no prophecy in Israel for about four hundred years, not since the prophet Micah. I am sure throughout this time there was no shortage of would-be prophets, but nobody listened. God had been silent for four hundred years in speaking to His people through an authentic prophet. But it was believed that prophecy would rise again when the Messiah was about to come. So, all Israel was waiting for one who might be that authentic prophet. John was such a prophet, and throngs came out to hear this one who might prove to be the harbinger of the Messiah.

Further, John was saying hard words, usually an indication of an authentic prophet. Somehow we know that those who speak for God do not offer us easy discipleship or cheap grace. Those things that are costly are ultimately the most worthwhile at any level. The Revolutionary War soldiers stayed at Valley Forge with no pay, no rations, and no chance of victory, because they believed in their cause. The Italian patriot Garibaldi called forth support by promising difficult conditions, long marches, no blankets, no food, no munitions. Jesus Himself kept warning those who heard Him that discipleship would be difficult; that while foxes had holes, He had no place to sleep.

In our church, we make membership difficult. Ten hours of classes are required plus a personal interview with the elders. The would-be member must turn in a pledge card promising not just financial support but also to work and pray and share the over-all ministry. Those who want to join in this pilgrim fellowship are promised no easy discipleship.

John demanded something of his hearers—repentance, change, belief, and works. Such demands honor others because one assumes they are capable of all this. Peter Drucker, one of the most highly

71

paid and brilliant management experts of our time, does seminars all over the land, primarily for business, but for the church as well. Drucker says, "Leadership is not magnetic personality. That can just as well be a glib tongue. It is not making friends and influencing people; that is flattery. Leadership is lifting a person's vision to higher sights, the raising of a person's performance to a higher standard, the building of a personality beyond its normal limitations." Drucker is describing John the Baptist's kind of leadership.

John came baptizing, and the idea of baptism was new for the Jews. Only the Gentiles, the outsiders who became Jews, were baptized. John was preaching that being born a Jew did not assure a right relationship with God; the Jews must be baptized just like the outsiders. Because of this unusual emphasis he was called John the Baptist.

John's essential message was simply that we be what we seem to be. If we want to seem godly, then we are to be godly, with no sham. He spelled out what that meant. He addressed himself in specifics to the ethics of the time: soldiers, don't intimidate and coerce; tax collectors, collect no more than is your due. He spoke of sharing with those in need. But this was not a new ethic. The rabbis had been saying all these things. But John was preaching that those ethics were to be a way of life. The crux of his message was, "God has told us what to do and be. Do it, and don't pretend to be something you're not."

But John raised another issue having to do with the old question of faith versus works. It is the same issue which touched off the reformation. Our faith is rooted in the mighty acts of God: the Incarnation, Atonement, Resurrection, His presence with us in the person of the Holy Spirit. But if those roots are genuine, they will bear fruits of goodness, generosity, compassion, and justice. John was calling for a faith rooted in repentance and belief which would bear fruit in the conduct of ordinary affairs. I am sure he was not urging his hearers to join holy orders and become Nazarites. There was no need for more long-haired prophets praying all day and eating grasshoppers. He was asking his hearers to return to their everyday lives, to where they had been planted, and to begin to bear fruit.

One Sunday I was to preach on this topic of "Holy Horticulture," and, hearing the title, a well-known botanist in our church was intrigued. He asked what I planned to say. I said, "I'm going to talk about you. If somebody hired you to plant a garden, would you ask them if they wanted all roots or all fruits? The faith versus works issue is that kind of a crazy question." God is engaged in holy horticulture. We are His creatures and He wants us to be whole people with strong roots and healthy fruits.

One of the tragedies of my generation was the gulf between the roots and fruits people. One group talked only about roots, the Bible, commitment, Jesus, prayer. They had little social concern and little involvement with the pain of the world around them. Those were the evangelicals. In the other camp were the liberals, who said doctrine and personal piety were incidental to a commitment to the cause of the disadvantaged and social justice. Those were and are the "fruits" camp. Now if all you have is roots with nothing visibly flowering from them, you have missed the point. But the other emphasis is cut-flower Christianity, and when the heat is on, those cut flowers are going to wilt. Right now, the liberal part of the Christian church seems to be shrinking. Without the great causes of the sixties and seventies, there seems no impetus to get out and do and care. John's message, the eternal message, is that we do not have the luxury of such a choice.

The people we honor, past or present—the St. Francises; the Schweitzers; Father Damien, the Roman Catholic priest in the leper colony in Molokai, Hawaii—these are people with deep roots who bore fruits of generosity, caring, and sacrifice. In the past one hundred years or more, Dwight Moody and Charles Finney, two great evangelists, called thousands to repentance and new life in Christ. But each of these famous preachers also started a school for the poor; Finney in Oberlin and Moody in Northfield, Massachusetts. They had a concern for deprived children who would otherwise get no education.

John's words to the Pharisees were scathing: *"Brood of vipers! Who warned you to flee?"* (v. 7). We have the image of a grass fire, and, as the fire spread across the field, all kinds of snakes began to slither in the other direction, away from the smoke and flames. John was saying, "You family of snakes! What are you doing here? Who warned you about the fire?" Apparently they came to hear and to be baptized and yet John did not welcome them. They did not come because they wanted to change but because they were fearful that John might be speaking the truth. And so—just in case—they came out to listen and to be baptized. They wanted to cover all the bases.

I'm reminded of an old army buddy of mine. All through combat he wore three different medals strung around his neck—a Protestant cross, a Catholic saint's medal, and a Jewish star of

cut flower frint

David. Asked about all of these, he would say, "I'm taking no chances." Well, that was the strategy of the Pharisees. They were taking no chances. John just might be right. Thomas Carlyle said of the poet Samuel Coleridge, "He has a look of anxious impudence in his eyes." I think that may be what John the Baptist perceived in these men, a look of anxious impudence. They came to hear and be baptized, but they had no intention of repenting.

There is a wonderful story about two men out fishing on a Wednesday evening somewhere up in the mountains. "You know, I feel guilty being here on prayer meeting night," confessed one. "Our pastor is trying so hard to get people to attend and, as deacons, we probably ought to be there tonight." His friend said, "I couldn't be there, even if I was at home. My wife is sick." Like the Pharisees, he was guilty, but not guilty enough to change. As the great Scottish preacher James Stewart has said, "It is very much easier to spend a dozen hours discussing religion than one half hour obeying God."

If you practice holy horticulture, your faith is rooted in the living Word, in a commitment to God and His people, and that will produce a measurable harvest of fruits that can be discerned. You can't say you'd rather have only fruits because, after all, roots get diseased and need fertilizing. Or, you can't opt for only roots to avoid the bother of pruning and plucking. One of the great Scottish preachers of the past is George Morrison, pastor of a great congregation in Glasgow. He told of a dream he had one night in which he died and went to heaven. In his dream he was standing before St. Peter, who asked, "Who are you?" He said, "I'm Morrison." "Who?" repeated St. Peter. "George Morrison, the preacher." "No record of you here, I'm sorry," answered St. Peter. "It can't be!" protested Morrison. "For twenty-five years I filled a great sanctuary twice on Sunday morning and every Sunday night, where I'm told I preached with power and beauty and poetry and brought people to conviction and conversion." Again St. Peter said, "I'm sorry. No record of you. What did you say your whole name was?" "George Herbert Morrison." "Oh," said St. Peter, "I do have a notation here. It says, 'One night he sat up all night long with somebody who was dying." The point is that even the great preachers, theologians, Bible scholars, and evangelists had better occasionally be putting their faith to work in specific and costly ways.

John destroyed people's sense of false confidence. This is just what Martin Luther did, and it touched off the Reformation. Luther said

74

that the practice of buying indulgences would not assure one's salvation or guarantee one a place in heaven. His great turning-point text was "The just shall live by faith." It is not far from what John was saying—that to get right with God, you have to admit you're not right with God. That's a paradox. Once you are aware you're not right with God you can be right with God.

But the crux of John's message was Jesus, not repentance. He said, *"One mightier than I is coming, whose sandal strap I am not worthy to loose"* (v. 16). In those days the rabbis had disciples who performed all sorts of menial tasks for them, *except* the removing of their sandals. In the Middle East of John's time, sewers were unknown and the waste products of humans and animals filled the streets. It was unthinkable that anyone else would handle your sandals after a day spent walking about in such conditions. But John says that the One who is coming is so great that he is unfit to perform even this lowly task for Him.

John told how they could prepare for this One who was coming by quoting the prophet Isaiah. Every valley should be filled and every mountain leveled, which was done for a visiting king in those days. They improved the roads, filled in the ditches and smoothed the hills so the king wouldn't have to go down to the river bed and back up over the mountains. A more level highway provided the king with a more comfortable trip. John predicts that a great king is coming and they'd better begin to get their personal and corporate lives straightened up.

And yet we are not saved by our works, but by grace. When the thief on the cross repented, Jesus said, "Today shall you be with Me in Paradise." He was saved by faith. He had no good works to commend him. But suppose the thief's life had been spared five more years? I think we could then expect his life to bear some fruit. If you repent and believe in your last hour you don't need fruits. But if you are living the life of faith you are bearing fruit.

God, you see, as has often been pointed out, has no grandchildren. The Pharisees thought their salvation was sure because of Abraham. John pointed out that God can raise up children from the very stones. Abraham's descendants were not His only avenue. Faith is not inherited. It doesn't matter how faithful and devout your mother and father were. It doesn't matter if you are a righteous Jew, claiming Abraham as your father. God has only children, and those children bear fruit.

T. S. Eliot writes about having the choice of being destroyed by fire or by fire. We can be destroyed by the fire of selfishness and self-indulgence or consumed by the fire John speaks of—a passion for the One who loves us with a passion. Henry Drummond, a scientist who wrote *The Greatest Thing in the World,* said once to a group of college students, "Gentlemen, I beseech you to seek the Kingdom of God first or not at all. I promise you a miserable time if you seek it second."

With John's ministry, the curtain was about to go up on the greatest drama that creation has ever witnessed, Jesus' three-year ministry. John tells us our faith must bear fruit, but if we rely on those fruits on Judgment Day we will be disappointed. John points us to the One who alone gives us the assurance of salvation, Jesus Christ.

21 When all the people were baptized, it came to pass that Jesus also was baptized; and while He prayed, the heaven was opened. 22 And the Holy Spirit descended in bodily form like a dove upon Him, and a voice came from heaven which said, "You are My beloved Son; in You I am well pleased."

23 Now Jesus Himself began His ministry at about thirty years of age, being (as was supposed) the son of Joseph, the son of Heli, 24 the son of Matthat, the son of Levi, the son of Melchi, the son of Janna, the son of Joseph, 25 the son of Mattathiah, the son of Amos, the son of Nahum, the son of Esli, the son of Naggai, 26 the son of Maath, the son of Mattathiah, the son of Semei, the son of Joseph, the son of Judah, 27 the son of Joannas, the son of Rhesa, the son of Zerubbabel, the son of Shealtiel, the son of Neri, 28 the son of Melchi, the son of Addi, the son of Cosam, the son of Elmodam, the son of Er, 29 the son of Jose, the son of Eliezer, the son of Jorim, the son of Matthat, the son of Levi, 30 the son of Simeon, the son of Judah, the son of Joseph, the son of Jonan, the son of Eliakim, 31 the son of Melea, the son of Menan, the son of Mattathah, the son of Nathan, the son of David, 32 the son of Jesse, the son of Obed, the son of Boaz, the son of Salmon, the son of Nahshon, 33 the son of Amminadab, the son of Ram, the son of Hezron, the son of Perez, the son of Judah, 34 the son of Jacob, the son of Isaac, the son of Abraham, the son of Terah, the son of Nahor, 35 the son of Serug, the son of Reu, the son of Peleg, the son of Eber, the son of Shelah, 36 the son of Cainan, the son of Arphaxad, the son of Shem, the son of Noah, the son of Lamech, 37 the son of Methuselah, the son of Enoch, the son of Jared, the son of Mahalalel, the son of Cainan, 38 the son of Enosh, the son of Seth, the son of Adam, the son of God.

—Luke 3:21–38

Beginnings and endings are always poignant. Our lives are marked by those times when we move from one phase to another.

Birth and death are the ultimate passages but in between are baptisms, graduations, marriage, parenthood. Our lives are full of new beginnings. And the key question to ask at the end of one passage and the beginning of the next is, "Who am I now? I'm not the person that I was before. Who am I now in this new beginning?"

One of the most poignant stories in my own past is the story of my mother, who made a new beginning at age fourteen. Her mother died when she was born; her father remarried and produced eleven more children with his second wife. She was the only stepchild. By her own admission, she was a very stubborn girl who made life difficult for her stepmother. And so she was sent off, against her will, to an unknown relative in America. At fourteen, she arrived in a new country, penniless and unable to speak the language.

When she left Sweden her father gave her a Bible, one she treasured always and which I now have, and in it he wrote these two verses. The first is 3 John 4: "I have no greater joy than to know that my children walk in the truth." The other is from the Gospel of John, "And Jesus said, 'I am the way, the truth, and the life" (14:6). I can only imagine what was in my grandfather's heart as, under pressure from his new wife, he sent his first-born away, suspecting rightly never to see her again. I am sure he wanted to give her something tangible to help her know who she was—a child of God.

In Luke's narrative we find Jesus at the point of a new beginning. He has been a carpenter, a faithful son of Mary and Joseph, living obscurely in Nazareth. Here He is about to begin his Messiahship and perhaps is at the place where He was questioning the rightness of His direction. It was the time to ask the question, "Who am I as I begin this, the greatest work in the whole universe?"

Luke, with his special interest in Jesus' prayer life, tells us that Jesus was praying. We might wonder that Jesus prayed at all, He who was so attuned to the will of His Father. In our own prayer life, much of the time we are asking for particular answers or interceding for other people. But if you're like me, the purpose of your prayers is the same as that of Jesus: we want to keep in a relationship with our Father. I find myself talking to Him in the shower or when I'm shaving. I talk to Him as I'm riding along the bike trail, and if there's nobody nearby, I talk right out loud. I talk to Him driving down the freeway alone in my car. I talk to Him in my office. The most important gift that God has to give us is

Himself: a relationship in which we belong to Him and He is our Father. Prayer, though it includes intercession or specific petition, is basically a means of reestablishing the relationship. We find Jesus in this kind of prayer as the Scripture begins.

We might ask why Jesus came to be baptized by John. Baptism was the outward sign of repentance from sin and Jesus was sinless. I think His baptism is further assurance that He was like us in every way except for sin and that therefore He submitted to baptism at John's hands. At that point, the Holy Spirit in the shape of a dove came down from heaven, the physical expression of God's power and presence. Incidentally, while the dove is the symbol of the Holy Spirit for us now, it was not any recognizable symbol for the Jews at that time. It was a strange symbol. With this heavenly apparition, a voice was heard saying, *"You are My beloved Son."* Jesus was baptized in the same manner as any other convert, but God, through these supernatural happenings, indicated Jesus was unlike anyone else who has ever lived.

But Jesus, the incarnate God, though unlike any of us, is like all of us. His specialness is, of course, that He is God's only begotten Son. But, on a human level, each of us is like everybody else and like nobody else. There's not a human being in the world, in whatever condition, who is not somewhat like you and me in loves and loyalties, hopes and fears. And yet God confirms in us, as He did with Jesus, that you are like nobody else that ever was. You are His special child.

Charles T. Leber, one of the great missionary leaders in the Presbyterian church, tells about being in Westphalia, Germany, at a clinic for very handicapped children. He arrived the day after a very wealthy businessman had visited, a man whom it was hoped would contribute money to the work. On his tour, he said to the doctor, "These are very pathetic children. What ratio of cures do you get? How many ever go back to a normal life?" "Well, about one in one hundred," was the reply. The businessman was surprised. "One in one hundred," he repeated. "It's not worth it." The doctor corrected him gently, "Yes, it is. If that one was your child it would be worth it." We are special to God. If you were the only person in the universe who responded, God would still consider the Incarnation, the Atonement, and the Resurrection worthwhile.

At His baptism, Jesus was given confirmation of His unique mission. We may or may not have had any such specific sign of our specialness. Blaise Pascal, the French scientist and Christian saint of two centuries ago, had such a sign. This man, who invented the

79

barometer and the adding machine and devised the first bus system in Paris, died at age thirty-three. After his death, a piece of paper was discovered which had been sewn in the lining of the jacket he always wore. It contained a description of an unusual night in his life when, as he was sitting in his room, he saw the fire of God come down. In the midst of this experience, he scrawled, "Fire, fire in the night; consuming me, all around, glory, wonder!" He never told anyone about that remarkable night. But he took that paper, with its incontestable message and sewed it in the lining of his jacket. In the years that followed, he could feel the crinkle of that paper and remember that mystical evening.

When I said yes to Jesus Christ as a young man in the Army, things happened to me that I have never shared with anybody. God demonstrably intervened in my life to let me know that the old was over and the new had begun. God wants to give most of us such signs.

I remember a friend in Connecticut who was being pressed by some friends at church who had gotten excited about the faith to make a new beginning with God. Her response was that she was too busy to become a serious Christian. She told them, "I have so many appointments, so many engagements to keep. I simply don't have time to make this kind of total commitment." To prove her point, she showed them her calendar and sure enough, the first clear day was seven weeks away. Half jokingly, she said, "I'll give Jesus that day. I can promise to do whatever He asks on that day. I have no other appointments." The day came, and, somewhat apprehensively, she said, "Jesus, I give you my life for today." That morning she was taken suddenly ill. The doctor came and proclaimed nothing seriously wrong. "Just stay in bed for several days," he said. "All you need is rest." The point came home. She said, "You know, I thought giving my life to Jesus would mean increasing my busy schedule. I discovered instead a God who cares about me, who knew I was too busy and forced me to slow down."

In verse 22 Jesus finds His unique identity. Luke doesn't tell us how many heard the voice. Perhaps only Jesus did and reported on it later. And then in that same verse we find the first foundations for the doctrine of the Trinity. The Father sends the Holy Spirit and says, "This is My Son." In one verse we find one God, three persons—Father, Son, and Holy Spirit.

Jesus' identity came from God, but His messianic role was confirmed by John the Baptist as He began a new phase of His earthly life. As you begin a new passage, people around you tell you who you are. One of the greatest sermons I ever heard was preached by Carlisle Marney, a Baptist preacher. He said that all of us are shaped by the people in our cellar and the people in our balcony. We learned about those cellar influences primarily from Freud, who said that we replay all the negative injunctions from early childhood and that these erode our self-confidence by reminding us of our weaknesses and failures. Through lengthy psychoanalysis we try to make peace with those negative forces, according to Freud.

But Marney's message was that all of us have people in our balcony as well; special people living or dead who are yelling down to encourage us and tell us who we really are. This group might include a parent or other relative, a special scout leader, a teacher, or a friend—someone who believed in us before we believed in ourselves and who said, "You can do it."

When Luke takes us through Jesus' genealogy, he is reminding us of all the people in Jesus' balcony. Luke begins the genealogy with Joseph, even though he has made it clear earlier that Joseph is not Jesus' real father. But Joseph was responsible for Jesus' psychogenetic inheritance. Psychogenetic inheritance, which is just recently being explored, emphasizes that we learn how to handle life from those with whom we live. They model certain behaviors for us, and from them we learn how to act and react, for better or worse. Even the shape of our bodies can be more psychogenetic than genetic. We are often fat or thin because of the eating habits of the people with whom we live. From our families we absorb a sense of hope or caring or the lack of either. Joseph taught Jesus how to be a faithful son, a man and a good Jew. Jesus could speak about God as a Father because he had a loving father who was a positive model.

As we read Jesus' genealogy, we are aware that all these marvelous heroes of Israel's history were His spiritual inheritance. They were His balcony people. As Christians we are the new Israel and therefore have all the great heroes of the faith in our balcony as well. Each of us has a psychogenetic inheritance from the faithful men and women of the Old and New Testaments. They are each giving us a special message, one that comes out of their pilgrimage with God. We can imagine Adam calling down to remind us when we are disobedient that God still loves and cares. Noah encourages us to follow our guidance and go against the crowd, even when they laugh at us as they did at him in the building of the ark. Abraham helps us to leave the safe and the familiar and to move out and trust God. We can take hope from Jacob, who got off to such a bad start in life and finally let God give him a new name. Esther models that women can get involved in the real world and make a difference.

The Bible says we are surrounded by a great cloud of witnesses. Let those special encouragers God is sending to you, now and in the past, tell you who you are. They believe in you.

CHAPTER TEN—THE UNHOLY TRINITY
LUKE 4:1–13

4:1 Then Jesus, being filled with the Holy Spirit, returned from the Jordan and was led by the Spirit into the wilderness, ² being tempted for forty days by the devil. And in those days He ate nothing, and afterward, when they had ended, He was hungry.

³ And the devil said to Him, "If You are the Son of God, command this stone to become bread."

⁴ But Jesus answered him, saying, "It is written, 'Man shall not live by bread alone, but by every word of God.'"

⁵ Then the devil, taking Him up on a high mountain, showed Him all the kingdoms of the world in a moment of time. ⁶ And the devil said to Him, "All this authority I will give You, and their glory; for this has been delivered to me, and I give it to whomever I wish. ⁷ Therefore, if You will worship before me, all will be Yours."

⁸ And Jesus answered and said to him, "Get behind Me, Satan! For it is written, 'You shall worship the LORD your God, and Him only you shall serve.'"

⁹ Then he brought Him to Jerusalem, set Him on the pinnacle of the temple, and said to Him, "If You are the Son of God, throw Yourself down from here. ¹⁰ For it is written:

'He shall give His angels charge over you,
To keep you,'

¹¹ and,

'In their hands they shall bear you up,
Lest you dash your foot against a stone.'"

¹² And Jesus answered and said to him, "It has been said, 'You shall not tempt the LORD your God.'"

¹³ Now when the devil had ended every temptation, he departed from Him until an opportune time.

—Luke 4:1–13

After Jesus' extraordinary baptism, Luke tells us He left Jordan and went into the wilderness for forty days, during which time He ate nothing. It's hard to imagine how hungry He might have been by that time. I can remember, as a small boy in the Chicago area, a bunch of us taking our Flexible Flyers to a distant hill on snowy, winter Saturdays. We would leave home early in the morning and coast all day long. It would be nighttime, dark and cold, before, one by one, we returned home, dragging our sleds behind us. I can still remember how hungry I was, not having eaten a thing since breakfast. And what wouldn't I have given for a cup of cocoa or my favorite food, a peanut butter sandwich? I'm like the little first-grader who had lunch in the cafeteria on a day when the school stove had broken down. In the emergency, they were serving peanut butter and jelly sandwiches. The first-grader left the cafeteria with this comment, "At last, a home-cooked meal!"

I can recall having heard sermons as a small boy on Jesus' temptations. I would think about being hungry for forty days and having Satan say, "Now, if you are the Son of God, turn this stone into a peanut butter sandwich." I didn't quite understand how Jesus could resist. Perhaps I understood more about Jesus' temptation then than I did years later after three years of seminary. Somehow, we have spiritualized these very earthly temptations. Medical specialists tell us now that it's possible for a healthy person to live forty days without food. The record says Jesus did. At the end of the time He was tempted.

Jesus had just had the experience of having God affirm who He actually was. He was clear about His mission as the Messiah, but now He had to deal with the question of strategy. Being who He was, called to redeem and reconcile a fallen world, how would He go about it? This is the whole focus of the temptations—the *how* of life. And the interesting thing is that during His encounter with the devil, the Scriptures were Jesus' resource. The answers that He gave to the devil in response to all three temptations came right out of Deuteronomy, the story of God's pilgrim people coming out of bondage, two from chapter 6 and one from chapter 8. As a good Jew, Jesus was steeped in the Scriptures, and I like to surmise that Jesus might have read Deuteronomy especially in preparation for His own mission, which was to lead the world out of bondage. Be that as it may, when Satan makes some suggestions in terms of a strategy for proceeding as the Messiah, Jesus is prepared with answers from the Old Testament.

What a gift God has given us in the Bible. Apart from the Bible, we would be ignorant of the nature of God and be unaware of the forces of evil at work in the world. But many of us, in spite of the clear message of Scripture, tend to make the devil a joke. There are countless stories poking fun at this idea of a personal devil. There's one about a woman who brings home a very expensive dress. The husband says, "Why did you buy that dress, dear? You know we can't afford it." She says, "Well, honey, the devil made me do it. I was trying it on in the store and he said to me, 'I've never seen you look more gorgeous than you do in that dress.'" "Well, why didn't you say, 'Get thee behind me, Satan'?" asked her husband. "I did," was the answer. "And he said, 'It looks great from behind, too.'" It's a cute joke except it makes the devil ridiculous and he is not. The Bible reminds us he is our ultimate adversary as he is God's. We make him out to be a simpleton, urging us to make some unnecessary purchase, but he has much more serious business with you and me.

Without the Bible we have a simplistic view of life and people. We think, for example, that education can make people good, or, that our problems can be solved by electing honest and sincere people to public office. We should know better. We want simple answers, but the Bible makes us face the complexities of life. I was told about a man who described to his friend the terrible hallucinations that had plagued him for a number of years. "I believed that there were wild, hideous animals hiding under my bed. Every night when the lights went out, they would come out, prowl all around the room and scare the stew out of me. But my brother finally solved my problem." "Oh, is he a psychiatrist?" asked his friend. "No, he's a carpenter. He sawed the legs off my bed." We'd all like some nice, simplistic ways to solve our problems, but the Bible reminds us that we are involved in a sophisticated contest with principalities and powers.

We are involved personally and globally in the struggle between the forces of light and darkness. I'm convinced that the devil doesn't worry much about atheists. Those who hold such a naïve view, philosophically, and psychologically, are unimportant in the devil's schemes. The devil is well aware that God exists, and I don't think he spends time dissuading us from a belief in God. If we read the biblical record, his basic strategy is to make us believe that God is not trustworthy. The basic lie is that we cannot trust God, for He wants to take all the fun out of life.

In the verses we are examining in this chapter, Luke describes Jesus wrestling with the basic issues of this struggle. During the three temptations the devil says to Jesus twice, "If you are the Son of God." He is trying to make Jesus doubt His Messiahship. Remember, Jesus has just heard God's voice declare, "You are My beloved Son." Satan says, "You don't believe that, do you? You'd better test it now. Turn these stones into bread." If we go back to the biblical record in the third chapter of Genesis, we find the account of the original struggle between good and evil. God made a cosmos, a world of lakes and seas, animals and plants. God the Creator was thrilled at what He had made, but He wanted somebody who could enter into the joy of His creation. There was no other reason for God to bring us into being, strange creatures that we are, except that He wanted to share His joy and His creation with us. And now we are collaborators with God and running the world that He made. In the cool of the evening God came down and walked with His creation. Life was meant to be like that—the Creator and the created together enjoying creation.

But the enemy entered into this creation in the form of a serpent. He said to Adam and Eve, "Do you really believe God is good? He has told you not to eat from that one tree because the moment you do, you will be as wise as He is. He's not your friend. He's holding out on you." They believed the serpent, and distrust began to grow and the relationship was broken. It's been broken ever since, and God has tried repeatedly to reestablish it through prophets, priests, judges, kings, and finally through His Son, Jesus Christ. He has gone to a great deal of trouble to let us know we can trust Him. This primal mistrust in the goodness of God is behind every problem that you and I experience.

John Claypool, one of the gifted preachers in our land today, tells a poignant story in *The Preaching Event* about identical twin brothers who never married because they so enjoyed each other's company. When their father died, they took over his store and ran it together in a joyful collaboration. One day a man came in to make a small purchase and paid for it with a dollar bill. The brother who took the dollar put it on top of the cash register and walked the customer to the door to say good-by. When he came back to get the dollar, it was gone. He said to his twin brother, "Did you take that dollar bill?" His brother said, "No, I didn't." That would have been the end of that except that in a few hours he brought the matter up again. "Surely, you took the dollar bill. There was nobody else in the store." His brother got angry and said, "I'm telling you, I did *not* take that dollar bill!" From that point mistrust grew until finally the two brothers could not work together. They put a partition right down the middle of the building and made it into two stores. They didn't speak for the next twenty years.

One day a stranger pulled up in a car and entered one of the two stores. "Have you been in business very long?" was his first question. "Yes, thirty or forty years," was the answer. "Good," continued the stranger. "I need to see you. I passed through this town twenty years

86

ago as an out-of-work vagrant. I got off a boxcar with no money and I hadn't eaten for days. I came by the alley outside and when I looked in and saw a dollar bill on the register I sneaked in and took it. I was raised in a Christian home and taught not to steal and I want to pay it back." He had no idea why the old storekeeper began to weep. "Would you mind coming next door and telling my brother that story?" he asked. Of course, with the second telling the two were reconciled amid many tears. Twenty years of broken relationship had been based not on fact, but on mistrust.

Our basic sin against God is mistrust. The devil hints that God is withholding something from us and he suggests ways in which we can take care of ourselves and get what is our due. In the temptations we read about here, Jesus is wrestling with this age-old issue. Will He trust God or will He give in to the easy successes promised by the devil?

In the first temptation the devil suggests Jesus will die if He doesn't eat. He must take care of Himself. The devil is still tempting us all in this area. The old maxim "If you don't take care of yourself, no one else will" is one version. The devil is saying to you and to me all the time, "Listen, take care of number one." That undermines our belief that we belong to God and that He can take care of us. We can begin to take care of ourselves in all sorts of ways—physically, financially, even sexually. The devil is telling the single, the widowed, those in unfulfilling marriages that sexual frustration is old-fashioned. Get with it, he says. Have your needs met.

Even in our dying, we are not beyond the temptations of the devil. I think of my mother who served God faithfully for ninety years. But in the last three years of her life, I saw her doubting God. She said, "I've lived too long. God should have taken me home. Why am I here?" It was hard to trust God with the timing of her death. The devil was telling her that if God had been trustworthy, she would not be old and lame and deaf. She would have died earlier.

A. J. Cronyn tells a story about a public health nurse in Wales who was the only medical resource in her whole area. She served tirelessly night and day, giving loving care. One day a doctor came to visit and inspect what she was doing. When he learned what her salary was, he said, "My dear, God knows you're worth more than you are being paid for this work." She replied without hesitation, "Well, that's enough." She believed God knew her needs and would take care of her.

In the second temptation, the devil promised Jesus success. He could have the world and rule it. All He need do was worship the devil and ignore what God required of Him. The end justifies the means. If your ambition is a worthy one, it's OK to break the rules that God has laid down for our conduct and behavior. To arrive at our goal, we need to cut a few corners. We are worshiping the devil when we ignore the moral and ethical absolutes that God has built into the universe. We worship the devil when we think that we are a special case and above the rules.

In the third and last temptation, the devil offered Jesus a strategy for popularity. Give the crowd something spectacular, he suggested. Throw yourself off the highest place in the temple, down four hundred feet or more into the Kidron Valley. When you land unscathed, people will be dazzled, and you'll be famous. This is an area in which we are still awfully susceptible. We want to be in the spotlight as president, chairman, speaker, preacher. Being an egotist, I find this a special temptation. For years I've had a sign in my office to help me with it: "There's no limit to the amount of good you can do if you don't care who gets the credit." If we are trusting God we don't need to throw ourselves off the temple roof or make the front page of the paper. We can ask God to show us the place He wants us to serve, and if we succeed, we can give the credit to Him.

In 1980, the world watched and cheered while Mother Teresa, a Yugoslavian nun, received her Nobel Peace Prize for her work among the suffering and dying poor people of Calcutta. The good news is that there are thousands like her all over the world who will never get a Nobel prize and who will never be in the spotlight. They are buried in obscure places, just doing the job without recognition or credit. But the temptation is still real. If nobody notices, why do it?

God is one. But we know His three faces as Father, Son, and Holy Spirit. Satan is one also. And he comes to us as an unholy trinity saying as he does to Jesus here, "Take care of yourself;" "Be successful;" and "Seek the spotlight."

We only know about the nature of Jesus' struggle with the devil because He told His disciples about it. The church is a family, a fellowship of strugglers. There is no private faith. We can share with each other our struggles and temptations. We can encourage each other to overcome as Jesus did in the ultimate fight. Verse 13 says the devil departed Jesus to wait for an opportune time. So he does with us. He may seize that opportune time today, this week. May we find, through the fellowship of believers, the determination to trust God instead.

CHAPTER ELEVEN—HERE AND NOW— OR NEVER

LUKE 4:14–30

14 Then Jesus returned in the power of the Spirit to Galilee, and news of Him went out through all the surrounding region. 15 And He taught in their synagogues, being glorified by all.

16 So He came to Nazareth, where He had been brought up. And as His custom was, He went into the synagogue on the Sabbath day, and stood up to read. 17 And He was handed the book of the prophet Isaiah. And when He had opened the book, He found the place where it was written:

18"The Spirit of the LORD is upon Me,
Because He has anointed Me
To preach the gospel to the poor;
He has sent Me to heal the brokenhearted,
To proclaim liberty to the captives
And recovery of sight to the blind,
To set at liberty those who are oppressed;
19To proclaim the acceptable year of the LORD."

20 Then He closed the book, and gave it back to the attendant and sat down. And the eyes of all who were in the synagogue were fixed on Him. 21 And He began to say to them, "Today this Scripture is fulfilled in your hearing." 22 So all bore witness to Him, and marveled at the gracious words which proceeded out of His mouth. And they said, "Is this not Joseph's son?"

23 He said to them, "You will surely say this proverb to Me, 'Physician, heal yourself! Whatever we have heard done in Capernaum, do also here in Your country.'" 24 Then He said, "Assuredly, I say to you, no prophet is accepted in his own country. 25 But I tell you truly, many widows were in Israel in the days of Elijah, when the heaven was shut up three years and six months, and there was a great famine throughout all the land; 26 but to none of them was Elijah sent except to Zarephath, in the region of Sidon, to a woman who was a widow. 27 And many lepers were in Israel in the time of Elisha

the prophet, and none of them was cleansed except Naaman the Syrian."

28 So all those in the synagogue, when they heard these things, were filled with wrath, 29 and rose up and thrust Him out of the city; and they led Him to the brow of the hill on which their city was built, that they might throw Him down over the cliff. 30 Then passing through the midst of them, He went His way.

—Luke 4:14–30

In these verses, Luke gives us the story of the beginning of our Lord's ministry. He tells us that Jesus returned to His hometown of Nazareth and went to the synagogue, so we conclude Jesus was a churchgoer. That's something to keep in mind when we are tempted to rationalize. "I can worship just as well at the eighteenth hole; I can worship on the lake in a sailboat; I can worship under the morning sun on the tennis courts." On the Sabbath day, Jesus went to church, however dull or interesting it was. On the Sabbath our Lord sought out the faithful people of God.

The synagogue was without clergy and, as was the custom, someone was selected each Sabbath to be the particular preacher or teacher. Often a visiting rabbi would be chosen. On this Sabbath, Jesus was the choice—local boy makes good. They had heard about this young man who was teaching in the synagogues and was *"glorified by all"* (v. 15). Now He was back home and the ruling elders had invited Him to speak. The synagogue was undoubtedly filled with friends, neighbors, and relatives. The custom then was to read the Word of God standing and to preach sitting down (not a bad idea from a preacher's point of view). Jesus stood and read the words of Isaiah and then sat down to make the astonishing claim we read in verse 21. *"Today this scripture is fulfilled in your hearing."* In this scene between Jesus and His fellow church members, it seems to me we find at least three pivotal new concepts.

New Credentials

The first is in the area of credentials. The elders who had heard great things about their hometown boy were undoubtedly asking, however subtly, "Now, who do you think you are? Give us your credentials." Jesus gave them the credentials of Isaiah and claimed them as His own, and they were all in the area of social concern. They were the same kinds of credentials He gave to the disciples of John the Baptist toward the end of John's life. These are still the authentic credentials of the people of God. God's Spirit is at work where personal and social concern are demonstrated. If we are God's people, we care about the physical, social, temporal needs of the world. Our authentic credentials are not primarily in the area of self-improvement, our spiritual maturity, or our knowledge of Scripture and theology. These are the kinds of credentials the elders were expecting. Jesus anticipated that and said, *"You will surely say this proverb to Me, 'Physician, heal yourself'"* (v. 23).

We still get hooked on the wrong kinds of credentials. Let's suppose for a minute that Mother Teresa was being examined by her spiritual superiors. They found that her nun's training did not include Greek and Hebrew, that she failed her Scripture-memorization course. They're concerned that she didn't speak in tongues and never attended a successful churchmanship seminar. Such a scene is ludicrous. Her credentials were that God was using her to care for the poor and the outcast. She needed no other credentials, nor do you and I. When the Spirit of God is upon us, these are our credentials.

A New Dimension

In these verses Jesus is communicating the basic idea that salvation is here and now. We used to live on a little island in Florida which had a well-known restaurant called "Scotty's Pub." Outside that pub was a sign promising "free beer tomorrow." We lived there for six years and in all that time not a drop of free beer was dispensed. If there is free beer tomorrow there is no free beer.

We Christians are sometimes accused of believing in pie in the sky by and by—some reward in the distant future. But eternity, that which is forever, has no future and no past. Eternity is now and it is endless. In this world we live in a very limited dimension—a time dimension with a past and a future. When we leave this world, we move into some other dimension, believers and unbelievers alike. We move into a timelessness with no past and no future. Eternity isn't lots of time. It is no time. And it starts now. This is all we have.

The synagogue had lost its relevance to the everyday and was concerned about the cultivation of mind and soul through study and praise. Unfortunately, the synagogue has become the model for all too many Christian churches. We come together to improve ourselves, to learn, to grow, to think. There is nothing wrong with that, but if that is the end product there is something very wrong with it.

Jesus stood up in the synagogue and talked about God in the present tense, and that is uncomfortable. It is much more comfortable to study about God and His mighty acts or to focus upon prophecy and the Second Coming. Prophecy and theology and church history are safe. It is much riskier to open your heart to God each day to listen and to ask, "Lord, what are you telling me today?" That plunges us into the now, which is the dimension Jesus introduces here. If God is not here and now there is no God. If we have only the God of history, the God of the apocalypse, and the God of eschatology, we have no God. Jesus said *today* this Scripture is fulfilled. The Bible is full of "nows." *Now* is the acceptable hour. *This* is the day the Lord hath made.

Inevitable Consequences

Jesus must have known the inevitable consequences of His message in the synagogue. There would be personal consequences. Dostoevsky said, "Men reject their prophets and slay them, but they love their martyrs and honor those whom they have slain." We all love the greats of the past who served God and humanity and are now comfortably dead. Martin Luther King is now greatly revered but, while living, he had many critics. Now that he's safely dead, we credit him with bringing in a new era of social justice. This is the history of the prophets. When Jesus began talking about the here and now, His hearers were uneasy. They found it surprising that their neighbor, Joseph's son, could be so full of wisdom and grace. Perhaps their reaction can be attributed to a form of self-hate. How can someone I know, from my town, be in any way special? We are so eager to see greatness in strangers. It's much harder to recognize it in our own colleagues and friends. This is precisely the attitude encountered by Jesus, stated in verse 24.

Jesus told His hearers there would be inevitable consequences for them as well. First He claimed that He was that very day the fulfillment of Isaiah's prophecy. Then He reminded them of the time when God passed over the Jews, His chosen people, to favor two Gentiles, a widow in Zarephath, and Naaman, the leper. The implication was that they would be judged in like manner for their rejection of Him. Enraged, they rose up to take Him out of the city and kill Him.

We're told that Jesus somehow mysteriously passed through the crowd. There is no indication of just how He did this. I'll make three suggestions. He might have escaped by supernatural means. Perhaps He miraculously became invisible and thereby walked right through this bloodthirsty mob. A second possibility is that His personal power was so awesome they dared not touch Him. They were intimidated by the aura that emanated from Him and in its path, they fell back like the waves of the sea. Voltaire said, "Life is a shipwreck, but we must not forget to sing in the lifeboats." Anybody who can sing in the lifeboats is a force to be reckoned with. And Jesus might have escaped the angry mob by the sheer power of His charisma.

But my favorite theory is that He walked right through the crowd simply because He was so ordinary. He was there someplace but indistinguishable. They couldn't pick Him out. How astonishing that God could be among us so anonymously. I have a feeling that if, by divine revelation, you were told Jesus would appear at your church some Sunday morning, you probably wouldn't be able to find Him. That's the miracle of the Incarnation.

So far as we know, Jesus never returned to Nazareth. You know, rejection can be irreparable. Our rejection of God is finally irreparable. I don't believe God ever sends anyone to hell. Hell is a chosen state. Having pursued us through a lifetime, God finally lets us have it our way. He doesn't fuss with us any more. We can have what we want.

The good news is that the life God offers us in Jesus Christ is here and now and calls for a response. You can't wait until you're more ready. We have no future. We have no past in the gestalt sense. The past is over and our memory of it is selective and untrustworthy. All of our past and all of our future is now. Now is all we have.

Chapter Twelve—What about Spiritual Healing

Luke 4:31–44

31 Then He went down to Capernaum, a city of Galilee, and was teaching them on the Sabbaths. 32 And they were astonished at His teaching, for His word was with authority. 33 Now in the synagogue there was a man who had a spirit of an unclean demon. And he cried out with a loud voice, 34 saying, "Let us alone! What have we to do with You, Jesus of Nazareth? Did You come to destroy us? I know who You are— the Holy One of God!"

35 But Jesus rebuked him, saying, "Be quiet, and come out of him!" And when the demon had thrown him in their midst, it came out of him and did not hurt him. 36 Then they were all amazed and spoke among themselves, saying, "What a word this is! For with authority and power He commands the unclean spirits, and they come out." 37 And the report about Him went out into every place in the surrounding region.

38 Now He arose from the synagogue and entered Simon's house. But Simon's wife's mother was sick with a high fever, and they made request of Him concerning her. 39 So He stood over her and rebuked the fever, and it left her. And immediately she arose and served them.

40 When the sun was setting, all those who had any that were sick with various diseases brought them to Him; and He laid His hands on every one of them and healed them. 41 And demons also came out of many, crying out and saying, "You are the Christ, the Son of God!"

And He, rebuking them, did not allow them to speak, for they knew that He was the Christ.

42 Now when it was day, He departed and went into a deserted place. And the crowd sought Him and came to Him, and tried to keep Him from leaving them; 43 but He said to them, "I must preach the kingdom of God to the other cities also, because for this purpose I have been sent." 44 And He was preaching in the synagogues of Galilee.

—Luke 4:31–44

In this last half of chapter 4, Jesus begins His healing ministry. It's a good time to raise the question, "What about spiritual healing?" Is the God we believe in able to deal with our physical, emotional, psychological problems? I'm sure the division of opinion on this subject is enormous. Some would say, "Spiritual healing is weird, cultish—it has nothing to do with the Christian life today." And some would consider it the most important aspect of a life of faith. All this was just as controversial in Jesus' time. Jesus' teaching and preaching were surprising enough, but in verse 36 we learn that His healing powers *"amazed"* them.

There is a wonderful story about Noah Webster, the father of all dictionary-makers and a great stickler for precise language. One day Mrs. Noah Webster opened the kitchen door to find Noah in the act of kissing their maid. She said, "Mr. Webster, I am surprised." "No, my dear," he corrected her. "You are amazed. I am surprised." The crowd reacted to Jesus here with both surprise and amazement. Even today, those with various credentials who engage in spiritual healing elicit such reactions.

Luke the physician describes a number of healings. In the first account, Jesus heals a man with demon possession. Thirty or forty years ago, most scholars thought this term was used to describe those suffering from epilepsy. We no longer believe that. Epilepsy is epilepsy. Demon possession is one possible explanation for bizarre behavior. Today even medical people do not dismiss the idea of demons entirely. There are documented cases that support the theory that sometimes strange beings inhabit us. The book *The Three Faces of Eve,* written by a psychiatrist, is the story of a woman inhabited by three different personalities. The New Testament gives us so many accounts of Jesus casting out demons, that we can only conclude it is a valid kind of mental illness, unlike the types of psychological or emotional breakdowns we are more familiar with. In this very first healing miracle, Jesus rebukes the demon and he comes out and the man is healed.

Next Luke records the physical healing of Peter's mother-in-law. We are told she had a high fever, another reminder that this account is written by a physician. (Other Gospel writers who report this event say only that she had a fever.) In this enlightened age of psychosomatic medicine, we could come up with a rational explanation for her sudden healing. She might have had what is called hysterical illness, the sort of thing that happens when we get frightened, upset or resentful, and our body reacts.

We sometimes forget that Peter had a house, a wife, a business, and a mother-in-law. And when Jesus said to Peter (as He does in the very next chapter), "Follow me," he was not talking to some student or some itinerant worker. Peter was a man with deep roots in his community. Jesus, who grew up in this same area, was getting ready to call His twelve disciples to share His ministry. Simon might very well have known Jesus all of his life, and possibly he was even beginning to believe that his neighbor might be the Messiah. We can imagine him coming home and saying, "Guess what Jesus did today? Let me tell you what He said today." His mother-in-law might have been justifiably dismayed about this turn of events. We can imagine her saying to her daughter, "Good grief, what's gotten into this man you married? I think he's lost his mind. He's neglecting his business. He's ignoring you." Perhaps this concern that her son-in-law might do something foolish as a result of his interest in Jesus had begun to affect her physically and caused her to take to her bed with a fever.

We can speculate on what happened when Jesus came to Simon's house. Suddenly this strange man, emanating the very love and presence of God, stood over this anxious woman and spoke to her. He dispelled her fears and immediately the fever left. Assuming her illness was psychosomatic, her healing is very explainable. But however much we might speculate on the causes of this woman's illness, the fact remains that she was genuinely ill and that she was instantly healed by Jesus.

Next, lest we think these two healings are only isolated incidents, Luke reports on the healings of many people—"all those who had anyone sick with various diseases" (v. 40). Luke is making sure we realize that Jesus was not a specialist. He could cure all diseases, not just demon possession and fever.

These three biblical accounts are in no sense at odds with modern medicine today. The four magic words being used just now (though sometimes couched in more medical terms) are *hope, love, joy,* and *faith.* Out there on the frontier of medicine there is an increasing awareness that human beings are basically spiritual and that the body will respond to these four positive attitudes and emotions.

The effects of hope and hopelessness are reported in an article by Dr. Sanford Cohen, chairman of psychiatry at Boston University of Medicine, in the *Handbook of Clinical Psychology and Pathology.* He believes a voodoo doctor or witch doctor actually has the power to kill someone by means of a hex—by "pointing the bone," as it is phrased: "The victim is convinced that he has been trapped and that death is the only escape and he dies of overwhelming hopelessness. . . . There is a striking similarity between westernized man dying from a fear of disease, from which there is no escape, and the aborigine who dies from an all-powerful spell."

Cohen also raises the question of self-willed death. This can happen after a doctor has diagnosed a fatal disease, say, cancer. In witchcraft terms, he has pointed the bone. So terrible is the blow that the patient may simply give up, and an autopsy will show a malignancy, but no reason why the patient should have died so soon. Scientists do not know what biological mechanism is at work in such cases, but Cohen says there is some evidence that a profound feeling of hopelessness triggers changes in levels of a brain chemical that plays a role in the transmission of the sympathetic nerve impulses. This is a scientific way of saying that hopelessness can kill you.

The next magic word is *love.* A lack of love is fatal, according to James Lynch, medical researcher at Johns Hopkins. He is convinced after years of medical research, written up in his book *The Broken Heart,* that loneliness is the number one physical killer in America. Those who are demonstrably lonely and unable to cope with it eventually die, though the diagnosed cause is cardiovascular disease or cancer.

Norman Cousins, in *Anatomy of an Illness,* promotes the idea that *joy* is salubrious. He describes how he cured himself of a fatal illness, one which the doctor gave him one chance in five hundred of surviving. He took his treatment into his own hands, left the hospital, and rented a hotel room. By way of treatment, he did some simple things like taking vitamin C and mending some of the broken relationships in his life. But realizing that the Bible speaks about joy and laughter as good medicine (Prov. 17:22), he programmed into each day several hours of belly-laughter. He practiced the therapy of joy and got well. We shouldn't be surprised. The doctors have been telling us for years that people aren't unhappy because they are sick. They get sick because they are unhappy. The presence of joy heals. And joy is one of the gifts of the Spirit, along with hope, love, and faith.

So much has been written on the inter-relatedness of faith and wellness. In his book *A Surgeon's Book of Hope,* William Nolen talks about the mysterious will to live. Doctors can't instill it, but its presence can reverse illnesses. Dr. Barry Wyke, a doctor in the

Royal College of Surgeons in London, has conducted studies to prove that a measurable physical change takes place in the body when you believe you are healed.

Hans Selye talked about the damaging effects of stress. You cannot avoid stress and inappropriately handled, it will kill you. Doctors can treat the results of stress but they can't deal with its cause. That's in the spiritual realm. The ultimate cure for stress is faith in a God who loves you, whom you can trust. Dr. Carl Simonton is doing research in Fort Worth on the causes and treatment of cancer. He takes only terminal cases and is getting incredible results. He asks his patients to imagine the body getting well and to believe it. This positive imagery begins to release healing forces. It's hard to believe such hard-nosed medical types are talking about the spiritual dimensions of illness in such specific terms.

Jesus' Priorities

Spiritual healing (which is not to be confused with faith healing) is a reality. But Jesus did not make it His major emphasis. He had other concerns. It's as if He were saying, "If you understood the spiritual nature of the universe and of man, you would understand that these things I do are not so unusual." Jesus' primary focus was on the kingdom of God. In verse 41 we read that when the sick came to Him He laid His hands on every one of them and healed them, but the next morning He departed quickly before more sick people appeared. Out of compassion Jesus healed the sick, and nobody, doctor or faith healer, did more healing in three years' time than our Lord. But invariably, as soon as the last person was healed, He left immediately and went to a quiet place.

It seems to me Jesus is saying that He came to proclaim a new kingdom of which He is the King. He came to introduce a new way to live. When we move into this new dimension of living, the very taproot of illness will be severed. Apart from that kingdom, illness will be like dandelions in the lawn in spring—everywhere. To spend one's life dealing solely with illness and treating pathology is an endless task. In the kingdom Jesus came to establish, it is more important to help people begin to find some new positive attitudes and behaviors. Jesus proclaimed a new king, a new center, a new direction, and new priorities. Incidentally, much of our illness has been dealt a death blow. But not all. We still live in a broken world.

Love, faith, hope, and joy—these clinical descriptions of wellness are the gifts of the Holy Spirit. They are the overflow of His presence in our lives. Their absence produces illness and their presence makes for health. Our primary focus is not on the elimination of illness or immorality but on righteousness. Righteousness is what you do. Righteousness is loving God with all your heart, soul, mind, and strength, and your neighbor as yourself. Righteousness is receiving the Spirit and the gifts of faith, hope, love, joy—the magic ingredients to wellness.

Chapter Thirteen—What to Do with the Rest of Your Life

Luke 5:1–11

5:1 So it was, as the multitude pressed about Him to hear the word of God, that He stood by the Lake of Gennesaret, 2 and saw two boats standing by the lake; but the fishermen had gone from them and were washing their nets. 3 Then He got into one of the boats, which was Simon's, and asked him to put out a little from the land. And He sat down and taught the multitudes from the boat.

4 When He had stopped speaking, He said to Simon, "Launch out into the deep and let down your nets for a catch."

5 But Simon answered and said to Him, "Master, we have toiled all night and caught nothing; nevertheless at Your word I will let down the net." 6 And when they had done this, they caught a great number of fish, and their net was breaking. 7 So they signaled to their partners in the other boat to come and help them. And they came and filled both the boats, so that they began to sink. 8 When Simon Peter saw it, he fell down at Jesus' knees, saying, "Depart from me, for I am a sinful man, O Lord!"

9 For he and all who were with him were astonished at the catch of fish which they had taken; 10 and so also were James and John, the sons of Zebedee, who were partners with Simon. And Jesus said to Simon, "Do not be afraid. From now on you will catch men." 11 So when they had brought their boats to land, they forsook all and followed Him.

—Luke 5:1–11

One of my earliest memories is going down one Saturday afternoon to the McVicar's Theater in Chicago with my father and seeing a movie called *Bring 'em Back Alive,* starring the fabulous Frank Buck. I never forgot that movie, and I am still in awe of Frank Buck. Very few of us would venture into the jungle even to shoot wild beasts, but this man went into the wilds of Africa to capture animals alive: to bring back elephants, tigers, and lions for our zoos and circuses. It boggled my mind.

Since I've been a pastor in Seattle, some members of our congregation similarly boggle my mind. Let me tell you about one. She is a tiny woman who lives in the University district. As part of her ministry she walks its unsafe streets in the night hours and frequently has her purse snatched. In it, the thief finds a note saying, "My dear friend, you must be in great trouble if you needed to steal this purse. I am sorry for you and I love you and I believe God loves you and wants to help you. So do I. Here is my address and phone number. Please come and see me." I consider her a present-day Frank Buck—out there at night in a dangerous area stalking the biggest game of all.

In these verses from chapter 5 we find Jesus proposing this kind of big game hunting, or to be more exact, fishing. He says, *"From now on you will catch men"* (v. 10). The story begins with the crowds pressing around Jesus eager to hear the Good News. Aware that crowding was becoming a problem, Jesus notices two boats by the Lake of Galilee (or, more accurately, the Lake of Gennesaret). He gets into Simon's boat and asks him to shove off a bit. And then He sits down to preach which, as we said earlier, was the custom in the synagogue. It's a custom we might consider emulating. I often think about that when I see TV preachers talk about the grace and love of God with much frantic waving and shouting and grimacing. I wish they'd try that sitting down. You've got to stand up for bombast, and the Jews must have realized that.

Have you ever wondered about Jesus' preaching style? I have a hunch there was much back-and-forth dialogue, with questions, pauses, and then, from time to time, a parable right out of the present (e.g., "As we all came down here this morning, did you notice that shepherd with his flock of sheep? Doesn't that remind you of God?")

Charles Finney, a converted lawyer and founder of Oberlin College, always drew large crowds, who came from great distances on foot or by horse and buggy to hear him preach. One man had come two hundred miles, and a reporter asked him why. He said, "Charles Finney talks about the things other men preach about." I think Jesus talked about God with such reality He didn't need to preach in the usual sense—no three-point sermons.

Finishing His sermon, Jesus said to Peter, "Let's go fishing." Did you ever get stuck with the preacher on Sunday afternoon? Perhaps it was your turn to take him or her to lunch and you found yourself frantically trying to think of some way to comment on the sermon. Peter and his friends had no such problem. As soon as this sermon from the boat was concluded, Jesus said, "Let's go fishing." He didn't change His suit or get out of His black robe. He fished in the same clothes He preached in.

Peter's reaction to this suggestion is interesting. When Jesus wanted to use Peter's boat for a pulpit, that was no problem. He was glad to shove off. When Jesus wants to use Peter's boat for fishing, Peter protests. We can hear him saying, "Wait a minute, now. We've been fishing all night. We caught nothing. In the morning, the sun's slanting rays hit the water and scare the fish. It's foolish to go out now." He is implying that while Jesus knows about preaching, he—Peter—knows about fishing!

Have you ever felt that way—that Jesus knows about spiritual things, the kingdom of heaven, God, prayer, but when it comes to practical affairs, running your business or your home, that's where *you're* the expert? Peter had that problem. He was skeptical about Jesus' helpfulness on a fishing trip. But he agreed to give it a try, and off they went. The results were astounding—one of the big fish stories of all time. We've all heard lots of those. I heard one about a lady who went on a fishing trip with her husband. Describing it to her neighbor, she said, "I did everything wrong. I was too noisy. I used the wrong bait. I reeled in too soon, and—I caught more fish than he did."

I'm sure that ever after, Peter enjoyed telling this particular fish story. I happen to believe that Jesus wants to make Himself negotiable to us in terms we can understand. How better could He have impressed Peter than with a record catch of fish? Peter may have been enthralled or intrigued by Jesus' teaching, but his attention must have been caught by Jesus' expertise and visible results in a field where Peter was a specialist.

I am reminded of a friend from the first church I served in New York State. He was the chief engineer at a laboratory that produces sound equipment. At a small prayer group meeting one night Sidney told us this story: "This week a strange thing happened. We produced two hundred amplifiers for a custom order, and when they came off our assembly line not a single one of them worked. We checked all the blueprints, all the parts, and could find nothing wrong. I went back into my office. I closed the door and I got on my knees and said, 'Lord, what's wrong with these amplifiers?' And while I was still kneeling the idea came to cross two particular wires. It didn't make sense to do so, but I went back and tried it. It worked. All those sets were delivered in perfect working order because Jesus demonstrated He knew even more about electronics than I did." It sounds miraculous, and many of us can report on similar miracles. Even though miracles are not the basis for our belief in God, He can use them to get our attention.

Some scholars have suggested the story here in Luke is simply an allegory. They tell us it really means that Peter would some day be catching great crowds of new converts. I don't believe it. I believe those were real fish. We're all too inclined to allegorize and spiritualize the Bible. I think Jesus revealed His power to Peter in the most relevant way possible.

Peter's reaction was to fall to his knees and worship Jesus. At last Peter realized that Jesus was the Messiah. Peter, who had heard Jesus preaching and teaching, was convinced by the miracle of the fish. He understood at that point that Jesus was more than a great teacher or preacher. And yet there are still those who insist that Jesus is just one among many spiritual greats. They are uninformed, to say the least. C. S. Lewis deals with this brilliantly in *Mere Christianity*. Lewis says that anybody who claims that he is God ("He who has seen me has seen the Father," John 14:9) is one of three things: he is a charlatan and a crook who is deliberately deceiving people, a loony who ought to be in an asylum, or—he is who he says he is and we fall at his feet and call him Lord. As a teacher, Jesus was not saying much that was new or unusual. Many of the rabbis of His time were saying similar things about life and ethics. Only Jesus said, "I and the Father are one."

Peter was overwhelmed by who Jesus actually was, and he fell down, saying, *"Depart from me, for I am a sinful man, O Lord"* (v. 8). And Jesus said, *"Do not be afraid. From now on you will catch men."* In response to Jesus' challenge those fishermen left everything and followed Him. It was a remarkable response to such an open-ended call. There was no time limit. Were they to follow Him for a week, a month, a year? They left *everything*—even the biggest catch of their lives. They left their boats and their families and they followed, and, as far as we know, not one ever went back.

They could not have known what they were called to at that point, but they might have had some understanding of what they were called from—perhaps from tedium or monotony. G. K. Chesterton said that Jesus Christ saves us from the degrading necessity of being the child of our time. We don't have to be the product of whatever time this is. We can be something original and different.

While there is an infinite variety of those things we are called *from,* we are all called *to* the same thing. We are called to big game hunting. We are called to go out and take people alive. The translation "to catch" is not really accurate. The actual Greek word Jesus used means "to take alive, as taking animals alive for a zoo or circus." It's a much more attractive image. In point of fact, nobody wants to be caught. Too much evangelism is conducted that way. We maneuver people into signing a decision card or accepting "the plan of salvation." Jesus was promising those early disciples that they would be taking people alive for the kingdom, and that's exciting business. The verb tense used here describes an ongoing process. It's not like deer-hunting, where you catch your limit for the season and quit until the next year. The taking people alive that Jesus speaks of is continuous and never-ending.

Sometimes we think there are two kinds of Christians: those who catch the animals for the zoo and those who come and look at them. It's not so. If we follow Jesus, He tells us we will be involved in big-game hunting. What could be more thrilling than to begin to stalk those who don't know Jesus and help them discover who He is in order that they might be saved from boredom or immorality or addiction or whatever their destiny would be apart from Him? Have you ever wondered what you are going to do with the rest of your life? We have a job beyond just church work. When Louis Evans, Sr., was pastor at Hollywood Presbyterian Church, he had a parishioner who was a new convert, a railroad engineer. One day this man asked Dr. Evans if there was a job for him in the church. Dr. Evans explained that they already had a surplus of ushers, teachers, and officers. But he did have a job for him. "Is your fireman a Christian?" Dr. Evans asked. "If he's not, that's your job."

Even preachers are called to this kind of big-game hunting. Samuel Shoemaker, well-known Episcopal preacher, now deceased, once told me about a vow he had made as a young priest in New York City. He understood that taking people alive for Jesus was central to the Christian's vocation, and he promised the Lord that he would never let a day go by when he wasn't "fishing for souls." Sometimes he'd come home after a long day's work of calling and sermon preparation. He'd be getting undressed for bed and realize that he hadn't talked to one person about the Lord that day. He'd put his clothes back on and go back on the street stalking big game.

I think that story reveals the underlying dynamic of this one man's widespread and fruitful ministry.

The church is not a spectator society in which we go to the zoo. We're all supposed to be out catching the animals, whoever we are. Jesus began with Peter, a rough fisherman, not a spiritual type. And he continues to call all sorts and conditions of people. Harold Hill, author of the book *How to Live like a King's Kid,* is an old friend of mine and one of the all-time big-game hunters. I once shared a cab with Harold on a trip to the Bermuda airport, a long drive from one end of the island to the other. Harold sat in front with the driver, talking the whole time about Jesus—the miracles, the excitement, the adventure. The cabby just kept driving, grunting occasionally. When we arrived at the airport, Harold turned to him, "Friend, can you think of any reason why you shouldn't turn your life over to Jesus?" The cabby couldn't, and right there in the cab we prayed with him about a new beginning.

There is no rule book for this kind of big-game hunting. One prerequisite is to love Jesus and to love the people you're talking to. Then pray for good things to overwhelm them. This is pre-evangelism. If their sick child is healed or their marriage is saved or if they catch enough fish, Jesus will have their attention. Then you can suggest they might want to meet the miracle worker Himself.

What to do with the rest of your life? The challenge is to spend it as a big-game hunter, taking people alive for Jesus. Don't settle for less.

Chapter Fourteen—Radical Christianity

Luke 5:12–39

Scripture Outline

EXPECTATIONS

12 And it happened when He was in a certain city, that behold, a man who was full of leprosy saw Jesus; and he fell on his face and implored Him, saying, "Lord, if You are willing, You can make me clean."

13 Then He put out His hand and touched him, saying, "I am willing; be cleansed." Immediately the leprosy left him.

14 And He charged him to tell no one, "But go and show yourself to the priest, and make an offering for your cleansing, as a testimony to them, just as Moses commanded."

15 However, the report went around concerning Him all the more; and great multitudes came together to hear, and to be healed by Him of their infirmities.

16 So He Himself often withdrew into the wilderness and prayed.

—Luke 5:12–16

Luke tells the story of two separate healings here, of the leper and the paralytic, after which he says they were all amazed and filled with fear, saying, *"We have seen strange things today"* (v. 26). God invariably surprises us with something unexpected, perhaps because you and I have so many false expectations of what life will hold for us. We're like the marine biologist I read about who crossed an abalone fish with a crocodile, hoping to get an abadile. Instead, he got a crocabaloney.

I enlisted in World War II full of patriotism and high ideals. Just one week in the army cured me of my false expectations. We all have false expectations as we enter into marriage. A friend of mine had been married just a year when he confided in me, "You know, marriage is wonderful, but it doesn't solve any of your problems." I think he had false expectations. As children, we have certain expectations about adulthood. As a kid I couldn't wait to grow up and have enough money to buy all the ice cream and candy and hot fudge sundaes I ever wanted without parental interference. Then you grow up and for some reason it's not as important any more—and besides, most of the time I'm weight-watching. I had false expectations.

What did you expect when you became a Christian? I'm sure Bishop Ridley, the courageous Bible translator of the sixteenth century, did not expect to be burned at the stake. Dietrich Bonhoeffer, German martyr under the Nazis, did not expect to be hanged at thirty-nine because of his unswerving faith in Jesus Christ. Alexander Solzhenitsyn did not expect, when he was confirmed in the faith, to spend years in prison because of his beliefs. Nevertheless, I am sure we all did have certain expectations when we became Christians.

In these verses, Luke is outlining a radical Christianity, "radical" meaning "root" or basic Christianity, and in doing so he shatters so many of our false expectations about the faith. Luke gives us a series of incidents which suggest that Jesus did not measure up to the expectations of the Jews in at least four areas: He performed the wrong kinds of healings, He preached the wrong theology, He kept the wrong company, and He had the wrong attitude. Let's look at those.

In the first incident, Jesus healed the leper. For the Jews, this was the wrong kind of healing because lepers were outcasts. It was believed at that time that those who were ill had sinned in some specific way. If you were a leper your sins were great, and you were especially to be avoided. We remember that at the beginning of His ministry, Jesus talked about setting the captives free. The lepers were the captives of society. In addition to coping with horrible and probably terminal illness, they were utterly isolated from normal social contact. They had only each other. Today leprosy is, for the most part, curable, and I don't think there is any comparable disease in our time. A present-day spiritual healer might be reluctant to tackle terminal cancer patients. But even that disease, dreaded as it is, cannot be compared to leprosy in Jesus' time.

By Jewish standards, Jesus performed a miracle on the wrong person and with the wrong methods. He did not yell "Be healed!" to this sufferer from some safe distance. Rather, He, a well person, physically touched a leper. The Jews believed that only God had the power to heal lepers. (In chapter 5 of 2 Kings, the king of Syria sends Naaman the leper to the king of Israel for healing. Outraged, the king of Israel reacts with these words: "Am I God, to kill and to make alive, that this man sends word to me to cure a man of his leprosy?") The leper's statement to Jesus, *"Lord, if You are willing, You can make me clean"* (v. 12), was actually a testimony of faith. He was saying, "You are God and You are able to do this." Jesus was willing, and He healed him with a warning to go and tell no one. In spite of that, the word went out.

THE WRONG THEOLOGY

17 Now it happened on a certain day, as He was teaching, that there were Pharisees and teachers of the law sitting by, who had come out of every town of Galilee, Judea, and Jerusalem. And the power of the Lord was present to heal them. 18 Then behold, men brought on a bed a man who was paralyzed, whom they sought to bring in and lay before Him. 19 And when they could not find how they might bring him in, because of the crowd, they went up on the housetop and let him down with his bed through the tiling into the midst before Jesus.

20 When He saw their faith, He said to him, "Man, your sins are forgiven you."

21 And the scribes and the Pharisees began to reason, saying, "Who is this who speaks blasphemies? Who can forgive sins but God alone?"

22 But when Jesus perceived their thoughts, He answered and said to them, "Why are you reasoning in your hearts? 23 Which is easier, to say, 'Your sins are forgiven you,' or to say, 'Rise up and walk'? 24 But that you may know that the Son of Man has power on earth to forgive sins"—He said to the man who was paralyzed, "I say to you, arise, take up your bed, and go to your house."

25 Immediately he rose up before them, took up what he had been lying on, and departed to his own house, glorifying God. 26 And they were all amazed, and they glorified God and were filled with fear, saying, "We have seen strange things today!"

—Luke 5:17–26

In these verses we find this radical Lord of ours preaching the wrong kind of theology from the viewpoint of the Jews. He didn't just heal diseases; He forgave sins. They could have overlooked the healing, but they believed that to pronounce that sins were forgiven was to commit blasphemy, for only God could forgive sins. When the Jews protested, Jesus gave them a choice. Since they took exception to His claim to forgive sins, He said instead, "Rise up and walk," and immediately the paralytic was healed.

Today, you and I have the power to pronounce that sins are forgiven in Jesus' name. The head of the psychiatric department at Duke University is a man named Bill Wilson, a Christian physician. I met a colleague of his some time ago who told me a story about Dr. Wilson. One of his patients was a Vietnam veteran who had been nonfunctioning for years. In the course of his Vietnam duties he had been responsible for the deaths of many people. The hospital staff felt convinced that his illness was the result of his inability to forgive himself. One day Dr. Wilson came in and asked to see this particular patient. He went into this poor man's room, sat on the bed and said, "I want to tell you that your sins are forgiven." "What did you say?" asked the patient. Dr. Wilson continued, "I have the authority to tell you through Jesus Christ that your sins are forgiven." That exchange marked the beginning of a healing, and the patient is now back functioning in society. Dr. Wilson performed a miracle of healing, not as a psychiatrist, but as a Christian.

It's been my observation that many of those seeking help in therapy groups or gestalt workshops are actually struggling with this whole problem of guilt. They have failed or hurt family and friends by acts of both omission and commission. How much they need to hear that their sins are forgiven. We Christians have the only answer for them. We have the authority to say, "Your sins are forgiven." We need not wonder to whom we should say those words. We are all already forgiven. Even those in hell, now or in the future, are already forgiven—they just refuse to accept it. We are free to say indiscriminately, "You are forgiven." However, those you say it to must believe in and appropriate that forgiveness.

THE WRONG COMPANY

27 After these things He went out and saw a tax collector named Levi, sitting at the tax office. And He said to him, "Follow Me." 28 So he left all, rose up, and followed Him.

29 Then Levi gave Him a great feast in his own house. And there were a great number of tax collectors and others who sat down with them. 30 And their scribes and the Pharisees complained against His disciples, saying, "Why do You eat and drink with tax collectors and sinners?"

31 Jesus answered and said to them, "Those who are well have no need of a physician, but those who are sick. 32 I have not come to call the righteous, but sinners, to repentance."

—*Luke 5:27–32*

Jesus kept the wrong company, and that was a further affront to the Jews. I have a special appreciation for Levi, who became Matthew, because he paid such a high price to follow Jesus. The fishermen who became disciples were middle-class businessmen. If this new venture ended in failure they could always go back to fishing. Levi/Matthew was a wealthy tax collector, and you couldn't give up tax collecting for the Romans on a whim and expect to ever return. He cut his ties. He gave up his wealth and privilege and position and did so gladly to follow Jesus. He was so elated about this decision he wanted to celebrate. He threw a great party and invited all his tax-collector friends. It was a feast the like of which few had seen in that time. He had found something of great price, and he wanted to share it with his old friends and colleagues.

My wife and I visited a well-to-do young California cotton merchant who is presently selling cotton to China. When two hundred Chinese dignitaries came to town on a cotton-buying mission, he invited them for dinner at his house. He and his wife set up small tables in the garden and at every table they planted a Christian neighbor to be a kind of leaven. All of those merchants from mainland China were introduced to some lively Christians at a party with good food and fun. It's a great way to evangelize. If that's your style, you can consider Levi your patron saint.

The Pharisees were upset because, in the East, table fellowship meant, and for the most part still means, full acceptance. To eat with someone is to say, "I have no reservations about you. We are one." Jesus sat down with these despised tax collectors, betrayers of the Jewish people. We might liken it today to sitting down with a Nazi collaborator in World War II. The Pharisees were understandably dismayed. In those times servants didn't eat with their masters. Only friends ate together. Jesus was demonstrating that these were his friends. He said, *"Those who are well have no need of a physician, but those who are sick"* (v. 31). He scandalized the Pharisees by indicating there are no good and bad people—only those who know they're bad and those who don't. To sin is man's condition. To pretend that he is not a sinner is man's sin.

THE WRONG ATTITUDE

33 Then they said to Him, "Why do the disciples of John fast often and make prayers, and likewise those of the Pharisees, but Yours eat and drink?"
34 And He said to them, "Can you make the friends of the bridegroom fast while the bridegroom is with them? 35 But the days will come when the bridegroom will be taken away from them; then they will fast in those days."
—*Luke 5:33–35*

The Jews could not forgive Jesus for His joyful attitude. Jesus and His disciples went through life rejoicing. Pierre Teilhard de Chardin, a great Catholic saint of the twentieth century, said that joy is the surest sign of the presence of God. But too much joy offends some people. Can you recall the Thanksgiving celebrations years ago as a kid when you couldn't wait to get to the groaning table to "pig out" on turkey and pie and all those good things? When dinnertime finally came, inevitably some older family member would pray, "O Lord, make us mindful of all those in the world who are starving right now." For me, it killed the whole thing. There is no shortage of doomsayers, those who love to rain on the parade. Jesus modeled a very different attitude.

The gospel is Good News. There is pain and suffering, but we can have inner joy. Writing of his conversion in his book *Surprised by Joy*, C. S. Lewis describes himself as the most reluctant convert in all England. He was dragged into the kingdom by his heels, kicking and screaming. He likens it to bracing yourself to dive into a cold mountain stream and finding it delightful. The religious people were convinced that Jesus had the wrong attitude. He suggested that while discipleship may cost you your life, the presence of God is cause for celebration.

SIPPING NEW WINE

36 Then He spoke a parable to them: "No one puts a piece from a new garment on an old one; otherwise the new makes a tear, and also the piece that was taken out of the new does not match the old. 37 And no one puts new wine into old wineskins; or else the new wine will burst the wineskins and be spilled, and the wineskins will be ruined. 38 But new wine must be put into new wineskins, and both are preserved. 39 And no one, having drunk old wine, immediately desires new; for he says, 'The old is better.'"

—Luke 5:36–39

There are so many ways in which we Christians want to hang on to the old wine and won't even try the new even in small things. Sometimes I suggest open-eyed grace at a restaurant and my companions are shocked. They say, "That's not the way we do it. We bow our heads." There's nothing in the Bible about closing our eyes to pray, but if that's our pattern we're reluctant to change. We all have a choice when it comes to trying the new wine, the new and fresh ways of serving God. We can be predictable religious types or we can be radical like Jesus Himself, associating with the wrong people, praying for the wrong miracles, refusing to conform to the heavy, joyless attitudes of the legalists. We can be radical saints filled with the Spirit of this radical Lord.

CHAPTER FIFTEEN—WORSHIP: DUTY, DIVERSION, OR DYNAMITE

LUKE 6:1–19

Scripture Outline

Observing the Sabbath (6:1–11)

Prayer and Worship (6:12–19)

OBSERVING THE SABBATH

6:1 Now it happened on the second Sabbath after the first that He went through the grainfields. And His disciples plucked the heads of grain and ate them, rubbing them in their hands. ² And some of the Pharisees said to them, "Why are you doing what is not lawful to do on the Sabbath?"

³ But Jesus answering them said, "Have you not even read this, what David did when he was hungry, he and those who were with him: ⁴ how he went into the house of God, took and ate the showbread, and also gave some to those with him, which is not lawful for any but the priests to eat?" ⁵ And He said to them, "The Son of Man is also Lord of the Sabbath."

⁶ Now it happened on another Sabbath, also, that He entered the synagogue and taught. And a man was there whose right hand was withered. ⁷ So the scribes and Pharisees watched Him closely, whether He would heal on the Sabbath, that they might find an accusation against Him. ⁸ But He knew their thoughts, and said to the man who had the withered hand, "Arise and stand here." And he arose and stood. ⁹ Then Jesus said to them, "I will ask you one thing: Is it lawful on the Sabbath to do good or to do evil, to save life or to destroy?" ¹⁰ And when He had looked around at them all, He said to the man, "Stretch out your hand." And he did so, and his hand was restored as whole as the other. ¹¹ But they were filled with rage, and discussed with one another what they might do to Jesus.

—Luke 6:1–11

Some time ago I heard about a pastor who was taking a Boy Scout troop on a tour of the church, explaining the meaning of the windows and some of the symbols. One of the scouts asked about a plaque displayed prominently in the narthex that listed a long roster of names. On being told that those were members of the church who died in the service, he asked what seemed the logical next question. "Which service, the 9:30 or 11?" We may laugh, but we have to admit that for the average small boy, and maybe a good many grownups as well, the Sunday morning services, though not exactly fatal, can seem pretty deadly. We preachers wear our black robes and speak in funereal tones, and it seems only the corpse is missing.

The sixth chapter of Luke gives us a surprising picture of our Lord's observance of the Sabbath, and the verses can illuminate for us the whole subject of worship. It seems to me we come to worship—I refer here to structured worship in the sanctuary—for one of three reasons: for duty, diversion, or dynamite. First of all, we may come out of duty. We love God and we owe Him something. We are His creatures and He requires homage. We come to say, "God, I am here because you're the boss." Second, we may come for a pleasant diversion. It's something to do on a rainy Sunday. The choir is not bad and sometimes the sermon is interesting. It's a harmless way to spend Sunday morning. Or, third, worship can be dynamite, which is exactly what God has promised us. Dynamite comes from the Greek word *dunamis,* which is the word used in Acts 1:8 when Jesus promises, "You will receive power *(dunamis)* when the Holy Spirit has come upon you."

So much of church history is puzzling unless we understand this concept of worship as an experience of power, or dynamite. The early Covenanters in Scotland, for example, were forbidden to be anything but Anglican, and yet whole families of them took to the hills to worship secretly. They would post armed watchmen all around, lest the English troops discover them. They courted death in order to worship. The pilgrims left their comfortable homeland and came to this uncivilized land to worship. You've got to say they must have found something in worship that a lot of us haven't found. We would scarcely risk our lives to worship if our motive is duty or diversion. But, if worship is dynamite, we can't exist without it. We come because we receive something from God Himself that we can receive in no other way.

Someone has said that faith over three generations—grandparent, parent and child—takes three different forms. For the first generation, faith is an experience of the living God. For the children of those believers, faith is a tradition they maintain to honor their parents. For the third generation, it's a duty to be performed. But actually, faith has neither children nor grandchildren. Faith is the outgrowth of a personal experience.

In this portion of Luke's Scripture, we read of the great confrontation between Jesus with His radical views of worship and the Pharisees and Scribes. It certainly cannot be said that the Pharisees and Scribes considered worship dull. Actually, for devout Jews, worship was a serious and sacred treasure. Worship was zealously observed even when they had no temple. Far from being indifferent, the Scribes and Pharisees were passionately devoted to maintaining a very precious tradition, a tradition they felt Jesus was somehow undermining and destroying.

Jesus went to the heart of all this when He questioned the *why* of worship. Did God create us in order to honor Him on the Sabbath? Do we exist to satisfy God's ego and to appease Him? Are we here to be expended in some process that He requires? If the Sabbath was made for man, that is a whole different perspective. Worship is a privilege. God has given us one special day in the week when in faith we come together as a family of brothers and sisters. He promises to be with us and that there will be *dunamis*—power to be healed, changed, convicted, guided, and blessed. The Sabbath is for us, and Jesus, believing that, saw it as a time for God to give good gifts to His people. If the Sabbath is for us, then it's okay for the hungry to eat grain. If the Sabbath is for us, then it's fitting that the sick be healed on that day.

Worship is a means of feeding the soul, and there are different ways of doing that, just as there are different ways of feeding the body. We may be fed at an old-fashioned Victorian dinner party with twenty-seven forks and knives and spoons and many courses. In that situation, we have to be aware of proper etiquette, the protocol of serving and clearing correctly. That's eating of one sort. On the other hand, you may be starving in a Third World country, without food for days, when an airlift drops down rations. Nobody cares about the proper fork or spoon. You tear open the package and you eat. In both cases you are eating, but in the first you eat as part of an elaborate pageant and in the other you eat for survival. We sometimes forget that the process of worship is a means of survival, and we can get caught up in the form. We criticize the procedures: "I don't think it's being done right. It was done much better several years ago (or twenty years ago). The

order of worship is not maximum. The music is not 'conducive'."
If we are desperately hungry for the food only God gives, we come
simply to eat.

The Pharisees, you see, were guardians of what used to be. They
missed the *now* of God—the sense of God in their midst. Jesus was
and is, through the Holy Spirit, the *now* of God, the present tense
of God. The Pharisees were archivists and historians. They were
traditionalists, which isn't all bad; it just misses the point. This is
the basic confrontation here. There are absolutes. The Ten
Commandments are absolutes. The grace of God is absolute. But
God, the Creator, is forever doing a new thing, and worship must
change as we change in our relationship to God. The traditionalists miss out on the drama of the God of the now interacting and
blessing us as we come to worship.

In almost every home we've lived in, we have displayed two
items together on one of the walls of the living room: a brass cross
given to us by friends in our first parish and a round barometer I
bought in Germany after World War II. I hang them side by side
to remind me that life is both absolute and variable. The cross is a
reminder of the changeless. Certain things are forever—the grace
of God, the redemption of your soul and mine in Jesus Christ. The
barometer, on the other hand, going up and down, heralding rain
and sun, reminds me that life is changing. The eternal God is
always changing in terms of His strategy with you and me.

I think that what Jesus is saying in these verses should revolu-
tionize all our ideas of worship. Worship, public or private, can be
the most exciting thing you and I engage in. The key to worship
is relationship. In the Old Testament, God hid behind the smoke
on the mountain to talk to His people because they didn't want a
relationship. It was too frightening. Instead they sent Moses to
report on what God had said. That can happen to present-day
preachers. They are expected to interpret what God is saying, and
their flock is then free to accept or reject that interpretation. But
since Pentecost there has been no such safe arrangement. At the
time the Scripture was fulfilled that "I will give my Spirit to all my
people" (Acts 2:17). From that point on, God made it possible to
enter into a relationship with Him and have dialogue.

Many of us have heard worship referred to as a time to get your
tank filled. Following that to its logical conclusion, we would come
on Sunday and get the tank filled. By Wednesday it would be half full
and by Saturday, almost empty, and time to come back again and
have the tank filled (or your battery charged). It's an unfortunate

analogy. There is no tank to fill and no battery to charge. God invites us into His presence, and we are either in that presence or we're not. No half tank, no half-charged battery. We either have a relationship or we don't, and worship is a means of reestablishing and reaffirming that relationship. Music, prayers, Scripture, and fellowship are all a means of heightening that relationship.

What is a right length of time for a worship service? We would conclude from our Western customs that one hour must be exactly right. Then there are the choices of what to do and what to sing and how often to pray and about what. I happen to have an aversion to printed bulletins outlining the order of service. We seem to be saying we know what God will do this Sunday morning and He had better not change His mind. If the Spirit has something fresh to say, He'll never get through. The program is set in concrete.

I heard a choice story about a Chinese holy man. He was very poor and living in a remote part of China, but he came to love God and to worship Him faithfully. As poor as he was, he understood that worship involves some sacrifice on our part. Food was his scarcest commodity, so every day before his quiet time of prayer and meditation he put a dish of butter up on the window sill as an offering to God. One day during this time, his cat came in and ate the butter. To remedy this, he began to tie the cat to the bedpost each day before his quiet time. The problem was solved permanently.

In time this man was so revered for his piety that others joined him as disciples and worshiped as he did. Generations later, long after the holy man was dead, his followers placed an offering of butter on the windowsill during their time of prayer and meditation. Furthermore, each one bought a cat and tied it to the bedpost. It was all part of the ritual. That's how tradition is created!

The question I have been asked most often by pastors at conferences over the years is, "How can I make worship more meaningful for my congregation?" My answer is simple. I suggest they plan an hour of worship that will be meaningful for them personally. We have to stop thinking of "them and us." We're all one. If you plan a service to meet your own need, after a hectic week of success and failure, grace and sin, it will meet the needs of almost everybody else.

Above all, worship is meaningful when we expect *dunamis.* In Isaiah 40:31 we read, "But those who wait on the Lord shall renew their strength; they shall mount up with wings like eagles; they shall run and not be weary; they shall walk and not faint." That is *dunamis*—power to heal, liberate, set free, transform, change values. Our expectations are the key to what we receive. Do you remember that Jesus in His own hometown of Nazareth could do no miracles because of their lack of expectation. So the best gift we can bring to worship is our own expectation.

I recently heard about two men who were walking down Fifth Avenue in New York. One stopped suddenly and said, "I hear a cricket." His friend scoffed. "How in the world can you hear a cricket on Fifth Avenue?" The first man explained that he was a naturalist and trained to hear crickets, and to prove his point, he reached in his pocket and took out a fifty-cent piece and dropped it on the pavement. Ten people stopped dead in their tracks. He demonstrated that we hear that which has meaning for us. In the same way, we can develop our sense of expectation and train ourselves to anticipate God's presence and intervention in our lives.

What can we legitimately expect in worship? First of all, we can expect to start or continue a relationship with God. In worship we have the opportunity to say yes to Him for the first time or for the hundredth time. We can expect a new beginning. Next, we can expect new freedom. The old values can be reexamined. We can let go of greed, pride, ambition. God can give us new values. Third, we can expect guidance. We may come saying, "What shall I do?" and find that, all of a sudden, a light bulb comes on to illumine our direction. That light comes from God. Finally, we can expect healing. In worship, we can be healed emotionally, physically, and relationally. God may speak to us about letting go of old resentments. All kinds of grace can be channeled our way if we don't stand on the hose. When we decide by God's power to love our enemies, healing forces are set in motion.

PRAYER AND WORSHIP

12 Now it came to pass in those days that He went out to the mountain to pray, and continued all night in prayer to God. 13 And when it was day, He called His disciples to Himself; and from them He chose twelve whom He also named apostles: 14 Simon, whom He also named Peter, and Andrew his brother; James and John; Philip and Bartholomew; 15 Matthew and Thomas; James the son of Alphaeus, and Simon called the Zealot; 16 Judas the son of James, and Judas Iscariot who also became a traitor.

¹⁷ And He came down with them and stood on a level place with a crowd of His disciples and a great multitude of people from all Judea and Jerusalem, and from the seacoast of Tyre and Sidon, who came to hear Him and be healed of their diseases, ¹⁸ as well as those who were tormented with unclean spirits. And they were healed. ¹⁹ And the whole multitude sought to touch Him, for power went out from Him and healed them all.

—Luke 6:12–19

After these two accounts of Jesus observing the Sabbath, Luke continues the story. In verse 12 he tells us Jesus went to the hills to pray and prayed all night. Was that worship? We cannot imagine he brought a prayer book or a hymnbook. How do you spend all night with God? Perhaps by simply being there, rejoicing, crying, talking, and listening. Spending time with God is the essence of worship. Everything else is stage setting. We can be in God's presence, corporately or alone, as Jesus was.

Jesus prayed all night, and on the following day God gave Him a family of twelve. God wants to give us a family of people who believe in us, pray for us, hold us accountable. Remember, Jesus chose twelve disciples, and one of them was Judas. That raises the question of whether or not Judas was an answer to prayer—one of the big theological questions of all time. God may give us some brothers and sisters who are not easy to love and who may even disappoint us and betray us, but the good news is that we need not be afraid of failure. God will be with us in our failures.

I love the famous story told by the nineteenth century Danish theologian Søren Kirkegaard about the state of the church in his time. It speaks as potently today about what we are called to be corporately. He tells of a barnyard full of big, fat, sleek geese, who had long since lost the ability to fly. But every seventh day they would waddle over to one corner of the barnyard and the biggest and fattest goose (probably in a black robe) would stand up on a stump and proclaim the glory of being geese. Occasionally, while this fat goose was talking, a honking would be heard overhead, the honking of a wild goose flying so high it couldn't even be seen. In hushed silence, the barnyard geese would stop for a moment to look and listen. Then the sermon would resume, extolling the joys of being geese.

As we think about programming worship, I wish we could do so, not for the fat barnyard geese, but for the wild geese among us who are meant to be lean and hard, to fly high, to take risks, and to live out there where God is. When we come to worship, we come down from the stratosphere, bloody, broken, and hungry. We feast, get up and go again as God directs our paths. Let's not leave worship rating the performance of the preacher or the choir. Let us leave asking, "What did God say to me? What would God do with me?" That's the dynamite we can expect as we gather in God's presence.

CHAPTER SIXTEEN—LIVING WITHOUT RULES

LUKE 6:20–49

Scripture Outline

Reacting to the Rules (6:20–36)

A New Rule (6:37–45)

Built to Last (6:46–49)

REACTING TO THE RULES

20 Then He lifted up His eyes toward His disciples, and
said:
    "Blessed are you poor,
    For yours is the kingdom of God.
    21 Blessed are you who hunger now,
    For you shall be filled.
    Blessed are you who weep now,
    For you shall laugh.
    22 Blessed are you when men hate you,
    And when they exclude you,
    And revile you, and cast out your name as evil,
    For the Son of Man's sake.
    23 Rejoice in that day and leap for joy!
    For indeed your reward is great in heaven,
    For in like manner their fathers did to the prophets.
    24 "But woe to you who are rich,
    For you have received your consolation.
    25 Woe to you who are full,
    For you shall hunger.
    Woe to you who laugh now,
    For you shall mourn and weep.
    26 Woe to you when all men speak well of you,
    For so did their fathers to the false prophets.
    27 "But I say to you who hear: Love your enemies, do
good to those who hate you, 28 bless those who curse you, and
pray for those who spitefully use you. 29 To him who strikes

you on the one cheek, offer the other also. And from him who takes away your cloak, do not withhold your tunic either. ³⁰ Give to everyone who asks of you. And from him who takes away your goods do not ask them back. ³¹ And just as you want men to do to you, you also do to them likewise.

³² "But if you love those who love you, what credit is that to you? For even sinners love those who love them. ³³ And if you do good to those who do good to you, what credit is that to you? For even sinners do the same. ³⁴ And if you lend to those from whom you hope to receive back, what credit is that to you? For even sinners lend to sinners to receive as much back. ³⁵ But love your enemies, do good, and lend, hoping for nothing in return; and your reward will be great, and you will be sons of the Most High. For He is kind to the unthankful and evil. ³⁶ Therefore be merciful, just as your Father also is merciful.

—Luke 6:20–36

The rules for living that Jesus gives us here are revolutionary. There is something fascinating about how we react to rules. We resist and resent rules and yet something in us demands rules. Adults pass on the rules of living to those younger, to children, students, or friends. They usually meet with a good deal of resistance. At our local department store, a teenager was overheard saying to a clerk, "I am crazy about this outfit, but may I exchange it if my mother happens to like it?" We all know that feeling. Somehow when someone in authority wants to guide us in matters of dress or behavior, we're a little rebellious.

Some of us seem to have more of a need for rules than others. I can remember at seminary how frustrated I was because my professors were unwilling to give us concrete rules. I was (and am!) a zealous evangelical, and I wanted the rules spelled out for me. In those days, I wanted answers to the question of whether or not Christians could smoke or use alcohol. And then there was dancing. Surely a nonintimate sort of square dancing was okay. Well, no one ever gave me rules for all those situations, and now I understand why. As a pastor and counselor, I try to resist the temptation to tell others what is right and wrong. If I do that I fail them. They need to get in touch with God who is the giver of life, and find His will in life's perplexing situations.

Assuming we understand clearly the rules outlined in this chapter, what then? First of all, we may feel overwhelmed and discouraged because we realize we can't possibly keep them. Or, we may be like the Pharisees and scribes we read about in Scripture who are pleased to hear the rules because they are smugly certain they have kept them since childhood. Then there are some of us who want to know the rules so that we can begin to look for the loopholes. We immediately try to decipher the fine print at the bottom of the contract. We think of God and His laws as some sort of celestial IRS and we look for ways to beat the system. We are like the man who was told to watch his drinking and now drinks only in bars with mirrors.

Knowing and keeping the rules can be a reason for excluding others. My knowledge of the rules makes me aware that *you* are not keeping them. Consequently, I am in and you're out. This was the attitude of the religious people of Jesus' time. They had an elaborate system of rules and enjoyed ferreting out those who did not adhere to them. Jesus refused to exclude people on the basis of whether or not they kept the rules. He hung out with tax collectors and sinners, the social and political outcasts. I am reminded of Edwin Markham's poem:

> They drew a circle that shut me out,
> Heretic, rebel, a thing to flout.
> But love and I had the wit to win,
> We drew a circle that took them in.

Luke gives us just four Beatitudes here, whereas in Matthew's account there are nine. According to Luke, Jesus said, *"Blessed are you poor,"* *"Blessed are you who hunger,"* *"Blessed are you who weep,"* and *"Blessed are you when men hate you and when they exclude you"* (vv. 20–22). Then, lest you miss the meaning, Jesus adds the four "Woe to you" statements that deal with the exact opposite behaviors. And while Matthew seems to spiritualize some of these rules in that he says, "Blessed are those who hunger and thirst for *righteousness,"* Luke simply speaks of actual hunger. The rules he reports deal not just with spiritual matters, but with the very basics of life.

When Jesus says, "Blessed are the poor," I don't believe He is saying that poverty is a good thing. And in saying, "Blessed are you that weep," He is not anti-joy. He explains later on that He came that we might have joy, that His joy might be in us and that our joy might be full. But there is an unreality about people who are always jolly and always laughing. A friend gave me a poem recently that speaks to this:

Have you been to the Land of Happy, where
    everyone's happy all day?
Where they joke and they sing of the happiest
    things, and everything's jolly and gay?
There's no one unhappy in Happy, there's
    laughter and smiles galore.
I have been to the Land of Happy—what a
    bore!

I think that's the kind of laughter our Lord is talking about—unreal and of no substance. But at the same time He is the source of a genuine joy that wells up inside us, a joy not dependent on circumstances.

All through the ages, wise people have understood the peril of seeking after riches. Shakespeare, for example, said, "If thou art rich thou art poor, for like an ass whose back with ingots bows, thou bearest thy heavy riches but a journey and death unloads thee." Martin Luther said, "Rich folks' children seldom turn out well. They are complacent, arrogant and conceited and think they need to learn nothing because they have enough to live on anyway." William James, the great pioneer Christian psychologist at the turn of the last century, said, "The desire to gain wealth and the fear to lose it are chief breeders of cowardice and propagators of corruption. There are thousands of conjectures in which a wealth-bound man must be a slave, whilst a man for whom poverty has no terror becomes a free man" (*Varieties of Religious Experiences,* p. 368).

But there are people in our time who say that the rules—the Ten Commandments and the even more difficult rules Jesus gives us here—are beyond our keeping. Therefore, forget the rules. According to this philosophy, the important thing is sincerity and good intentions. Ten years ago we heard a lot about situational ethics—that morals and values varied, depending on the circumstances.

But in fact, there are absolutes, those things that are true now and always. One of our great psychiatrists, Dr. Karl Menninger, brought a book out a few years ago entitled, *Whatever Became of Sin?* He says we suffer personally and corporately because of our lack of absolutes. We assume that those guilty of criminal behavior must be insane, and we put them in mental hospitals. He says that there is no way someone diagnosed criminally insane can repent. But if your behavior is a matter of choice, you can choose to live differently.

Somehow our "no rules" or "things are all relative" approaches have put terrible burdens on society. Whether or not we can always keep them, the rules are stars to steer by. Stars are fixed and absolute and boats have crossed great oceans because of those fixed absolutes. And the moral and biblical absolutes, including those that Jesus gives here, are true, and we steer our lives by them, no matter how often we get off course. Without absolutes there is no sense of sin, nor need for repentance. We are told that the unforgivable sin is the sin against the Holy Spirit. Because we know the rules, the Holy Spirit points out those dishonest and sinful areas in our lives, and we can be forgiven and come back to life. If there are no rules, then I can't repent. I am lost in my sin. The sin against the Holy Spirit is to say I am innocent when He says I am guilty.

A NEW RULE

37 "Judge not, and you shall not be judged. Condemn not, and you shall not be condemned. Forgive, and you will be forgiven. 38 Give, and it will be given to you: good measure, pressed down, shaken together, and running over will be put into your bosom. For with the same measure that you use, it will be measured back to you."

39 And He spoke a parable to them: "Can the blind lead the blind? Will they not both fall into the ditch? 40 A disciple is not above his teacher, but everyone who is perfectly trained will be like his teacher. 41 And why do you look at the speck in your brother's eye, but do not perceive the plank in your own eye? 42 Or how can you say to your brother, 'Brother, let me remove the speck that is in your eye,' when you yourself do not see the plank that is in your own eye? Hypocrite! First remove the plank from your own eye, and then you will see clearly to remove the speck that is in your brother's eye.

43 "For a good tree does not bear bad fruit, nor does a bad tree bear good fruit. 44 For every tree is known by its own fruit. For men do not gather figs from thorns, nor do they gather grapes from a bramble bush. 45 A good man out of the good treasure of his heart brings forth good; and an evil man out of the evil treasure of his heart brings forth evil. For out of the abundance of the heart his mouth speaks.

—*Luke 6:37–45*

There are some pitfalls in this whole business of rules. We make up our own rules for Christian conduct and measure others by them. There are Christians who make missions and missionary efforts their test for orthodoxy. For others, evangelism is the only valid priority. Or, we can test the commitment of others by their concern for the poor or by what we consider sound biblical doctrine. I have resisted all of these rules, convinced that there are no rules but the law of love. But I have found that you can make a rule of no rules. If the new rule is love, then I find myself excluding people who don't love. You see, there is no hiding place. In verse 41, Jesus tells us to examine our own eye and not to look for the speck in another's eye. Jesus is calling us to live beyond the rules. That's what the law of love is actually all about.

Jesus is saying that the rules for love are beyond any kind of a simple test. We are tested by our day-to-day actions and by the quality of our relationship with the maker of the rules. If we are honest, we confess that much of the time we don't keep His rules. Nevertheless, our emphasis is on keeping a relationship with the rule-giver, who is our Creator. Obviously, there are no rules to cover most of life's situations. We can't find rules to tell us how to be a lover or how to be God's person in every situation.

At the beginning of the ecumenical movement between Catholics and Protestants, I led a conference for a group of Catholic nuns. We had a marvelous week together, but at the final communion I was told that the priests had ruled I could not partake of the Eucharist because I was a Protestant. The nuns were incensed and delivered an ultimatum. "If our brother Bruce can't come to our Lord's table, we will not come." The priests were in a tizzy, but they reconsidered the matter and decided to break the rules for that one occasion. That was a long time ago, and it is unlikely such a situation would arise today. But it pointed out to me that God's law of love goes far beyond "keeping the rules."

BUILT TO LAST

46 "But why do you call Me 'Lord, Lord,' and not do the things which I say? 47 Whoever comes to Me, and hears My sayings and does them, I will show you whom he is like: 48 He is like a man building a house, who dug deep and laid the foundation on the rock. And when the flood arose, the stream beat vehemently against that house, and could not shake it, for it was founded on the rock. 49 But he who heard and did nothing is like a man who built a house on the earth without a

foundation, against which the stream beat vehemently; and immediately it fell. And the ruin of that house was great."

—*Luke 6:46–49*

In this story of the house built upon a rock, that rock is not the rock of rules. The house is built upon the Giver of life, our Redeemer, Jesus Christ. The house built on the sand is as costly as the house built on the rock. But one stands and the other does not. When we build our lives on rules, rules that justify ourselves and exclude others, we are building on the insubstantial.

Watchman Nee tells about a new convert who came in deep distress to see him. "No matter how much I pray," said the man, "no matter how hard I try, I simply cannot seem to be faithful to my Lord. I think I'm losing my salvation." And Nee said, "Do you see this dog here? He is my dog. He is house-trained; he never makes a mess; he is obedient; he is a pure delight to me. Out in the kitchen I have a son, a baby son. He makes a mess, he throws his food around, he fouls his clothes, he is a total mess. But who is going to inherit my kingdom? Not my dog; my son is my heir. *You* are Jesus Christ's heir because it is for you that He died." So it is with us. We are Christ's heirs, not through our perfection but by means of His grace.

Scripture Outline

Faith That Works (7:1–17)

A Confrontation (7:18–23)

Not Having to Win (7:24–35)

FAITH THAT WORKS

7:1 Now when He concluded all His sayings in the hearing of the people, He entered Capernaum. 2 And a certain centurion's servant, who was dear to him, was sick and ready to die. 3 So when he heard about Jesus, he sent elders of the Jews to Him, pleading with Him to come and heal his servant. 4 And when they came to Jesus, they begged Him earnestly, saying that the one for whom He should do this was deserving, 5 "for he loves our nation, and has built us a synagogue."

6 Then Jesus went with them. And when He was already not far from the house, the centurion sent friends to Him, saying to Him, "Lord, do not trouble Yourself, for I am not worthy that You should enter under my roof. 7 Therefore I did not even think myself worthy to come to You. But say the word, and my servant will be healed. 8 For I also am a man placed under authority, having soldiers under me. And I say to one, 'Go,' and he goes; and to another, 'Come,' and he comes; and to my servant, 'Do this,' and he does it."

9 When Jesus heard these things, He marveled at him, and turned around and said to the crowd that followed Him, "I say to you, I have not found such great faith, not even in Israel!" 10 And those who were sent, returning to the house, found the servant well who had been sick.

11 Now it happened, the day after, that He went into a city called Nain; and many of His disciples went with Him, and a large crowd. 12 And when He came near the gate of the city, behold, a dead man was being carried out, the only son of

his mother; and she was a widow. And a large crowd from the city was with her. 13 When the Lord saw her, He had compassion on her and said to her, "Do not weep." 14 Then He came and touched the open coffin, and those who carried *him* stood still. And He said, "Young man, I say to you, arise." 15 So he who was dead sat up and began to speak. And He presented him to his mother.

16 Then fear came upon all, and they glorified God, saying, "A great prophet has risen up among us"; and, "God has visited His people."

17 And this report about Him went throughout all Judea and all the surrounding region.

—Luke 7:1–17

Perhaps you have had the experience of attending church with a friend and finding afterward that while you found the sermon dull and irrelevant, your friend thought it was powerful and exactly to the point. It's an experience that points up the fact that no single sermon touches all the hearers alike. I was thinking of this about a month ago as I was driving in southern Indiana through lovely Brown County, where roads had been built right through the limestone cliffs exposing geologic strata that had been evolving for eons.

The gospel is like that—a road that slices right through life. Abraham Maslow, one of our great pioneer psychologists, talked about our different levels of conscious need: survival, security, belonging, and status. If these four needs are met, we move up to the level of self-actualization, which is our need to be and do that which is rewarding and fulfilling. All of us, he says, are at one of these levels at any one given point in life. But Jesus Christ is the eternal word for us at all of these levels. If you are facing death—your own, or that of someone close to you—He says to you, "I am the resurrection and the life. He that believes in me shall never die." If you are at the security level, He says, "Seek first the kingdom of God and all the things you need will be added unto you." In terms of belonging, He has said, "You are my friends."

The words of Scripture we read here could prompt a sermon on any number of subjects addressed to any of these levels of need. Chapter 7 of Luke deals with death, faith, compassion, and love.

The first thirty-six verses of Luke 7 deal with power in various forms. They deal with Christ's power over illness and death as well as His power over the political and relational dimensions of life. They provide a prism which reveals the totality of our Lord's authority.

In verses 1–10, we find a centurion who, though a Gentile, understood who Christ was and is. It is a story that would especially interest Theophilus, Luke's Gentile reader. But the story is significant not just because this Gentile has faith. He has a remarkably mature faith.

In life, evolution is from the complex to the simple. I happen to live in Seattle, the home of one huge branch of the aviation industry. The first airplanes built by Boeing were propeller planes with a vast number of parts. Next they manufactured prop jets, which are less complicated. The next step produced the pure jet, which is even more simple. Today, we have the rocket, the most sophisticated form of aviation, and yet the simplest of all these concepts and the one requiring the fewest parts.

The centurion's faith is simple but not simplistic. The centurion understands that all authority comes ultimately from God. With his military background he is familiar with a chain of command. Orders are received and then channeled to others, peers and subordinates alike. The centurion realizes that God's own power resides in Jesus, and he suggests that this power could flow through his own faith to heal his faithful servant. The centurion is a model for all of us. He wants to be a channel, open at both ends—open to receive power from God and eager to let that power flow out to others.

The healing that Jesus performs in this instance can be explained logically by modern researchers. Their studies indicate, for example, that witch doctors do actually have the power to kill simply by means of suggestion. If the object of a hex attributes supernatural powers to the witch doctor, then the hex or curse is taken very seriously and his body begins to deteriorate. On the other hand, positive encouragement from a physician in whom we have put our faith can reverse disease and enable the healing process. The centurion had complete faith in Jesus' power and his faith could provide the channel for the healing of his servant. We Christians ought not to be surprised by Jesus' healing powers, then or now. We also have His promise that the things that He does, we shall do also (John 14:12). We need to receive that mysterious healing power in order to transmit it to those around us who are suffering physical or mental illness.

In verses 11–17, Jesus raises the son of the widow of Nain from the dead. Only Luke tells this story. The Gospels give us three accounts of Jesus raising the dead. One is the story of Lazarus, raised after being dead three days. Another is the daughter of Jairus, who is presumed to have died on her sickbed. Later on, in verse 22, we read that "the dead being raised" is one of the authentic marks of the Messiah. This particular miracle is an example of the unusual compassion that Jesus demonstrated throughout His ministry to the disenfranchised, the outcast, and the poor.

A widow in those days was in a totally vulnerable position if there were no male relatives to protect her. This particular woman had lost first her husband and now her only son. The only social security in those days was having some man provide for you. This woman's future was bleak indeed.

In His compassion for the widow, Jesus restored her dead son to life. Verse 16 indicates that fear seized all those who witnessed this event. Throughout the Gospels, this was a common reaction when Jesus demonstrated His messianic powers. It seems to me it is a pattern indicative of the ambivalence in all of us. We want to believe, and we do not want to. When the angels appeared to the shepherds over Bethlehem's fields, the message was, "Fear not." These heavenly messengers were aware that the shepherds would need to overcome their fear in order to believe. Dramatic signs, whether they be angels in the sky or raising the dead, do not automatically produce belief.

A CONFRONTATION

¹⁸ Then the disciples of John reported to him concerning all these things. ¹⁹ And John, calling two of his disciples to *him,* sent *them* to Jesus, saying, "Are You the Coming One, or do we look for another?"

²⁰ When the men had come to Him, they said, "John the Baptist has sent us to You, saying, 'Are You the Coming One, or do we look for another?'" ²¹ And that very hour He cured many of infirmities, afflictions, and evil spirits; and to many blind He gave sight.

²² Jesus answered and said to them, "Go and tell John the things you have seen and heard: that *the* blind see, *the* lame walk, *the* lepers are cleansed, *the* deaf hear, *the* dead are raised, *the* poor have the gospel preached to them. ²³ And blessed is *he* who is not offended because of Me."

—Luke 17:18–23

Now let us zero in on the confrontation between Jesus and the disciples of John. This is an example of the kind of power struggle we're all familiar with. On the heels of these events—the healing of the slave (vv. 1–10) and the raising of the widow's son from the dead (vv. 11–17)—John the Baptist sends two of his disciples to inquire about Jesus' authenticity (7:18–23). John wants to know if Jesus is really the Messiah or if he has baptized the wrong person and should look for another.

We might wonder how, with all the evidence coming in, this great man of God could have doubts. One explanation might be that John was suffering a midlife crisis. A good many people in our culture have gone through this. They come to a place in life when they wonder, "Is this all there is? Must I settle for this?" As a youngster I may have had dreams of being a brain surgeon, an airline pilot, a champion skiier, a rodeo star. Suddenly, all of these things are out of reach and I'm stuck with a routine job, an unexceptional family, and an unexciting life. With the realization that this is all there is, panic sets in. That's what midlife crisis is all about. You come to the place where your options have begun to shrink and you must settle for what is.

Perhaps this is what happened to John. His mission was to prepare the way for the Coming One, the Messiah, his cousin Jesus, and he was concerned about what he saw happening. Now John did not mind being number two in the kingdom. He had said, "One mightier than I is coming whose sandal strap I am not worthy to loose." But John must have been concerned that Jesus did not conform to his concept of the Messiah.

First of all, he had a hard time believing that someone committed to serving God could be so joyful. Second, he expected the Messiah to deal harshly with all the evildoers. Certainly John had. He had spoken out against the king and called the Pharisees a generation of vipers. That was the game plan, according to John, and I'm sure he believed that the one coming after him would drive the Romans out of the land, convert all the hypocritical Pharisees, shake the foundations, and clean the place up.

Instead, Jesus came celebrating life. He went to parties, He enjoyed people, He drank wine. Beyond that, He taught that we are to love our enemies and turn the other cheek. No wonder John thought he might have baptized the wrong person. When John sent his messengers to Jesus, it was a time of confrontation between these two powerful men, the prophet and the Messiah.

But you see, John was doing what all of us do. We have a scenario in life for those around us. We have stereotyped ideas about how others are going to behave. That's the basic cause of the generation gap. I'm reminded of the old New Englander who was sitting in front of the general store when a carload of young wise guys from the city pulled up. "Hey, pop, how long has this town been dead?" one called. Thinking a minute, the old man retorts, "Well, it can't be very long. You're the first buzzards I've seen." It's a typical putdown encounter.

The power game is never more apparent than in the eternal battle between the sexes. Blondie and Dagwood are the classic caricatures of this very real conflict. Blondie is constantly conniving to get more money than her budget allows to buy some hat in the local department store. As for Dagwood, he has a never-ending series of schemes to sneak out and play poker or to go bowling with the boys. The game is to get one's way by tricking the other party. Each party has a need to win. When lovers marry, we say, "These two shall become one." They may spend their remaining years figuring out "which one?" The battle of the sexes is fought in many arenas. There is the issue of time. One partner is almost compulsively punctual while the other seems to engage deliberately in dallying and delaying tactics. Perhaps the power game is even more apparent in the area of money—how much is spent and for what.

One wife I know has chosen to make tuna fish the issue of her power struggle. It seems her husband said at the time of their wedding, "Listen, dear, I will eat anything except tuna. I hate it. Please, please, never serve tuna." Thirty years later she boasted to me that she had been serving him tuna regularly, fixed in twenty-eight different ways, and he was unaware he had eaten it. It's become a game, but one with revealing implications.

Adler and Freud, two colleagues in psychoanalysis, couldn't agree on the single most important basic human drive. Freud said it was sex, while Adler considered it the need for power. But sex can be an extension of power. For many married couples the real issue is not when or how often they have sex or in what position. The crux of it all is who decides, who says, "Tonight is the night."

NOT HAVING TO WIN

24 When the messengers of John had departed, He began to speak to the multitudes concerning John: "What did you go out into the wilderness to see? A reed shaken by the wind? 25 But what did you go out to see? A man clothed in soft garments?

Indeed those who are gorgeously appareled and live in luxury are in kings' courts. 26 But what did you go out to see? A prophet? Yes, I say to you, and more than a prophet. 27 This is *he* of whom it is written:

'Behold, I send My messenger before Your face,
Who will prepare Your way before You.'

28 For I say to you, among those born of women there is not a greater prophet than John the Baptist; but he who is least in the kingdom of God is greater than he."

29 And when all the people heard *Him,* even the tax collectors justified God, having been baptized with the baptism of John. 30 But the Pharisees and lawyers rejected the will of God for themselves, not having been baptized by him.

31 And the Lord said, "To what then shall I liken the men of this generation, and what are they like? 32 They are like children sitting in the marketplace and calling to one another, saying:

'We played the flute for you,
And you did not dance;
We mourned to you,
And you did not weep.'

33 For John the Baptist came neither eating bread nor drinking wine, and you say, 'He has a demon.' 34 The Son of Man has come eating and drinking, and you say, 'Look, a glutton and a winebibber, a friend of tax collectors and sinners!' 35 But wisdom is justified by all her children."

—*Luke 7:24–35*

Jesus reminded the multitude that John came playing the funeral game, saying, "Life is hard and doom is at hand." And they said, "Boo!" Jesus came saying, "Life is a celebration," and they were similarly hostile. He told them they were like children in the marketplace. They refused to play funerals and they would not dance or celebrate. John didn't please them and the Son of Man does not please them.

Jesus' remarks about John give us insight into dealing with the struggle for power. First of all, He honors John. He says, *"I say to you, among those born of women there is not a greater prophet than John the Baptist. But,"* He adds, *"he who is least in the kingdom of God is greater than John"* (v. 28). Jesus came to bring a new kingdom and a new way to live. As for us, instead of struggling for power in life, in the church, in our relationships, we can come into a kingdom where Jesus, the King, provides a new center to our lives. As we move into our varied situations and relationships, we need not struggle for power. We are there as ambassadors for a kingdom. In each situation, we can say, "Lord, what would You have me do here? You are the model."

We read that the meek will inherit the earth, but meekness from weakness is no blessing. We all have a sphere of influence from which we can wield tremendous power, and, beyond that, as Christians, we have the power of the Holy Spirit. We are powerful people. We are not meek because we are frightened or weak. If we are meek, it is because we choose to be. If you and I are under orders as ambassadors, winning is no longer the issue. In most relationships, if you win, you lose. You can insist on your rightness at the expense of the relationship. Is it that important to win? Perhaps you will have achieved a pyrrhic victory like that of the king of Epirus, who defeated the Romans in battle but lost 80 percent of his troops. He was astute enough to realize that one more victory like that would finish him. Jesus has a new strategy. He says, "Love your enemies." Sometimes you confront them and sometimes you give up even when you are right.

Disraeli, master politician and past prime minister of England, once said that, next to knowing when to seize an opportunity, the most important thing is to know when to forego an advantage. The strategy of the kingdom, it seems to me, is to let the other person save face—as over against saying, "I told you so." Jesus didn't confront individuals with their sins, and, by letting them save face, they entered the kingdom. Some of us still remember the Cuban missile crisis of the sixties when John F. Kennedy was wise enough, like Disraeli, to let the Russians save face and choose to withdraw their missiles.

The power thus goes to the one who knows when *not* to win. In our overwhelming need to convince the other person that we are right and they are wrong, let's remember that the prodigal son's father never said, "You stupid boy, I knew you'd come to your senses." Instead, he said, "I'm so glad you're home. I've missed you." The King welcomes us into the kingdom in the same way, with no recriminations.

The ultimate power game is the game we play with God Himself. And hell is that place where God finally says to us, "Have it your way. You've won." But we can have it *His* way. The King welcomes us into the kingdom and as we move out to strangers, friends, and family, He gives us the power to live as He would have us, to defer to our enemies, and not to have to win.

Chapter Eighteen—Unconditional Love
Luke 7:36—8:3

Scripture Outline

An Extravagant Act (7:36–50)

The Women Around Jesus (8:1–3)

AN EXTRAVAGANT ACT

36 Then one of the Pharisees asked Him to eat with him. And He went to the Pharisee's house, and sat down to eat. 37 And behold, a woman in the city who was a sinner, when she knew that Jesus sat at the table in the Pharisee's house, brought an alabaster flask of fragrant oil, 38 and stood at His feet behind Him weeping; and she began to wash His feet with her tears, and wiped them with the hair of her head; and she kissed His feet and anointed them with the fragrant oil. 39 Now when the Pharisee who had invited Him saw this, he spoke to himself, saying, "This Man, if He were a prophet, would know who and what manner of woman this is who is touching Him, for she is a sinner."

40 And Jesus answered and said to him, "Simon, I have something to say to you."

So he said, "Teacher, say it."

41 "There was a certain creditor who had two debtors. One owed five hundred denarii, and the other fifty. 42 And when they had nothing with which to repay, he freely forgave them both. Tell Me, therefore, which of them will love him more?"

43 Simon answered and said, "I suppose the one whom he forgave more."

And He said to him, "You have rightly judged." 44 Then He turned to the woman and said to Simon, "Do you see this woman? I entered your house; you gave Me no water for My feet, but she has washed My feet with her tears and wiped them with the hair of her head. 45 You gave Me no kiss, but this woman has not ceased to kiss My feet since the time I came in. 46 You did not anoint My head with oil, but this woman has anointed My feet with fragrant oil. 47 Therefore I say to you, her sins, which are many, are forgiven, for she loved much. But to whom little is forgiven, the same loves little."

48 Then He said to her, "Your sins are forgiven."

49 And those who sat at the table with Him began to say to themselves, "Who is this who even forgives sins?"

50 Then He said to the woman, "Your faith has saved you. Go in peace."

—Luke 7:36–50

Thomas Carlyle once said, "The great law of culture is to let each one become all that he was created capable of being, expand if possible to his full growth and show himself at length in his own shape and stature, be these what they may." I would propose that the kingdom of God has the same goal. You and I are not cannon fodder for the kingdom. We are invited to enter the kingdom in order that we might become everything that God had in mind when He thought of us—even before we were conceived. That is central to our faith.

Last year a beloved brother and senior elder in our church died. With only two days' notice, the funeral service was packed with mourners from all over the world. His son told me about collecting his dad's belongings at the hospital after his death. "All he had I could put in one hand—a pen and a pencil, a ring, a pocketknife, and a wallet." This man, eminently successful in business, did not collect a surplus of things. Like Abraham, he was God's friend. He carried a Bible with him wherever he went. He loved people. Another son told me about the many loans his father had made which remain unpaid to this day. He spent a good part of his life helping people who couldn't pay him back. It was a lesson to me in the essence of life—which is to love God and your neighbor.

Funerals are often occasions to make most of us rethink our ideas on the essence of life. Someone has said, "Just because you can't take it with you doesn't mean you won't get what's coming to you." Just what is coming to us and what does God want to give us?

These verses we read here, it seems to me, deal with the very essence of the gospel. A religious leader invites Jesus to his home for a party. Earlier in this chapter we read that John was wary of

Jesus because he seemed to like parties. Here we find him at yet another party. Now, a party in those days was a public event. Homes had open courts, and the uninvited could stand around and observe the guests and the festivities. They ate, as the Romans did, with a table in the middle and many couches. Lying with heads at the table and their feet out, the guests would form a pattern that resembled a great big star. Jesus was reclining in this manner at the home of Simon when a woman in the crowd came up and wept over Him. Her tears washed His feet, and she dried them with her hair. In those days it was forbidden to unbind your hair and only loose women did so. After all this, she poured expensive ointment over His feet.

Simon's reaction reveals a good deal about who he was and his reasons for asking Jesus to the party. He did not invite Jesus as a social equal and he did not provide the usual amenities for Him: the anointing of oil for the head, the ritual footwashing, and a kiss of greeting. He invited Him as a curiosity. He had heard that Jesus was a prophet and he wanted to see for himself who this questionable celebrity was.

In Simon's opinion, Jesus flunked the first test. Simon said to himself, *"This man, if He were a prophet, would know who and what manner of woman this is who is touching Him."* And Jesus, reading his heart, said, *"Simon, I have something to say to you,"* and He pointed out that this woman had done the things that Simon did not do. Because she had been forgiven so much, she washed His feet with her tears; dried them with her hair; anointed not His head but His feet with expensive ointment. Her sins, which were many, were forgiven because she loved much.

We don't know how Simon reacted, but he is exposed. He knew everything about religion, liturgy, theology, ethics, temple worship, and the law. He knew all about the things of God but somehow he missed the essence of it all, which this woman captured. The woman knew how sinful she was. Simon's problem was that he thought he was better than he was and he misunderstood the nature of God who is the giver of unconditional love.

The essence of the gospel is *agápē*, which is the Greek word for the love of God, a love unlike any other love. Every other kind of love is to some degree conditioned. It's a trade-off: "I will if you will." God's love is very different. Through Jesus, God is saying that He loves you just the way you are now. There's nothing you can do that can make Him love you more than He does right now. If you will respond to His love and give Him your life, He is not going to leave you as you are. You are a mess, obviously. He will reprogram you, make you transparent, set you free. All these strange quirks in you are going to go—in one year or in five thousand years. But when you are what He intended when He thought of you, He will not love you one bit more than He does now. That kind of love is the most powerful force in the world.

In psychology now, they are discovering that the vital ingredient in effective therapy is the ability of the counselor to love those whom he counsels. The term used is not love. That would be too spiritual. The quality is called "nonpossessive warmth." But when the therapist does not try to manipulate the other person into being good or responsible but relates in love, healing happens.

I can think of a few times in my own life when I received unconditional love. My father had a great love affair with automobiles. They were introduced in his lifetime, and he never got over his delight in them. In the depression years he bought a car about once in ten years, and that car represented affluence and freedom and adventure. We had an old DeSoto, and one evening I borrowed it for a high school dance. Some of the students got a little wild, and when I came out with my date, my dad's beloved car was tipped on its side in the school parking lot. Friends helped me right it, but it was badly scraped. I drove it home and told my father what happened. I protested my own innocence, and I don't know to this day if he believed me. But the point is he never said, "How could you let this happen to my car?" He just listened, and loved me. I had damaged his most prized possession, but there were no recriminations.

I can remember a similar experience of unconditioned love some years ago when our children were young. We bought a baby parakeet—a poor, bald thing with no feathers. However, Jeremiah (his name) grew into a very beautiful and talented bird. He could say "Give me a kiss, baby" and "I'm a Presbyterian." This bird had the run of the house, and on one sunny day I walked out into our back yard, only to discover Jeremiah on my shoulder. I turned immediately to go back in, but off he flew, never to be seen again. Jerry had been a member of the family for eight years, and I thought my kids would blame me for my carelessness. But they never once said, "How could you?" They loved me, and felt sorry for me. Those are rare moments—when we are forgiven much. I think this is the heart of the Christian program that God has in mind for us. We are to receive His unconditional love and transmit it to others, however undeserving or unworthy. That's the proof of our faith.

THE WOMEN AROUND JESUS

8:1 Now it came to pass, afterward, that He went through every city and village, preaching and bringing the glad tidings of the kingdom of God. And the twelve were with Him, 2 and certain women who had been healed of evil spirits and infirmities—Mary called Magdalene, out of whom had come seven demons, 3 and Joanna the wife of Chuza, Herod's steward, and Susanna, and many others who provided for Him from their substance.

—Luke 8:1–3

These three verses are especially interesting. We said earlier that Luke's Gospel is, among other things, the Gospel of women. Here he tells us that Jesus and His disciples were largely supported by women. Certainly this was not because they needed to be. You remember, God provided the Israelites with manna for forty years in the wilderness. Jesus might have chosen to do miracles and turn stones into bread. But unconditional love also knows how to receive. During His three years of ministry, our Lord received the generosity of those women who had been healed, liberated, and forgiven.

The whole act of love consists of giving and receiving. First we receive from God Himself. We are loved just the way we are. Because of that assurance, we move out to love a handful of people to whom we are accountable. Next, we begin to reach out beyond our usual spheres to those, rich or poor, who are in need. Finally, we are free to receive the love others need to give, and to enjoy it.

CHAPTER NINETEEN—LEARN TO LISTEN

LUKE 8:4-21

Scripture Outline

Taking Heed of What We Hear (8:4–15)

Marks of the Kingdom (8:16–21)

TAKING HEED OF WHAT WE HEAR

4 And when a great multitude had gathered, and they had come to Him from every city, He spoke by a parable: 5 "A sower went out to sow his seed. And as he sowed, some fell by the wayside; and it was trampled down, and the birds of the air devoured it. 6 Some fell on rock; and as soon as it sprang up, it withered away because it lacked moisture. 7 And some fell among thorns, and the thorns sprang up with it and choked it. 8 But others fell on good ground, sprang up, and yielded a crop a hundredfold." When He had said these things He cried, "He who has ears to hear, let him hear!"

9 Then His disciples asked Him, saying, "What does this parable mean?"

10 And He said, "To you it has been given to know the mysteries of the kingdom of God, but to the rest it is given in parables, that

'Seeing they may not see,

And hearing they may not understand.'

11 "Now the parable is this: The seed is the word of God. 12 Those by the wayside are the ones who hear; then the devil comes and takes away the word out of their hearts, lest they should believe and be saved. 13 But the ones on the rock are those who, when they hear, receive the word with joy; and these have no root, who believe for a while and in time of temptation fall away. 14 Now the ones that fell among thorns are those who, when they have heard, go out and are choked with cares, riches, and pleasures of life, and bring no fruit to maturity. 15 But the ones that fell on the good ground are

those who, having heard the word with a noble and good heart, keep it and bear fruit with patience.

—*Luke 8:4–15*

One of the greatest gifts that God can give us in life is the gift of listening. Listening is the key to success and perhaps even survival in most relationships. We have all seen beautiful double-page magazine ads in which reputable business systems companies claim that they will teach the members of your firm how to listen. They suggest that the art of listening leads to business success. I don't know if they can deliver what they promise, but I am convinced that every year many businesses will fail, not because their product is faulty or their service poor, but because management and workers are not listening to each other. I am convinced that every year some marriages will fail because two people, though lovers, do not know how to listen to each other. Even the one who looks so strong and adequate may be trying to communicate, "Help me. I'm frightened. I'm lonely." Every year there are parents and children who will begin an irreparable breach because of feelings that can't be put into words. Family members speak past each other and a relationship diminishes.

A recent research project at the University of Nebraska indicates that the loneliest group of people in our society are not the unmarried or the recently bereaved, but teenagers. How much parents need to listen for that deep loneliness and provide a climate for communication.

In the church, we affirm the ministry of every believer and that makes us responsible for the well-being of the friends around us. Do we really hear what they are saying?

A pastor friend named Bruce Evans has written something that addresses this very real problem:

> Who'd have known she was coming unglued?
> Every hair was neatly placed, no slip showed,
>   nor thread hung
> Colors blended as did words, pleasing both eye
>   and ear;
> Style embraced form, concealing and revealing
>   female ripeness;
> Delicate perfume, yet firm, intertwined and
>   matched the carefully wafting, casual con-
>   versation;

No blood, no sweat, no tears.
So who would have known a lost soul plods
    the walls of hell's depression while years
    of building lay in heaps unseen?
She was so appealing. Who'd have known she
    was coming unglued?

Learning to listen to our friends and families and, beyond that, to God, is essential to any good relationship.

The lesson in these verses is clear; not all will be saved. Some will be lost. And yet the Word of God, the spoken word, the Word made Flesh, does not vary. Jesus says, "It's the same sower and the same seed." The idea of the Word being seed was an old rabbinical teaching. The seed is the same, but the soil into which the seed falls is what makes the difference. And I suggest that depends on our ability to hear what God is saying. Verse 18 says, *"Take heed how you hear."*

Jesus describes four kinds of soil, an analogy so basic and simple, and yet so hard for some to understand. There are those who have become like the asphalt or concrete of our highways. They see and experience something of the wonder of God. They hear the message and see it lived out and yet they say, "It can't be so. It's too simple. It's too easy." Their cynicism results in a hardness of heart, and the Word cannot find a lodging place.

Then there are those impressionable ones who hear the Word and have an instant and positive response. They join all the groups, buy all the books, come to all the courses. They never miss worship. But in a few years, where are they and what has happened to them? A great beginning and no finish. One of my friends in seminary was a gifted evangelist who while still in seminary converted thousands. He could preach and expound Scripture with dazzling skill. Today he is a militant unbeliever. A great beginning and no finish. You know people like that. They made a showy beginning that for some reason was shallow, and when the heat (or the pressure or the adversities) came, there was no power to finish.

And then there are the people who hear the Word gladly. They are sincere believers, and they make a solid beginning in the life of faith. Then God begins to bless them. They prosper. They have children and grandchildren. They succeed in their jobs, pursue many hobbies, acquire lands, summer homes, many friends. They join clubs and receive honors. The first thing you know, all these good things choke out their primary commitment. They are just too caught up in the good things of life to be concerned about the things of God.

But finally, there are those special ones who for some reason hear and respond, either because of circumstances or their spiritual sensitivity, I don't know. The Word of God, Jesus Himself, takes root in their lives. Suddenly, life opens up now and forever, world without end. How do you account for that? They have been given the gift of being able to listen to God and to understand, beyond head reasoning, the mystery of the kingdom of God.

One Sunday morning a young woman came up to speak to me after the Sunday service. She and her husband and daughter were passing through on a week's vacation. "You spoke about experiencing God's love," she said, "and I've never done that. My husband has tried to help me. Seminary professors have tried to explain it. I've read all the books and I believe, but I've never experienced this love God has for us." I said, "Well, it's one thing to believe in marriage, and it's something else to get married. Have you ever given your life to the Person who is at the center of the kingdom? And if not, would you like to right now?" She said yes, and she did. Somehow she was ready, and the seed took root in her heart.

Missionaries tell us about preaching the love of God and the mystery of the kingdom to isolated tribal people who have never heard before, and there are those who seem prepared to understand and respond immediately. Helen Keller was like that. Though blind, deaf, and dumb, when communication was finally established and she was told about Jesus, she said, "I always knew there was such a person."

Luke records that Jesus said, "Be careful *how* you hear." Mark reports something quite different. According to Mark, Jesus said, "Be careful *what* you hear." What is the message? It seems to me there are three basic messages that we can hear from most Christian pulpits, and I would categorize them as: him, her, or it. Him is Jesus. We can preach about the kingdom of God with Jesus as the King. "Her" refers to the church. We can preach about the church—what the church was and is now; her rules and regulations. All Christians are part of the church, but preaching the church is not the same as preaching the kingdom. The "it" would be Christianity, whatever that means—the rules, the lifestyle. "It" centers in how Christians behave, how they handle problems.

But effective preaching centers in the "Him." We proclaim that there is One among us who is the King, who says to us, "Seek ye first my kingdom, and everything you need now and forever will be added unto you." It's hard to believe that when we seek first His kingdom, God will deal with all of our needs, our loneliness, grief, unemployment, illness. To believe that becomes the test of faith for you and me.

MARKS OF THE KINGDOM

16 "No one, when he has lit a lamp, covers it with a vessel or puts it under a bed, but sets it on a lampstand, that those who enter may see the light. 17 For nothing is secret that will not be revealed, nor anything hidden that will not be known and come to light. 18 Therefore take heed how you hear. For whoever has, to him more will be given; and whoever does not have, even what he seems to have will be taken from him."

—Luke 8:16–18

We have in these verses some of the characteristics of the kingdom. First of all, there is no socialism. There is no equal distribution of goods or talents. If you hear and listen well, everything is yours and more, and you are to give away what you have as fast as you get it. But there are people who never have enough because they can't hear the Good News. So there is somehow a great inequity in the kingdom. Second, there are no secrets. These verses tell us that our lives will be like lamps on a stand and that there will be no hidden places. It's frightening to live in a kingdom where everything you have thought and are thinking and will think will some day be exposed. It's difficult to believe there is mercy and grace even for some of those grungy thoughts that you and I have from time to time, and that we can claim forgiveness.

19 Then His mother and brothers came to Him, and could not approach Him because of the crowd. 20 And it was told Him by some, who said, "Your mother and Your brothers are standing outside, desiring to see You."
21 But He answered and said to them, "My mother and My brothers are these who hear the word of God and do it."

—Luke 8:19–21

Jesus assures us here that to be in the kingdom is to become a part of His family. He says that His earthly mother and blood brothers are not His only relatives, but that whoever has heard the Word of God and does it enters His kingdom. Those are His mother and brothers. So learn to listen. Be careful how you listen. Most of all, listen to the Holy Spirit. You and I can do all things through Christ, who strengthens us. Don't listen to your doubts; don't listen to your fears; don't listen to the minimizers and detracters. Listen to the Holy Spirit who points the way to the King, and take your place as part of the family of God.

CHAPTER TWENTY—JESUS AND THE NEW PSYCHIATRY

LUKE 8:22–39

Scripture Outline

Confronting the Storm at Sea (8:22–25)

Dealing with Madness Ashore (8:26–29)

Identity and Integration (8:30–33)

The Marks of Wellness (8:34–36)

High-Priced Health (8:37–39)

CONFRONTING THE STORM AT SEA

22 Now it happened, on a certain day, that He got into a boat with His disciples. And He said to them, "Let us cross over to the other side of the lake." And they launched out. 23 But as they sailed He fell asleep. And a windstorm came down on the lake, and they were filling with water, and were in jeopardy. 24 And they came to Him and awoke Him, saying, "Master, Master, we are perishing!"

Then He arose and rebuked the wind and the raging of the water. And they ceased, and there was a calm. 25 But He said to them, "Where is your faith?"

And they were afraid, and marveled, saying to one another, "Who can this be? For He commands even the winds and water, and they obey Him!"

—Luke 8:22–25

As they must have done many times before, Jesus and His disciples are crossing Lake Gennesaret, the Sea of Galilee. It is a lake surrounded by high hills and therefore subject to sudden storms. The wind spirals down through those ravines and makes this fairly small body of water extremely tempestuous. Crossing the lake in such a storm in a small fisherman's boat, the disciples waken Jesus and He stills the storm. It is a phenomenon that we find hard to explain. Did Jesus actually have control over nature and the elements? One explanation is that He simply calmed their fears. In their panic they lost control and by waking Jesus, a calming effect took place and they had confidence to get through the storm.

We all know people like that—those we would like to have with us in a tight spot. They manage to raise our hopes when, through stupidity or circumstances, it looks as if we were at the end. One of our children is like that. We have been boaters for a good many years, and on more than one occasion we've been in some sticky situations from which we could not reasonably expect to be delivered. Our youngest son is always optimistic. When the rest of the family is saying, "How did you get us into this mess, Dad?" or "Run for the lifejackets," he is the one with the calming word. "Don't panic," he will say. "It looks bad, but we're going to make it." Certainly there aren't enough of those people in the world— the ones who handle impossible situations with grace and style. This ability is something we might aspire to. Disaster is bound to happen, but we can be the encouragers, the voices of hope.

But as plausible as this interpretation of events is, it is not what Luke says happened. The disciples woke Jesus. He stood up and rebuked the wind and the waves, and there was a calm. In his Gospel, Mark enlarged upon this story, using two different Greek verbs to describe the disciples' fear. When the storm came upon them, Mark says, "They were afraid." But *after* Jesus stilled the wind and waves, they were *"greatly* afraid." What manner of man was this? It may seem difficult to believe that Jesus had the power to change the elements, but it is no more incredible than the fact of the Incarnation. The cosmic Creator with all power, became Jesus and lived among us. But Jesus' ultimate power is demonstrated not in stilling the storm, as awesome as that is, but in the events of the next verses.

DEALING WITH MADNESS ASHORE

26 Then they sailed to the country of the Gadarenes, which is opposite Galilee. 27 And when He stepped out on the land, there met Him a certain man from the city who had demons for a long time. And he wore no clothes, nor did he live in a house but in the tombs. 28 When he saw Jesus, he cried out, fell down before Him, and with a loud voice said, "What have I to do with You, Jesus, Son of the Most High God? I beg You, do not torment me!" 29 For He had commanded the unclean spirit to come out

of the man. For it had often seized him, and he was kept under guard, bound with chains and shackles; and he broke the bonds and was driven by the demon into the wilderness.

—*Luke 8:26–29*

Here Luke, our medical man, talks about mental illness, a serious problem in his time and perhaps our number one problem today. More people are hospitalized with various kinds of mental illnesses than with any other one ailment. So what we read here about the healing of the demoniac can be of enormous help to us today.

Luke describes demon possession, and in our present sophistication we presume he meant some form of mental illness. Today, psychiatrists, physicians, and psychologists seem to have a new name for an age-old problem. Whether the diagnosis is demons or paranoia or manic-depressive or schizophrenia, the problem is the same and just as difficult to solve. One school of thought is that schizophrenia is a result of chemical changes in the body and that drugs can significantly affect those changes. But even the medical profession doesn't know whether those discernible chemical changes are the cause of the illness or whether the illness has produced chemical changes. Even with our new understanding and our new labels, mental illness is a mystery.

The demoniac is living in the tombs all by himself, certainly not a place anyone in his right mind would choose to live in. In Alameda County, when the team of Sine and Burkeman did a nine-year study of seven thousand people, they discovered that there is absolute correlation between mortality and the degree to which people are alienated or lonely. Lonely people become ill far more often than those who live in family units or with friends. Jesus comes upon a man who has become somehow estranged and lonely and who chooses to live in a place that symbolized that state.

Does it seem strange to you that the conversation begins with the demoniac crying out, "Do not torment me"? It seems an odd request of someone he calls "Son of the Most High God." Perhaps it's not so puzzling. Those who really love us can sometimes seem to be tormenting us. The people who have no special concern for us often make us feel good. Our real friends tend to ask hard questions and expect mature responses. They hold us to our best. Sometimes we're less than grateful. Also, I am sure the demoniac sensed that this encounter would produce a radical change in his life, and most of us are ambivalent about dealing with radical changes.

IDENTITY AND INTEGRATION

30 Jesus asked him, saying, "What is your name?"

And he said, "Legion," because many demons had entered him. 31 And they begged Him that He would not command them to go out into the abyss.

32 Now a herd of many swine was feeding there on the mountain. So they begged Him that He would permit them to enter them. And He permitted them. 33 Then the demons went out of the man and entered the swine, and the herd ran violently down the steep place into the lake and drowned.

—Luke 8:30–33

After Jesus commands the demons to come out, he asks this man, "What is your name?" This is a profound question on the whole matter of identity and one that modern psychiatry deals with—who do you perceive yourself to be? The man replies with great insight, "My name is Legion." A legion was comprised of 6,000 soldiers. In biblical times, the degree of mental illness was measured by the number of demons living in the sufferer. (Mary Magdalene had seven demons.) The demoniac, in claiming to be inhabited by 6,000 demons, is telling Jesus, "I am really sick. I don't know who I am."

This is sometimes a problem for even the most stable of us. Benjamin Franklin, a genius inventor and architect of our government, was reputed to be a petty and mean man within his own family. Which was the real Ben Franklin? Thomas Jefferson, who wrote that "all men are created equal" kept slaves until the day he died. Which was the real Thomas Jefferson? We revere Tolstoy as one of the great Christian writers and statesmen of his time. And yet his wife said of him that he never gave her a kind word or a cup of water. Again, will the real Leo Tolstoy please stand up? Even the apostle Paul, in Romans 7:19, 24, speaks of a divided self: "For the good that I will to do, I do not do; but the evil I will not to do, that I practice. . . . O wretched man that I am." It seems all of us are potentially schizophrenic.

And so with the demoniac in the tombs—his own identity has been lost, and many different personalities are dividing him. He is lost and lonely living on the outer edges of normal society. Jesus was the answer to his problems. The same Jesus who stilled the storm is also the One who can heal mental illness. Jesus, very God of very God, can save us from all of the situations that, however unwittingly, we get ourselves into. This Ultimate Being, God Himself, is our friend. C. Raymond Beran gives us this description of a friend:

> A friend . . . is a person with whom you dare to be yourself; your soul can be naked with him. He seems to ask you to put on nothing, only to be what you are. He doesn't want you to be better or worse. When you are with him you feel as a prisoner feels when he is declared innocent. You do not have to be on your guard. You can say what you think, so long as it's genuinely you. He understands those contradictions in your nature that lead others to misjudge you. With him you breathe freely. You can avow your little vanities and indecent hates, your meanness and absurdities and in opening them up to him they are lost, dissolved in the white ocean of his loyalty. He understands. You do not have to be careful. You can abuse him, neglect him, tolerate him, it makes no matter. He likes you. He is like fire that purges to the bone. He understands.

When I read that I am aware that I have never had a friend like that . . . nor been a friend like that! But that's just the point. Jesus *is* such a friend, One who says, "Tell me about it," and you can begin to reveal who you are and to say, "I failed in my marriage." "I've alienated my children." "I betrayed my best friend." In His presence we find integration and become one person.

THE MARKS OF WELLNESS

34 When those who fed *them* saw what had happened, they fled and told *it* in the city and in the country. 35 Then they went out to see what had happened, and came to Jesus, and found the man from whom the demons had departed, sitting at the feet of Jesus, clothed and in his right mind. And they were afraid. 36 They also who had seen *it* told them by what means he who had been demon-possessed was healed.
—*Luke 8:34–36*

When the townspeople came out to see this man who had lived among them all these years as a lunatic, they found him healed. Luke's description of his new state gives us three basic ingredients of health and wholeness that are applicable for any age. They found the man from whom the demons had departed sitting at the feet of Jesus, clothed and in his right mind. That's exactly what the new psychiatry, the post-Freudian psychiatry, is all about—these three signs of wholeness.

First of all, the demoniac is sitting at the feet of Jesus. He is under authority and has chosen now to act responsibly. He is no longer free to do his own thing. Doing his own thing had made him ill. He did his own thing when he was running about in a frenzy, tearing off his clothes and living like an animal. He has chosen now to submit his life to authority, the authority of Jesus. Christian freedom is a paradox. When you submit to the lordship of Christ, you are most free. Martin Luther said, "A Christian man is the most free lord of all and subject to no one. A Christian man is the most dutiful servant of all and subject to everyone." We lose our freedom to find a new freedom.

Second, the demoniac is clothed, which is another mark of wellness. He is no longer shameless. His nakedness symbolized shamelessness, a flaunting of all morals and absolutes. This is a common disease today. There are those who tell us everything is relative and, if it feels good, do it. But under Jesus' lordship, the demoniac puts on clothes with a new sense of what is decent and proper.

The last phrase in Luke's description is that the demoniac is now in his right mind. He sees the world as it is. He is not paranoid, convinced that everybody is out to get him. Those of us who suffer from those feelings need to remember that most of the world doesn't even know we exist. On the other hand, being in your right mind means coming to grips with the fact that everybody does not love you. They don't. You have enemies. In his right mind, the demoniac sees life as it actually is.

HIGH-PRICED HEALTH

37 Then the whole multitude of the surrounding region of the Gadarenes asked Him to depart from them, for they were seized with great fear. And He got into the boat and returned.

38 Now the man from whom the demons had departed begged Him that he might be with Him. But Jesus sent him away, saying, 39 "Return to your own house, and tell what great things God has done for you." And he went his way and proclaimed throughout the whole city what great things Jesus had done for him.

—Luke 8:37–39

Finally, it seems that this remarkable healing took place at a great cost to the townspeople, the cost of a herd of pigs. The demons asked and received permission to go into the pigs and, as a result, the pigs ran into the sea. When the townspeople arrived they were distressed about what had happened to the pigs. They weighed the situation. One of their neighbors, who had been a dangerous lunatic for years, was now well, but at the cost of some very expensive property. They concluded that the cost was too high. They said, in effect, "Would you please leave us, sir? We'd rather have a few crazies around than have our property destroyed. If that's the cost of healing, no thanks. We don't want it."

It's easy to condemn those townspeople, but suppose, for a minute, that herd of pigs represents a year's salary in today's terms. Let's imagine that a friend of yours had a serious emotional breakdown and that in your prayer time God spoke to you and said, "If you will quit your job and spend a year with that person, he or she will get well." Would you do it? I'm not sure I would. I might say, "Aren't there places for people like that? We have asylums and institutions. Let them go there." It's easier to warehouse our ill and to give them drugs than to invest our own lives and time. Before we condemn the Gadarenes, let's understand that the cost is often high for a person-to-person ministry.

The reaction of the healed man is very understandable. He wanted to join the parade. Now that he was well, he wanted to join the twelve and travel with Jesus. Instead, Jesus sent him back home to minister and to witness. For the most part, that's where He sends us—to be a part of the whole healing process, which is one of the marks of the kingdom of God.

CHAPTER TWENTY-ONE—THE DIFFERENT TOUCH

LUKE 8:40–56

40 So it was, when Jesus returned, that the multitude welcomed Him, for they were all waiting for Him.

41 And behold, there came a man named Jairus, and he was a ruler of the synagogue. And he fell down at Jesus' feet and begged Him to come to his house, 42 for he had an only daughter about twelve years of age, and she was dying.

But as He went, the multitudes thronged Him. 43 Now a woman, having a flow of blood for twelve years, who had spent all her livelihood on physicians and could not be healed by any, 44 came from behind and touched the border of His garment. And immediately her flow of blood stopped.

45 And Jesus said, "Who touched Me?"

When all denied it, Peter and those with him said, "Master, the multitudes throng and press You, and You say, 'Who touched Me?'"

46 But Jesus said, "Somebody touched Me, for I perceived power going out from Me." 47 Now when the woman saw that she was not hidden, she came trembling; and falling down before Him, she declared to Him in the presence of all the people the reason she had touched Him and how she was healed immediately.

48 And He said to her, "Daughter, be of good cheer; your faith has made you well. Go in peace."

49 While He was still speaking, someone came from the ruler of the synagogue's house, saying to him, "Your daughter is dead. Do not trouble the Teacher."

50 But when Jesus heard it, He answered him, saying, "Do not be afraid; only believe, and she will be made well."

51 When He came into the house, He permitted no one to go in except Peter, James, and John, and the father and mother of the girl. 52 Now all wept and mourned for her; but He said, "Do not weep; she is not dead, but sleeping." 53 And they ridiculed Him, knowing that she was dead.

⁵⁴ But He put them all outside, took her by the hand and called, saying, "Little girl, arise." ⁵⁵ Then her spirit returned, and she arose immediately. And He commanded that she be given something to eat. ⁵⁶ And her parents were astonished, but He charged them to tell no one what had happened.

—Luke 8:40–56

In the crowd waiting at the lakeshore were two people for whom Jesus performed miracles. If we believe that Jesus is who He said He is, we have no problems with the miracles. The mystery is that in that crowd there were only two. Albert Einstein once said, "The most beautiful thing we can experience is the mysterious. It is the source of all true art and science."

These two healings are mentioned in all four Gospels, but only Luke tells us that this was Jairus's only daughter. If you have one child or many, I suppose they are equally loved. But when there is just one, that child is very special.

The two people involved in these two healings could not be more different. Jairus is a man of substance, rich and socially powerful. He was religiously prominent. In the synagogue, he decided who would preach, what Scripture would be read, and what hymns would be sung. The woman who suffered the issue of blood was not even allowed to set foot in the synagogue. She was ceremonially unclean. She was at the other end of the social and religious spectrum.

When Jesus returns by boat from the country of the Gadarenes, a crowd is waiting for Him. Jairus comes forward in faith and begs Jesus to come to his house where his daughter lies dying. Jesus sets off with him, and meanwhile the crowd is pressing in. Amid all this touching and jostling, Jesus says these remarkable words, *"Somebody touched me, for I perceived power going out from me"* (v. 46). Someone had touched Him with a different touch, a touch that drew power from God Himself. We read, *"She touched the border of His garment."* (v. 44).

This unclean woman, forbidden by law to have any social intercourse with anybody, defies the law and reaches out to Jesus. She dares not touch His person, but she believes that if she can just touch the border of His garment, she will be made well. It is noteworthy that Jesus perceives immediately that a transaction has taken place. That would lead us to believe that when God answers our prayers discernible power goes out from Him. The Bible evidence points to the fact that there is a reservoir of power available and that when we ask in faith there is a transfer of that power to you and me.

At the Syracuse Upstate Medical Center, they are operating on the theory that well people have a reservoir of power that can be tapped to bring healing to the sick. A course is offered in the laying on of hands, the premise being that healthy people have a life force called "prana" that can be transferred to the ill. This course is being taught as a strictly somatic, secular technique. We are wondrously made indeed, and Jesus, who was totally human, was well aware of the power He possessed, and that power was noticeably diminished as someone drew upon it.

In asking *"Who touched Me?"* Jesus insisted that the one who touched Him come forward. I can think of a couple of reasons why He did this. First of all, it might have taken a long time for this social and religious outcast to convince her friends and neighbors that she was well, had Jesus not publicly pronounced her so. She was immediately restored, not just to health but to an active place in normal society. Beyond that, Jesus wanted her to know that her *faith* had made her well. There was nothing magical about touching His garment. Jesus honored her imperfect faith, which was perhaps mixed up with some superstitious expectations.

The lesson for us here, it seems to me, is that imperfect faith is far better than an enlightened cynicism. Sometimes those of us who think we're sophisticated tend to judge the simple and devout who are lighting candles, kneeling before statues, reciting set prayers, going through all sorts of little mechanical rituals as if those were the things that pleased God. But we had better be careful about feeling superior to all this. It's better to have a superstitious type of faith that works than to be theologically sophisticated and ineffectual.

About a dozen years ago my wife and I made several trips to England with different teams of lay witnesses. On one trip, the famous Redcap 42, Ralston Young, was with us. Years ago he was written up in *Reader's Digest* in their "most unforgettable character" section. Ralston ministered for many years in an extraordinary way in Grand Central Station. He would often say, "You know, everybody going through Grand Central isn't going to a honeymoon or a party. Many are going to funerals, the hospital, even to prison." He began to minister to the people whose bags he carried, and he affected many lives.

On a later trip to England, we stayed in a home where Ralston had previously been a guest. I was surprised to find a Thom McAn shoehorn displayed prominently on a table in the bedroom. I asked my host where he got it. He was a little embarrassed. "Ralston left that behind when he was here," he explained. "And you know, we've kept it as a kind of religious icon or relic. It reminds us that a man of God was here who brought us a new dimension of faith." These sophisticated Anglicans wanted a tangible reminder that a special person had passed through their lives. In our imperfect faith, we sometimes need those reminders of God's presence and power.

The circumstances of the two healings in these verses are so different. In a crowd full of people, many of whom have faith, there is one special woman of faith. In a faith ambience, a person of faith touches Jesus differently, and the miracle takes place. But after that healing, Jesus goes on to a home where there is a no-faith ambience. A man comes to tell Jairus, the master of the home and ruler of the synagogue, "Don't trouble the master. Your daughter has died." The implication is, the Healer didn't get here in time; he ought to make faster house calls. Jesus says, *"Do not be afraid"* and *"Do not weep; she is not dead, but sleeping"* (vv. 50, 52). He is laughed at. Those who were there did not believe that He had power over life and death. He had just healed a faith-filled person in a faith-filled crowd. But in this situation, the little girl was incapable of faith and she was already dead. Furthermore, she was surrounded by unbelievers, skeptics, and cynics who laughed at Jesus.

The next verses are especially significant. Jesus allowed no one in the room except the parents and three of His disciples. He gave the little girl a negative-ectomy. We all know what an appendectomy is. In this negative-ectomy, Jesus cut out all the unbelievers around the little girl's bedside. Their lack of faith was blocking the mighty acts of God. Taking the little girl's hand, Jesus says the same words her mother must have used countless times to waken her in the morning, "Beloved little girl, wake up." And she does. All of us are subjected to all too many negative influences. We are surrounded by cynics who don't believe in God or in the possibility of positive change in our jobs, homes, families, neighborhoods. That's why Sunday worship is so important. For at least an hour a week we sit in a congregation of believers. We are in a faith ambience just like the one Jesus created around this little girl.

Finally, Jesus says, "Give her food." It seems mundane, but I'm sure the parents were so awe-struck that they might have stood immobilized all day, unable to deal with practical needs. Jesus' words underscore the reality of her healing. This was not some spooky miracle. The dead girl was restored to life, and life must be nourished and sustained.

These healings are only two of the many miracles recorded in the Gospels. As I reflect on all these miracles, I find myself bothered by the non-miracles of our present-day lives. I am reminded of the man who bought a parrot hoping to teach it to talk. For months he would say to the parrot each morning on his way to the bathroom, "Good morning. How are you? Have a nice day." The parrot never said a word. One morning the man overslept and rushed into the bathroom without speaking to the bird. "Well," said the parrot, "what's the matter with you this morning?" The real mystery is not why the parrot spoke, but why it was silent all those months.

But there are still miracles taking place. There are those reaching out with a different touch even today. In my present parish, miracles sometimes occur during Sunday worship. One man went home after a service and removed a back brace he had worn for months, and he hasn't needed it since. Within the faith ambience of a worshiping congregation, periodically someone reaches out with a different touch and leaves restored. One Sunday a husband and wife came to church separately. She sat downstairs in front and he in the balcony. They hadn't spoken for weeks, but they left together. They reached out and touched Jesus, and He healed their relationship. These incidents don't surprise me. I'm just surprised that they don't happen even more often in a faith-filled crowd.

A friend of mine is a successful businessman with three young children and a wonderful wife. He is an officer in his church and has led retreats for men all over the Southeast. Three years ago, he was told he had leukemia and was given nine months to live. Most of his friends had very little hope for him. But Bill is still here and never looked better. He explains it like this: "I thought I would stop putting off those things I've always wanted to do. I spent more time with my wife and kids. I began to do those things I felt God would have me do. I decided to put down death and take up life." My friend Bill reached out with a different touch.

What are the ingredients of a different touch? Exhaustion? Desperation? You've blown it and have no place to turn? The one constant in the equation is Jesus who is there, who loves us, who has the power. Verse 50 of our Scripture has a good word for us. Jesus says, *Do not be afraid; only believe.* Today or tomorrow, whatever you face, your own mistakes and failures, loneliness, ill-ness, grief, do not be afraid. Only believe that Jesus, the constant, is there.

CHAPTER TWENTY-TWO—WHEN TO TAKE CARE OF YOURSELF

LUKE 9:1–17

Scripture Outline

Christian Lifestyle—A Puzzling Dilemma (9:1–6)

Who Is This Jesus (9:7–9)

Unexpected Resources (9:10–17)

CHRISTIAN LIFESTYLE—A PUZZLING DILEMMA

9:1 Then He called His twelve disciples together and gave them power and authority over all demons, and to cure diseases. ² He sent them to preach the kingdom of God and to heal the sick. ³ And He said to them, "Take nothing for the journey, neither staffs nor bag nor bread nor money; and do not have two tunics apiece.

⁴ "Whatever house you enter, stay there, and from there depart. ⁵ And whoever will not receive you, when you go out of that city, shake off the very dust from your feet as a testimony against them."

⁶ So they departed and went through the towns, preaching the gospel and healing everywhere.

—Luke 9:1–6

There are many opposing views of the Christian lifestyle. On this particular occasion, Jesus is sending His disciples out, advising them to take nothing for their journey—neither staff, bag, bread or money: not even an extra tunic. There are Christians who take this passage literally. They don't believe in making provisions for the future, are contemptuous of insurance, forego bank accounts, and even avoid a steady income. They say, "I'm going to trust God to take care of me." On the other side of the spectrum are the extremists, the Christian survivalists, who are building camps in the woods, laying in supplies for the upheaval to come, and amassing an arsenal to defend themselves and their goods. They consider themselves God's remnant, and they are taking every precaution to insure that they will survive the great tribulation ahead.

Even missionaries are divided over this matter of preparedness. One of my oldest friends was head of the largest independent faith mission in the world for many years. His group sent out workers with a minimum of training and very little support, believing that if God had called them to these far places, He would take care of them. Often these workers would be floundering, ill, and without money in some foreign field, only to be rescued and helped by missionaries from the mainline churches who had been sent out with careful training and responsible financial backing. My faith-missions friend would say, "You see, God did take care of them through these other church-supported workers."

In the early years of our country's history, there were two different approaches to evangelism by two of our great denominations. The Methodist Church felt the West was expanding so fast that there wasn't time to thoroughly equip and train preachers and lay evangelists. They sent out anyone who had the call, and the West was evangelized by Methodist circuit riders. The Presbyterians felt the gospel was so important it could be entrusted only to seminary graduates with a background in Greek and Hebrew. They never caught up with the Methodists in claiming the expanding frontier for the kingdom of God. One could make a case for either point of view.

We Christians are divided in our opinions on military preparedness. There are Christians who consider our nation's arms buildup senseless. They'd like to emulate the Quakers, who have traditionally been pacifists, refusing to bear arms. Incidentally, we're told that in those wild frontier days there is no record of any Quaker being molested or killed by Indians or bandits, yet they never locked their doors or carried guns. Other Christians follow the admonition "to be wise as serpents." They see American military might as the only means of insuring righteousness, peace, and justice for all the world.

In these verses Jesus seems to be saying that there is an urgency that precludes detailed plans. During World War II, General MacArthur once asked his chief engineer how soon he could get a bridge across a certain river. "About three days," was the reply. The engineer was told to go ahead and draw the plans. Three days later MacArthur asked for those plans. The engineer seemed surprised. "Oh, the bridge is ready. You can cross it now. If you want plans, you'll have to wait a little longer. We haven't finished those yet." Sometimes we devote so much time to planning that the job doesn't get done.

Jesus is saying here that the time is short. The twelve were to go immediately without making provision for the future. But let's remember that His advice is for that particular journey. He is not giving us a strategy for all time. Later on, when the church understood that Christ's return was not imminent, Paul urged believers to live responsibly. Anyone who didn't work shouldn't eat. Apparently some of those early Christians wanted to go floating along until the Second Coming. Paul advised them to go out and get a job and build for the common good. The point is that there's a time for responsible preparation and a time to move out and capture the moment with no thought for the details.

A doctor in our church went out to the Far East thoroughly prepared to be a medical missionary. However, through unforeseen circumstances, he and his wife were moved to Somalia, not to practice medicine but to oversee a refugee camp of eighty-three thousand people. They were totally unprepared and untrained for that, but God was there enabling them. There is a lesson here. Sometimes we spend too much time getting ready for every contingency. Somebody has said that "life is what happens to you while you are planning the next thing."

It seems to me this part of our Scripture helps us all with this by zeroing in on the *what* and the *how*. The *what* in the case of the twelve was to preach the kingdom of God and heal the sick. Next Jesus outlines the *how* for them, a strategy that includes a minimum of encumbrances. If the job to which you are called requires low pay or no pay, then poverty is a blessing. Poverty for poverty's sake is no blessing. I've had friends who have given their money away as a spiritual discipline. It's a means of testing God, to see if He will provide for them. I don't commend that to anyone. The issue is, *what* are you called to? If it is something that may require poverty, then God will take care of you and the *how* is incidental.

WHO IS THIS JESUS?

7 Now Herod the tetrarch heard of all that was done by Him; and he was perplexed, because it was said by some that John had risen from the dead, 8 and by some that Elijah had appeared, and by others that one of the old prophets had risen

again. ⁹ Herod said, "John I have beheaded, but who is this of whom I hear such things?" So he sought to see Him.

—Luke 9:7–9

Herod is wondering who Jesus is. Who is this teacher-prophet-healer of whom he hears such remarkable things? That's still the crucial question—deciding who Jesus is. There are many groups today with their own answers to that question: Christian Scientists, Mormons, Moonies, Jehovah's Witnesses, and many more. Each group wants to tell us who Jesus is. We orthodox Christians don't agree with them. Like Herod, we must find our own answer to that question. As we seek to see and know Jesus, He can guide us in finding the *what* and *how* for our lives, a strategy as specific as the one outlined here for the twelve disciples.

UNEXPECTED RESOURCES

¹⁰ And the apostles, when they had returned, told Him all that they had done. Then He took them and went aside privately into a deserted place belonging to the city called Bethsaida. ¹¹ But when the multitudes knew it, they followed Him; and He received them and spoke to them about the kingdom of God, and healed those who had need of healing.

¹² When the day began to wear away, the twelve came and said to Him, "Send the multitude away, that they may go into the surrounding towns and country, and lodge and get provisions; for we are in a deserted place here."

¹³ But He said to them, "You give them something to eat."

And they said, "We have no more than five loaves and two fish, unless we go and buy food for all these people." ¹⁴ For there were about five thousand men.

Then He said to His disciples, "Make them sit down in groups of fifty." ¹⁵ And they did so, and made them all sit down.

¹⁶ Then He took the five loaves and the two fish, and looking up to heaven, He blessed and broke them, and gave them to the disciples to set before the multitude. ¹⁷ So they all ate and were filled, and twelve baskets of the leftover fragments were taken up by them.

—Luke 9:10–17

The Feeding of the Five Thousand is the only miracle recorded in all four Gospels. In an attempt to offer a logical explanation for this amazing story, the theory has been advanced that many in the crowd had brought a bag lunch or picnic hamper and those were taken out and shared. The four Gospel writers don't leave much room for such an interpretation. They tell us that the disciples were concerned that there was no food available. They had some practical solutions, like sending the multitude into town for provisions. In other words, "Let's refer them to the delicatessens, the grocery stores, the supermarkets. Let's refer them to someone who can help them." Jesus said to them as He does to us, *"You* feed them." As people come to us with their needs, let's believe that we have the resources to meet those needs—psychological, emotional, relational, or physical.

As a pastor, I am often asked by concerned parties to intervene and counsel some friend or relative. I usually say, "No. God sent that person to *you,* not to me. Let's talk about how you can provide the necessary help." Invariably, they find that they do have the insight and authority to deal with that troubled person. Jesus says to the disciples here, and to us, to believe that God has given us the resources to meet the needs with which we are presented.

In this incident, Jesus provided bread for five thousand people. They ate until they were filled. Yet when He was hungry in the wilderness at the beginning of His ministry, He did not turn the stones into bread. This could provide a rule of thumb for us. When do we take care of ourselves, defend ourselves, fight for our rights? What we read here would indicate that if doing so is in our own interest, it's questionable. If it's for someone else, it's probably in order. Jesus was always concerned about the other person. He trusted the Father for His own needs.

In terms of knowing when to take care of yourself, there is no clear answer. We are to take care of the people God has entrusted to us. You and I have the power and authority to turn stones into bread for other people. There is a very poignant story about Bobby Burns, the famous Scottish poet. He was never honored in his lifetime, but when he died the world proclaimed him a genius, a great man, "a poet among us." His mother outlived him and was invited to a great celebration to honor his memory. In the midst of the proceedings, she stood up and cried aloud, "Oh, Bobby, you asked for bread and they gave you a stone." How many people there are now living on stones who need the bread of praise, affirmation, support, and gratitude. You and I have it in our power to turn those stones into bread.

God does perform miracles, but we can't rely on them. Remember that after the Feeding of the Five Thousand, they gathered up the leftovers. They were thrifty Jews and there was no assurance that God might do this again. They were not going to waste any part of the miracle. If there were no miracle tomorrow, those leftovers would make some tasty casseroles or bread pudding.

When we find out *what* God has for us, we can trust Him for the future. We need not live so timidly. Too many of us tend to give cautious advice to our children and our young people. We tell them they need tenure and pensions and security and insurance. God is urging us to launch out and do the *what* He has called us to, and He will take care of us.

I heard a story about Wilfred Grenfell, the great medical missionary to Labrador. On one occasion, he was back home talking about his life in Labrador and the early hardships when a woman said to him, "Oh, I'm so sorry, Dr. Grenfell." "Oh, no," said he, "I must have miscommunicated. Don't be sorry. I was having the time of my life."

Recently a lady in our parish had a serious car accident involving several other cars. She was to blame for the accident and she knew it. How do you take care of yourself in that situation? We are advised to clam up, admit no guilt, and let the insurance company deal with the problem. But this woman had an acute sense of responsibility for the multi-car collision. She was full of remorse and did not take care of herself. She wrote a letter of apology to all the other people involved. Here is an excerpt from one reply:

> You've been much in our thoughts these days, but it's with a loving and wistful feeling of wanting you to be somehow cheered and calmed in your troubled heart. Probably not a single person Saturday evening felt any anger toward you, dear friend. Certainly, there is nothing to forgive you for. People are always making mistakes, all of the time, only usually they don't look so distraught afterwards. (Isn't that right?)
>
> Friend, we were all standing by the street telling each other we were happy to be safe and alive after such a devastating experience. We should have been more careful to comfort you. . . . We feel as though we were introduced to a whole new set of very nice people we would not have met otherwise. Do take care and know that we

don't think badly of you at all. It could have been any of us in your place. Call if you like. You have friends here.

My parishioner did not act in her own best interest. She did the risky thing, and in reaching out she received in return the mysterious gift of friendship.

In verse 5 Jesus gives us a wise word. Don't waste time trying to convince the unconvincible. Jesus' advice is that if you come in love and openness and you are not received, you are to shake the very dust from your feet. Some people make a career of skepticism. In these verses Jesus gives us permission to move on. There are others out there who are ready, who want to enter the kingdom and who will hear us gladly.

18 And it happened, as He was alone praying, that His disciples joined Him, and He asked them, saying, "Who do the crowds say that I am?"

19 So they answered and said, "John the Baptist, but some say Elijah; and others say that one of the old prophets has risen again."

20 He said to them, "But who do you say that I am?"

Peter answered and said, "The Christ of God."

21 And He strictly warned and commanded them to tell this to no one, 22 saying, "The Son of Man must suffer many things, and be rejected by the elders and chief priests and scribes, and be killed, and be raised the third day."

23 Then He said to them all, "If anyone desires to come after Me, let him deny himself, and take up his cross daily, and follow Me. 24 For whoever desires to save his life will lose it, but whoever loses his life for My sake will save it. 25 For what profit is it to a man if he gains the whole world, and is himself destroyed or lost? 26 For whoever is ashamed of Me and My words, of him the Son of Man will be ashamed when He comes in His own glory, and in His Father's, and of the holy angels.

27 But I tell you truly, there are some standing here who shall not taste death till they see the kingdom of God."

—Luke 9:18–27

My wife and I went to see the movie *Raiders of the Lost Ark* with another couple. Three of our group thought it was disgusting—violent, shallow, and two-dimensional—but *I* loved it. I guess I'm addicted to adventure stories. The plot, you may remember, revolved around two archaeological teams during World War II racing across the Egyptian desert to find the ark of the covenant. One team wanted to capture it for Hitler, and the other, headed by a renegade American archeologist, wanted it for the free world. It's interesting to me that movie producers would bet on public interest in the ark of the covenant. The Jews believed, in Old Testament times, and even now, that the ark is the symbol of God with us. The ark represented the presence of God Himself.

The movie builds up to the moment when the ark is opened and all hell (or judgment) breaks loose. But I consider it theologically unsound. If someone could find the ark, which I hope happens someday, and it is opened, I don't think anything would happen. Just as the ark was a sacramental symbol of God's old covenant with His people and represented God's presence with us, Jesus is the new ark of the covenant, and one of His names is Emmanuel, which means God with us. We worship the new ark of the covenant. God has given us His power and presence in His Son.

In these verses, the disciples are aware suddenly of that presence and power. It is a moment of truth. There is an increasing awareness of the inevitable clash between the temple authorities and Jesus. With the moment of confrontation imminent, Jesus asks His disciples, *"Who do you say that I am?"* Peter says, *"The Christ of God,"* in other words, "God with us, the Messiah."

Often we see most clearly in adversity. We are blinded in times of peace and prosperity. Sometimes we need to have something disastrous or ominous impending to give us a clear vision. I recently talked to a man whose marriage is crashing in. His wife is about to leave him. Suddenly he has perceived the whole relationship in a new light. What can he do? Is it too late? Clarity comes about a gift taken too lightly.

The central issue of our life today is the person of Jesus. In verse 18 he asks His disciples a question that we could answer in all sorts of ways. We could report what movies or books or sermons say about Jesus. We could repeat what we hear about Jesus on TV. But the question remains, "Who do *you* say that I am?" Some would say He is the best of the bunch. Of all the great prophets, teachers, leaders, Jesus is the wisest and the kindest and the most loving. For others, He is, in point of fact, the ark of the covenant, God with us. That's the watershed.

To recognize that Jesus is the Christ implies some response. Isaiah, when he saw the Lord, responded, "Here am I. Send me." His own agenda was no longer important. God has an agenda for us as well. In these verses Jesus says to His disciples that now that they know who He is, they must make a response. They are to take up their cross and follow Him.

In verse 26 Jesus says, *"Whoever is ashamed of Me and My words, of him the Son of Man will be ashamed when He comes."*

I still bear the scars of being ashamed of someone I loved. I was a ten-year-old boy with a seventy-year-old father who spoke with a very heavy Swedish accent. On the occasions when school friends came home to play with me, they would often remark that my grandfather had a funny way of talking. I was ashamed to admit that he was my dad. My father was aware of this, and one day he said, "Son, I understand that you're embarrassed about me, and it's okay. I know that you love me." Jesus gives us a warning about those times when we are tempted to feel ashamed of Him.

The agenda He has for us seems clear here. We are to pick up our cross and follow Him. The cross He has for us should not be confused with the thorns of life, our common human inheritance. The cross is chosen willingly. We tend to say of those who are ill, bereaved, or suffering financial difficulties that they "have their cross to bear." But those unfortunate happenings are not crosses. Those are the thorns we have *not* chosen. In 2 Corinthians 12:7 Paul writes about having a thorn in the flesh. There is much speculation about what it was. He had some physical ailment that was uncomfortable and unpleasant. Mental and physical afflictions are to be expected in this life.

Thorns are unchosen suffering. Christ came to alleviate suffering. We can be burden-bearers with each other in our suffering. But suffering in itself is not noble. It is simply part of life. When you are able to endure a painful thorn in the flesh by the grace of God, you are a profound witness to your contemporaries. I know any number of people who have borne some of life's most difficult thorns with courage. A couple in our parish lost their daughter and her entire family in a plane crash—an enormous tragedy. But they have been witnesses to God's grace in the midst of the worst possible circumstances. What a vast resource for witnessing and ministering we have in each other because of our thorns, those unchosen mishaps and misfortunes.

But bearing your cross is quite a different matter. Your cross is not like Jesus' cross. His cross was a literal one and He died on it to forgive our sins. He says to His disciples here and He says to us today to take up our cross daily. Our cross is that difficult thing we choose to do because we are His people. We receive grace to be brave and uncomplaining through our thorns but the glory comes as we pick up our cross for His sake. We choose a hard place, a difficult relationship, a thankless job. We serve on a committee, or get involved with a neighbor. We do the things we don't have to do because we feel it is God's agenda for us. We say, like Isaiah, "Here am I. Send me."

What does the cross look like? It looks like Calcutta for Mother Teresa. It looked like Lambarene for Albert Schweitzer. It looked like Africa for David Livingstone, the leper colony at Molokai for Father Damien. It was the slums of Tokyo for a crazy little Japanese saint named Toyohiko Kagawa. A friend of mine heard him speak once at a university in Vermont. He said, "You know, he had nothing new or startling to say. But I saw those great thick glasses and I remembered that he had lost his sight because of a disease he contracted living in a packing crate in the slums of Japan. This man had picked up his cross, and his lack of oratorical skills seemed unimportant."

When John Gardner, founder and former head of Common Cause, spoke in our city, he described one of the heroes of his life. He is a cheerful old man, who, on meeting someone new, always asks, "What have you done that you believe in and are proud of?" That's a good question. It's far more relevant than asking someone what he or she does for a living. Like Paul, we all have our tent-making. Our answer to this question is a good indication of whether or not we have picked up our cross and followed Jesus. God's grace is seen in His people, in the way we carry our thorns and survive, not somehow, but triumphantly. But God wants to share His glory with us, and that happens when we pick up our cross.

CHAPTER TWENTY-FOUR—THE GLORY OF THE ORDINARY

LUKE 9:28–62

Scripture Outline

The Glamorous Mountaintop (9:28–42)

The Unglamorous Realities (9:43–48)

Handling the Opposition (9:49–56)

Costly Discipleship (9:57–62)

THE GLAMOROUS MOUNTAINTOP

28 Now it came to pass, about eight days after these sayings, that He took Peter, John, and James and went up on the mountain to pray. 29 As He prayed, the appearance of His face was altered, and His robe became white and glistening. 30 And behold, two men talked with Him, who were Moses and Elijah, 31 who appeared in glory and spoke of His decease which He was about to accomplish at Jerusalem. 32 But Peter and those with him were heavy with sleep; and when they were fully awake, they saw His glory and the two men who stood with Him. 33 Then it happened, as they were parting from Him, that Peter said to Jesus, "Master, it is good for us to be here; and let us make three tabernacles: one for You, one for Moses, and one for Elijah"—not knowing what he said.

34 While he was saying this, a cloud came and overshadowed them; and they were fearful as they entered the cloud. 35 And a voice came out of the cloud, saying, "This is My beloved Son. Hear Him!" 36 When the voice had ceased, Jesus was found alone. But they kept quiet, and told no one in those days any of the things they had seen.

37 Now it happened on the next day, when they had come down from the mountain, that a great multitude met Him. 38 Suddenly a man from the multitude cried out, saying,

"Teacher, I implore You, look on my son, for he is my only child. [39] And behold, a spirit seizes him, and he suddenly cries out; it convulses him so that he foams at the mouth; and it departs from him with great difficulty, bruising him. [40] So I implored Your disciples to cast it out, but they could not."

[41] Then Jesus answered and said, "O faithless and perverse generation, how long shall I be with you and bear with you? Bring your son here." [42] And as he was still coming, the demon threw him down and convulsed him. Then Jesus rebuked the unclean spirit, healed the child, and gave him back to his father.

—Luke 9:28–42

One of my favorite philosophers is the late Erma Bombeck. She once wrote an article in a law journal. I don't know how she happened to appear in a law journal, but here's what she said:

Someone asked me the other day if I had my life to live over would I change anything? My answer was no, but then I thought about it and changed my mind. If I had my life to live over again I would have waxed less and listened more. I would never have insisted the car windows be rolled up on a summer day because my hair had just been teased and sprayed. I would have invited friends over to dinner, even if the carpet was stained and the sofa faded. I would have eaten popcorn in the good living room and worried less about the dirt when you lit the fireplace. I would have taken time to listen to my grandfather ramble about his youth. I would have burnt the pink candle sculptured like a rose before it melted while being stored. I would have sat cross-legged on the lawn with my children and never worried about the grass stains. I would have cried and laughed less while watching television and more while watching real life. I would have eaten less cottage cheese and more ice cream. I would have gone to bed when I was sick instead of pretending the earth would go into a holding pattern if I weren't there for the day. I would never have bought anything just because it was practical, wouldn't show soil and was guaranteed to last a lifetime. When my child kissed me impetuously I would never have said, 'Later, now go wash up for dinner.' There would have

been more 'I love yous,' more 'I'm sorries,' more 'I'm lis-
tenings,' but mostly given another shot at life I would
seize every minute of it, look at it and really see it, try it
on, live it, exhaust it, and never give the minute back
until there was nothing left of it.*

Erma Bombeck is talking about seizing and enjoying the ordinary events of life. Most of us are victims of the media-hype of our
time. We have a fatal fascination for the fabulous. Religiously
speaking, we are hooked on spiritual ecstasy. We are programmed
to expect the big, the unusual, and the spectacular, and we miss
the glory of the ordinary.

The seven events we read about here seem to fit into a pattern. First
of all, there is the transfiguration of Jesus on the mountain. Peter and
James and John saw Jesus in a new light. Did you ever look at someone you love and suddenly understand for the first time the wonder
of that person? How did you miss it before? Just a few verses earlier,
Peter had declared Jesus to be the Christ and the Son of God. But he
and James and John are dazzled to see Him in the company of the
superstars of the Old Testament, Elijah and Moses. They were convinced He was the Son of God and Messiah, but it had not occurred
to them that He was in the same league with Elijah and Moses.

In the midst of this supernatural experience, Peter reacts with a
sophomoric suggestion. Even Luke is embarrassed by it and makes
excuses for him. Peter suggests they build three booths and stay
there forever, enjoying the light and the glory and the ecstasy (v.
33). Instead, they return the very next day to the valley and the
needy crowds. That's where Jesus felt He belonged, and that's
where you and I belong. We can't live on the mountaintop. Jesus
moved from the mountaintop to the valley of need because that's
where the gospel is relevant.

Peter presumed himself to be an expert in liturgical matters,
proposing to design an altar with three parts for the worship of
Elijah, Moses, and Jesus. I'm sure he could have drawn up an
appropriate order of service complete with hymns and prayers.
But he and the other disciples failed when confronted with a
father whose small son had alarming and dangerous seizures.
There is nothing wrong with proper prayers in the sanctuary, but
if they are not instruments for God's help and healing in the
everyday hurts and needs of life, they are rightly questionable.

* From AT WIT'S END by Erma Bombeck.©1981 Field Enterprises, Inc. Courtesy
of Field Newspaper Syndicate.

Sometimes I am taken to task by members of my congregation who want more biblical preaching. Since I have been going through one of the Gospels verse by verse in the last year, I try to press them to explain. It seems they object to my emphasis on applying the Bible to our everyday lives and behavior. They would like the Word exegeted in some isolated context. But the living Word must be taken down into the valley, where it belongs. The gospel is most extraordinary as we see it applied to the ordinary events of our lives.

THE UNGLAMOROUS REALITIES

43 And they were all amazed at the majesty of God.

But while everyone marveled at all the things which Jesus did, He said to His disciples, 44 "Let these words sink down into your ears, for the Son of Man is about to be betrayed into the hands of men." 45 But they did not understand this saying, and it was hidden from them so that they did not perceive it; and they were afraid to ask Him about this saying.

46 Then a dispute arose among them as to which of them would be greatest. 47 And Jesus, perceiving the thought of their heart, took a little child and set him by Him, 48 and said to them, "Whoever receives this little child in My name receives Me; and whoever receives Me receives Him who sent Me. For he who is least among you all will be great."

—Luke 9:43–48

When Jesus mentions His coming death, the disciples are horrified. Did you ever stop to think that if He had come two thousand years later and the establishment had put Him to death, He would have hung from a gallows or been electrocuted? Those Christians who presently wear crosses around their necks would be wearing a little electric chair or a tiny gallows. The cross is not a beautiful object. It represented death. Jesus somehow transformed this most gruesome method of execution into something glorious.

"Who is the greatest?" the disciples then demanded to know. They seemed to want some extraordinary reward, the promise of ecstasy. Jesus said, *"Whoever receives this little child in My name receives Me."* It's still true. Somehow there is glory in receiving children, caring for them, holding them, nurturing them, teaching them. We find the glory and wonder of Jesus through them.

HANDLING THE OPPOSITION

[49] Now John answered and said, "Master, we saw someone casting out demons in Your name, and we forbade him because he does not follow with us."

[50] But Jesus said to him, "Do not forbid him, for he who is not against us is on our side."

[51] Now it came to pass, when the time had come for Him to be received up, that He steadfastly set His face to go to Jerusalem, [52] and sent messengers before His face. And as they went, they entered a village of the Samaritans, to prepare for Him. [53] But they did not receive Him, because His face was set for the journey to Jerusalem. [54] And when His disciples James and John saw this, they said, "Lord, do You want us to command fire to come down from heaven and consume them, just as Elijah did?"

[55] But He turned and rebuked them, and said, "You do not know what manner of spirit you are of. [56] For the Son of Man did not come to destroy men's lives but to save them." And they went to another village.

—Luke 9:49–56

Again, the disciples are caught up in the excitement of fighting a theological battle (vv. 49–50). They were the guardians of the truth and they wanted to stamp out the unorthodox. In His reply, Jesus seems to be indicating, "We need all the help we can get." After World War II a group of Christians offered to come to Russia to help rebuild hospitals and orphanages. The Russians were puzzled, especially when the Christians suggested they would be coming to help them with God's work. They were shocked by such an idea. Yet God can be working in the world through all sorts of people, even some who seem to us antireligious. But it's much more stimulating and exciting to engage in theological skirmishes than to affirm and support the good that we see.

Later, James and John urge a course of action that is dramatic and exciting. They want to destroy the town that has refused to receive Jesus, but Jesus rebukes them. The calling down of fire and brimstone still has appeal. Those churches who take a strong stand against all the evils of life are prospering. They are against sin, the devil, alcoholism, pornography, communism (you can make your own list). People will flock to join the "against" churches—those with a negative thrust. It's much more difficult to attract a following for a positive program, one for God and for our neighbors. That's too ordinary and unexciting.

COSTLY DISCIPLESHIP

57 Now it happened as they journeyed on the road, that someone said to Him, "Lord, I will follow You wherever You go."

58 And Jesus said to him, "Foxes have holes and birds of the air have nests, but the Son of Man has nowhere to lay His head."

59 Then He said to another, "Follow Me."

But he said, "Lord, let me first go and bury my father."

60 Jesus said to him, "Let the dead bury their own dead, but you go and preach the kingdom of God."

61 And another also said, "Lord, I will follow You, but let me first go and bid them farewell who are at my house."

62 But Jesus said to him, "No one, having put his hand to the plow, and looking back, is fit for the kingdom of God."

—Luke 9:57–62

These are poignant stories of people who want so much to follow Jesus, but somehow they can't pay the price. They've got to go home first and get ready or take care of some pressing matter. The first man is caught up in a burst of zeal: *"I will follow You wherever You go."* He thinks discipleship will be a glamorous life. Jesus corrects this impression. He tells him that discipleship is not easy. It's a difficult life with no place to call home. It means putting your hand to the plow and doing the ordinary, hard work. It is in this unexciting everyday discipleship that the glory is found.

In my overseas tour in World War II, I still remember going for days and even weeks, sleeping on the ground without blankets. I'm a compulsively clean person and for six weeks I didn't even bathe. Lack of creature comforts was worse than the fear of death. I vowed at that time that if I ever got out alive I would settle for a leakproof roof over my head, a warm bed, enough food, a hot shower, clean clothes, and coffee as the morning sun comes up. Nothing else seemed necessary or even desirable at that time. And though that was long ago, whenever I start complaining I remember those days of deprivation when my vision was so clear. When I had nothing, I was convinced that the real wonder of life is in the ordinary, everyday comforts that many of us take for granted.

Sometimes it is more difficult to see God in the ordinary, but the miracle of the Incarnation is that God became one of us in Jesus and Jesus was so ordinary in appearance that the Sanhedrin had to hire one of the twelve to point Him out in the Garden of Gethsemane lest they get the wrong man.

The Last Supper was an occasion when God exalted the ordinary. Jesus took the ingredients of a typical supper, the bread and the wine, and transformed them into our present communion elements. We have since romanticized those elements as we have the Cross. I am convinced that if Jesus came today He might even use coffee and doughnuts. He took those things common to a meal in any household and said, "This is My body and My blood. Eat and drink in remembrance of Me." Our present communion traditions vary greatly. Most Protestants observe the sacraments only every few months. Roman Catholics or traditional Anglicans celebrate mass every Sunday. The Quakers hold no formal communion at all. They say every meal is a sacrament.

You may have read the well-known little book, *The Practice of the Presence of God,* written by Brother Lawrence, a monk of the seventeenth century. When he joined the monastery, he was put in charge of the kitchen. There he learned to commune with God, cleaning the pots and pans, buying cabbages, cooking soup. He began to be annoyed by the frequent calls to prayer. He had to interrupt his time with God to go into the chapel and pray formally. He found that God was more real in the ordinary and everyday chores.

Blaise Pascal, the great French saint and scientist, once said that the more intellectual people are, the more originality they see in others. As we see with God's vision, no one is ordinary. We see His glory in every person, and as we go about our everyday lives, we find Him in every circumstance.

CHAPTER TWENTY-FIVE—THE KEY TO EVERYTHING
LUKE 10:1–42

Scripture Outline

A Missionary Journey (10:1–24)

The Shape of Love (10:25–37)

A Matter of Focus (10:38–42)

A MISSIONARY JOURNEY

10:1 After these things the Lord appointed seventy others also, and sent them two by two before His face into every city and place where He Himself was about to go. 2 Then He said to them, "The harvest truly is great, but the laborers are few; therefore pray the Lord of the harvest to send out laborers into His harvest. 3 Go your way; behold, I send you out as lambs among wolves. 4 Carry neither money bag, knapsack, nor sandals; and greet no one along the road. 5 But whatever house you enter, first say, 'Peace to this house.' 6 And if a son of peace is there, your peace will rest on it; if not, it will return to you. 7 And remain in the same house, eating and drinking such things as they give, for the laborer is worthy of his wages. Do not go from house to house. 8 Whatever city you enter, and they receive you, eat such things as are set before you. 9 And heal the sick there, and say to them, 'The kingdom of God has come near to you.' 10 But whatever city you enter, and they do not receive you, go out into its streets and say, 11 'The very dust of your city which clings to us we wipe off against you. Nevertheless know this, that the kingdom of God has come near you.' 12 But I say to you that it will be more tolerable in that Day for Sodom than for that city.

13 "Woe to you, Chorazin! Woe to you, Bethsaida! For if the mighty works which were done in you had been done in Tyre and Sidon, they would have repented long ago, sitting in sackcloth and ashes. 14 But it will be more tolerable for Tyre

and Sidon at the judgment than for you. 15 And you, Capernaum, who are exalted to heaven, will be brought down to Hades. 16 He who hears you hears Me, he who rejects you rejects Me, and he who rejects Me rejects Him who sent Me."

17 Then the seventy returned with joy, saying, "Lord, even the demons are subject to us in Your name."

18 And He said to them, "I saw Satan fall like lightning from heaven. 19 Behold, I give you the authority to trample on serpents and scorpions, and over all the power of the enemy, and nothing shall by any means hurt you. 20 Nevertheless do not rejoice in this, that the spirits are subject to you, but rather rejoice because your names are written in heaven."

21 In that hour Jesus rejoiced in the Spirit and said, "I thank You, Father, Lord of heaven and earth, that You have hidden these things from the wise and prudent and revealed them to babes. Even so, Father, for so it seemed good in Your sight. 22 All things have been delivered to Me by My Father, and no one knows who the Son is except the Father, and who the Father is except the Son, and the one to whom the Son wills to reveal Him."

23 Then He turned to His disciples and said privately, "Blessed are the eyes which see the things you see; 24 for I tell you that many prophets and kings have desired to see what you see, and have not seen it, and to hear what you hear, and have not heard it."

—Luke 10:1–24

In Sanibel, Florida, I lived across the street from Sidney Simon, a pioneer figure in the educational world. He is a professor at the University of Massachusetts and the father of something called "values clarification." He claims that if you know which things in your life are negotiable and which are absolutely essential, you have a great advantage. All decisions are simplified once you know what is important to you. It seems to me that clarifying our values would help all of us in the watersheds of life.

I heard of a man who was praying in church rather audibly, "O Lord, make me successful but keep me humble." His wife overheard his prayer and was prompted to respond, "O Lord, You make him successful. I'll keep him humble." At any rate, this man had a clear understanding of what he wanted most from God. For him, success was the essential ingredient of life. Sir James Barrie, author of *Peter Pan,* said, "Charm is the essential thing. If you have it you don't need to have anything else, and if you don't have it, it doesn't much matter what else you have." Well, certainly there are people who have built a life around being charming. In our present culture, we have an increasing number of physical fitness devotees who are building their lives around exercise and proper diet. And in every age, there are those driven by the desire to be wealthy or famous or powerful. As we read these next verses perhaps we can discover what it is we really need from God. What exactly is the "key to everything"?

On this occasion Jesus is sending out the seventy, much as the twelve were sent out earlier. "Why seventy?" you might ask. No one knows for sure, but the conjecture is that in Genesis 10, the seventy nations of the world are named, and therefore Jesus sent out seventy to symbolize the sending of the message to all the known world. The first twelve symbolized the sending of the message to the twelve tribes, the House of Israel. But on each occasion, we can assume Jesus had a reason for sending out a particular number.

The instructions are very much the same as those given the twelve (Luke 9). First He sent them out in pairs. It seems to me there is a synergy—a spiritual energy—released when two or more are involved in the same ministry. The seventy are told to take no luggage and to get going without delay. Jesus says that their mission will be a dangerous one. They will be lambs among wolves. He says again, as He said to the twelve, that they are not to bless the unwilling. That's still wise advice. Don't waste your time on people who yawn or get angry or want to argue. Jesus advises us to tell the exciting news to those who are eager to hear. He says, "Do not go from house to house" socializing. In other words, the seventy were not to stop and engage in chit-chat: "Hello. How are you? How's your mother? Is your daughter still in school?" They were to live simply, heal the sick, and proclaim the kingdom of God.

God gives this same commission to us if we are His people. As He sent the seventy, so He sends us out with the same authority and the same commission. When the seventy return, they are filled with joy. They can't believe what's happened to them. They say, *'Even the demons are subject to us through Your name"* (v. 17). They are delighted by the visible results of their mission. Their powers are not just spiritual.

In verse 21, Luke says Jesus *"rejoiced"* upon hearing this news. This is the only place where this particular word is used to describe Jesus' emotions. He is beside Himself with joy when He hears their report. It's mind-boggling to realize that we have the power to make God rejoice by our fruitful ministry. It was the beginning of a whole new day. Up to that point, the battle was between Satan and Jesus. Because of the works of the seventy, Satan experienced a mighty fall. Jesus says, *"I saw Satan fall like lightning from heaven."*

It seems a grandiose claim in the face of what actually occurred. Seventy people went out—some of their hearers responded, some didn't. Some cities rejoiced and some didn't. Some were healed; a few more entered the kingdom. It would all seem less than spectacular. Nevertheless, it was the start of a new era. It was the beginning of the royal priesthood that Jesus has created to do His work in the world. The seventy discovered they had the power of Jesus to help and heal and liberate, and we who are believers are the descendants of those seventy. This missionary journey of the seventy symbolized the geometric increase in the ministry of Jesus Christ and ultimately in the kingdom of God.

In verse 20, Jesus cautions the seventy. He tells them that even though He has given them great power, a still more precious gift is theirs. They are loved eternally. Some day the world will pass away. They will all die. All these marvelous events that thrill them now will some day be inconsequential. The eternal fact is that their names are written in the Lamb's Book of Life and they will live eternally— home free forever and ever. That assurance is the real source of joy. Incidentally and temporally they had great power.

I saw a sign in someone's kitchen:

> The book of life is short,
> And when a page is read,
> Only love remains.

All wisdom, all power, all cleverness will someday pass away (1 Cor. 13). The one remaining truth is the fact that we are loved by God Himself, and His love goes on and on. In His joy, Jesus immediately turns to God in prayer. He says, *"All things have been delivered to Me by My father, and no one knows who the Son is except the Father, and who the Father is except the Son, and the one to whom the Son wills to reveal Him."* It's an astounding statement. If all things belong to Jesus Christ then He is the means of meeting all our needs, whatever they are—physical, emotional, relational, and spiritual. He is the "key to everything" we spoke of earlier.

THE SHAPE OF LOVE

25 And behold, a certain lawyer stood up and tested Him, saying, "Teacher, what shall I do to inherit eternal life?"

26 He said to him, "What is written in the law? What is your reading of it?"

27 So he answered and said, "'You shall love the LORD your God with all your heart, with all your soul, with all your strength, and with all your mind,' and 'your neighbor as yourself.'"

28 And He said to him, "You have answered rightly; do this and you will live."

29 But he, wanting to justify himself, said to Jesus, "And who is my neighbor?"

30 Then Jesus answered and said: "A certain man went down from Jerusalem to Jericho, and fell among thieves, who stripped him of his clothing, wounded him, and departed, leaving him half dead. 31 Now by chance a certain priest came down that road. And when he saw him, he passed by on the other side. 32 Likewise a Levite, when he arrived at the place, came and looked, and passed by on the other side. 33 But a certain Samaritan, as he journeyed, came where he was. And when he saw him, he had compassion. 34 So he went to him and bandaged his wounds, pouring on oil and wine; and he set him on his own animal, brought him to an inn, and took care of him. 35 On the next day, when he departed, he took out two denarii, gave them to the innkeeper, and said to him, 'Take care of him; and whatever more you spend, when I come again, I will repay you.' 36 So which of these three do you think was neighbor to him who fell among the thieves?"

37 And he said, "He who showed mercy on him."

Then Jesus said to him, "Go and do likewise."

—Luke 10:25–37

Once we have found this great central truth in life, that we are loved by God now and forever, we can behave like the Good Samaritan and say, "Whatever is mine is God's and whatever is God's belongs to my neighbor because my neighbor belongs to Him." The Good Samaritan is not trying to keep the rules. He isn't even doing his duty. He is doing what is instinctive and natural because of who he is. Scholars cannot agree on how much money he gave the inn keeper. Some say two weeks' worth of board.

Others say two months. The point is that he paid the innkeeper a considerable amount of his own money to take care of this unknown, injured man.

Jesus says to us, "Love your neighbor as you love yourself." Love of self is instinctive and involuntary. If you're in trouble, you never wonder if you're worth helping. When you're queuing up for a movie or a ball game, it would never occur to you to surrender your place to someone else. You get in line early and feel entitled to be there. Jesus says in the kingdom that's how you love your neighbor. You feel he/she is worthy and deserves preferential treatment. There is no legalism. The lawyer who asks Jesus the question, "Who is my neighbor?" is trying to find a new rule, a new law. In the Good Samaritan story, Jesus indicates that the law of love puts an end to legalism. No more laws, no more rules. We are simply to love one another as He has loved us.

A friend of mine was building a home in the mountains of Vermont in a place where it's very difficult to get water. He asked an old Vermonter to come over and divine the source of water on his property with a stick. Sure enough, this old-timer found the appropriate spot. "Just dig fourteen feet straight down here and you'll find an underground river," he told my friend. "When you hit the water, pump it out every day." My friend followed the instructions and found the river. He pumped it out the first day and more water came in. In the next few days, the water rose to four feet, then six feet. At eight feet it seemed stationary, so he left it. Returning some months later when the house was finished, he immediately turned on the water. The first day there seemed to be plenty, but by the next day there was none at all. The well was empty. In spite of his efforts to revive it, my friend ended up having to dig an artesian well at a cost of three thousand dollars.

Much later he ran into the old Vermonter in town and told him the disappointing story. "Did you pump it out every day?" was the question. "No," said my friend. The Vermonter shook his head. "You fool! An underground river is made up of thousands of little capillaries running underground. As you pump the water you enlarge those capillaries and more water comes. Once you stop, the water backs up, the capillaries close and the river is formed somewhere else." Our life in Jesus is like that. As we give our time, our love, our money, the well is always filled. When we begin to believe "What's mine is mine" somehow our lives dry up and we've lost the key to everything.

A MATTER OF FOCUS

38 Now it happened as they went that He entered a certain village; and a certain woman named Martha welcomed Him into her house. 39 And she had a sister called Mary, who also sat at Jesus' feet and heard His word. 40 But Martha was distracted with much serving, and she approached Him and said, "Lord, do You not care that my sister has left me to serve alone? Therefore tell her to help me."

41 And Jesus answered and said to her, "Martha, Martha, you are worried and troubled about many things. 42 But one thing is needed, and Mary has chosen that good part, which will not be taken away from her."

—Luke 10:38–42

I've always regretted all the controversy over Mary and Martha, those two sisters who were Jesus' beloved friends. Bible students can't help taking sides on which one is more admirable, the spiritual type or the practical one. But they both have excellent qualities, and I thank God for Marthas and Marys, then and now. It seems to me that the story really deals with our goals in life. What has our attention most of the time? Martha is focused on her own goal. She is so busy being gracious and polite and a good hostess that she has no time to be with the Lord. We may say that all we have—time, life, money—is the Lord's, but does He have our attention? We may be too busy doing good works.

The priest and the Levite in the story of the Good Samaritan were doing the right thing. This injured man might possibly be dead, and touching him would render them ceremonially unclean. They would be unable to enter the synagogue to teach and preach. Theological propriety kept them from acting in love. Martha's social proprieties kept her from focusing her attention on Jesus and His agenda for her life.

You and I can lose sight of who we are and whose we are very easily. The good things in life—family, job, community service, even good works—can begin to choke out God's life in us. As we make God and His presence in our lives our primary focus, we find He is the key to everything.

CHAPTER TWENTY-SIX—LEARNING TO PRAY

LUKE 11:1–13

11:1 Now it came to pass, as He was praying in a certain place, when He ceased, that one of His disciples said to Him, "Lord, teach us to pray, as John also taught his disciples."

2 So He said to them, "When you pray, say:
Our Father in heaven,
Hallowed be Your name.
Your kingdom come.
Your will be done
On earth as it is in heaven.
3 Give us day by day our daily bread.
4 And forgive us our sins,
For we also forgive everyone who is indebted to us.
And do not lead us into temptation,
But deliver us from the evil one."

5 And He said to them, "Which of you shall have a friend, and go to him at midnight and say to him, 'Friend, lend me three loaves; 6 for a friend of mine has come to me on his journey, and I have nothing to set before him'; 7 and he will answer from within and say, 'Do not trouble me; the door is now shut, and my children are with me in bed; I cannot rise and give to you'? 8 I say to you, though he will not rise and give to him because he is his friend, yet because of his persistence he will rise and give him as many as he needs.

9 "So I say to you, ask, and it will be given to you; seek, and you will find; knock, and it will be opened to you. 10 For everyone who asks receives, and he who seeks finds, and to him who knocks it will be opened.

11 If a son asks for bread from any father among you, will he give him a stone? Or if he asks for a fish, will he give him a serpent instead of a fish? 12 Or if he asks for an egg, will he offer him a scorpion? 13 If you then, being evil, know how to give good gifts to your children, how much more will your heavenly Father give the Holy Spirit to those who ask Him!"
—Luke 17:1–13

There is a story that I hope is true about a man working the four to midnight shift every night. He walked home and his route passed a cemetery. One night he was in a particular hurry, and since the moon was full, he decided to take a short-cut through the middle of the cemetery. The route lopped five minutes off his walk, and soon it became his regular path. But on one particularly black night, he had an unfortunate mishap. He fell into a freshly dug grave. He wasn't hurt but the hole was so deep he was unable to get out. He began to yell, but nobody heard him. Resigned at last to simply wait for morning, when his plight would be discovered, he pulled his coat up around his neck and huddled in a corner to try to sleep. He was awakened in an hour or so by the noise of a falling body. A second unfortunate man had stumbled into this unexpected hole. Sleepily, the first arrival watched his companion trying frantically to crawl out. After a few minutes, he felt obliged to comment, "You'll never get out that way." Well—he did!

The story illustrates whimsically that all of us have undiscovered and unexpected powers—powers we didn't know we had. One of the most effective ways to appropriate that power is through prayer. In these verses, we find a shortened version of the Lord's Prayer. Bible experts tell us that this is perhaps the most authentic version. The fuller and more familiar version provided by Matthew is thought to be a later expanded one.

It seems to me that Jesus models three things about prayer in this Scripture. First of all, prayer is to be brief and real. The effectiveness of our prayers has nothing to do with their length or their so-called "spirituality." How little we find in this prayer Jesus gives us that could be considered "spiritual." This reduced and simple prayer deals with the very basics of your life and mine—with reality.

Second, Jesus emphasizes persistence. He tells the story of the man awakened by his friend's knock. At first, he is reluctant to respond. We need to remember here that a parable teaches only one lesson. This parable teaches us to be persistent in prayer. It is not a story about the nature of God. God is not in bed with His children, asleep and reluctant to answer our prayers. Jesus is telling us to approach God boldly as we would a neighbor and to ask repeatedly without giving up. God will reward our perseverance.

Third, Jesus tells us to pray expectantly. We are to expect answers and miracles because of the nature of the One to whom we pray. If your earthly father wants to give you whatever you ask for, how much more does your Father in heaven want to give you the desires of your heart?

I have often wondered why the disciples waited so long to ask Jesus to teach them to pray. They had been with Him for months, perhaps even years. They had watched Him praying each day. They saw Him withdrawing alone to pray. The Messiah's life was a life of prayer and they must have been aware of that. I don't understand why they waited so long to ask, "What is it you are doing? Teach us how to do it." Perhaps they were intimidated. Most of us are hesitant to ask each other about the important things of life. Apparently the disciples were.

I also feel certain that Jesus would never have taught the disciples this prayer if they hadn't asked Him to. I don't believe, personally, that it was ever Jesus' intention to teach a rote prayer. He was not indicating that they should use these exact words whenever they prayed. I think He was suggesting a pattern. They insisted on a model prayer, and somehow along the way we have adopted His very words, as though they were some magical formula, rather than trying to understand their underlying spirit.

Certainly prayer is essential to the life of faith and, had I been Jesus, I probably would have made an issue of it at the very beginning with the disciples. ("Now, get this, and get this good. Prayer is the center of our ministry. I want to teach you to pray. Get your notebooks and write down after Me, 'Our Father, who art in—' Are you getting this? Repeat after me—") I would have made sure that everybody knew the right way to pray. Instead, Jesus simply prayed. He just prayed and prayed until they eventually asked, "How do You do it?" By way of answer, He said, "Try this." It was so important He didn't insist they learn to pray until they themselves perceived they were missing something.

The pattern for prayer Jesus gives us here has six separate ingredients. It occurred to me that one way to remember them is to think of the six letters in the name of the author of the prayer—C-H-R-I-S-T. This formula has been a real help to me in my personal prayer life.

"C" represents *concentrate.* Concentrate on the Person you are praying to, and not on the prayer. Someone has said, "Don't pray hard. Pray easy. Prayer doesn't do it; God does it." Prayer is simply a way of tapping into God Himself. You need not be a spiritual type in order to pray. You may say, "Well, I don't feel like prayer." Think about the One you're talking to, the One who has promised to be available to you as you talk and listen in dialogue. Suppose you were told that God was on the phone asking to speak to you. Can you imagine saying, "I don't feel much like prayer today"? You'd say,

"Give me that phone!" The point is, if you concentrate on the Person you're talking to, you don't need to be an experienced pray-er. You can have real conversation with your heavenly Father.

Jesus says we can call God "Father." We can call the Creator of the universe "Daddy." We can crawl up on His lap on good days or bad days and talk to Him. And, Jesus tells us here, if your earthly father would not give you a stone if you asked for bread, how much more will your heavenly Father give you all things that you need.

For many of her readers, Dear Abby was the national resident psychotherapist. One column featured a letter signed by "Fed-up Mamma." It said, "Dear Abby: My nineteen-year-old son got into trouble with the law, drinking and stealing. He served some time, but I think the judge let him off easy, considering he cussed out a cop and broke probation and now he's back again in jail. It serves him right. Let him pay for running his smart mouth. Every day he calls up his daddy and puts in his order. It's always two cartons of cigarettes a week. Yesterday he asked for Tang breakfast drink, a big bag of chocolate chip cookies, a quart of milk, two Big Macs and a large order of fries. Today he asked for a bucket of Kentucky Fried Chicken, a bag of Doritos, some beef jerky and some more cookies. His daddy takes him whatever he asks for, and I keep fighting him about it. All I buy the boy is cigarettes. I say he put himself in jail; let him live on what they feed him there. Am I wrong to feel the way I do, Abby? Please send me your advice."*

I won't tell you Abby's advice. But I would raise a pertinent question. Is our God more like that boy's mother or his father? Shocking as it seems, Jesus suggests that God, like this father, loves you whether you deserve it or not. He wants to give you the desires of your heart because He loves you. The first guideline Jesus gives us for prayer is to concentrate, concentrate on the Person who is willing and eager to talk to you, who loves you, and whom you can call Daddy, and who wants to give you everything you need.

"H" is for *Hallelujah.* Jesus says, Hallowed be thy name, meaning, "Holy" be thy name. Hallowed defines the person of God. To this ultimate, holy person, we respond with "Glory, Hallelujah!" At this point in your prayer, if you have the gift of tongues, you can use this strange language to say, "Praise, celebration, glory, hallelujah." If you don't have the gift of tongues you can praise Him just as joyfully. You can invent ways to celebrate His glory. Driving down the freeway, in the shower, or in your quiet time,

* Taken from the Dear Abby column. © 1981, Universal Press Syndicate.
Reprinted with permission. All rights reserved.

try new ways of expressing praise. You might try leading cheers for Him, saying, "Yay, God!" or "Rah, rah, rah!" Take time through the day to celebrate the fact that God is a person, holy and wonderful, and find ways to say "Hallelujah!" We read that "the joy of the Lord is my strength," and that "God dwells in the praises of His people." Doctors affirm the verse in the Old Testament that "a merry heart is good medicine." The more time we spend praising God and saying, "Glory, Hallelujah," the better we will feel, physically and emotionally.

"R" stands for *ruler.* Jesus simply says, "Thy kingdom come." God is the ruler of that kingdom. He is going to rule all things some day. He rules the cosmos now. In this world His kingdom is growing. We can extend the kingdom by our gifts and our prayers and by the sacrifice of our lives every day. The kingdom will come in fullness some day. Right now it's here in part. Through our prayer, we say, "Let me be a part of building Your kingdom." We also reiterate our belief that all things will ultimately be the Lord's. Therefore, believe in miracles. There is nothing that cannot be if you are talking to the Ruler of the universe. The Bible abounds with miracles wrought by prayer.

"I" is for *I* need and *I* feed. Jesus says, "Give us this day our daily bread." We are praying, "God, give me what I need. God, feed me." We feed on Him for the things we need. And apart from Him, we are impoverished. I need bread—daily sustenance. My family and friends need sustenance. God gives us bread. I need help, perhaps in some basic areas. I need money. I need a job. I need healing. I need strength. I need love.

I asked someone who came to see me recently, "What do you need most?" He said, "A friend. I don't have a single friend." I believe that's a basic need just like bread, and the two of us prayed that God might supply his need. We pray, "Give us this day the things we need," and God, being who He is, wants to give us those very things. He wants to meet our relational needs and our sexual needs. He wants to give wisdom and guidance. All these things comprise our basic daily needs.

One of my all-time favorite hymns is a Welsh one called, "Guide Me, O Thou Great Jehovah," written in 1745. It has just one flaw. In one verse, the English translation reads, "Feed me 'til I want no more," which means feed me 'til I'm fed up. It suggests there will be a time when we'll be so full we won't need the Lord. In the original Welsh of William Williams, that line is, "Feed me now and evermore." Being God's children, we never cease needing Him. We stand in His presence now and eternally, and He feeds us continually. And so we have the *I* of the Lord's Prayer—*I* need; *I* feed.

"S," the fifth letter, is for *Saviour*. When you pray, affirm that God is your *Saviour* in Jesus Christ. Jesus says in His prayer that God will forgive us for our sins. We cannot live a single day without sinning by omission or commission. We confess those in prayer and ask for forgiveness. By the blood of Christ, we are forgiven. But the ultimate sin is our unwillingness to forgive someone who has sinned against us. Jesus is not suggesting we can make some sort of a trade-off, for example, "I have forgiven all those people who have hurt me, God, so deal with me the same way." If that was my prayer, I would be in big trouble. When I'm aware of how much the Lord has forgiven me, I can only be magnanimous toward those who have misused me.

A friend of mine once told me that the most significant person in his life was his grandfather. The grandfather ran a feed and grain store during the Depression, and he gave credit to so many customers who never did pay that he eventually declared bankruptcy. It took him years to earn enough to repay all the liens against his business. But on the day when the last creditor was finally paid, this old gentleman took his books, including all the records of the people who had owed him money, and burned them in a huge bonfire. Incidentally, the amount totalled $40,000, a lot of money in those Depression years. With that $40,000 bonfire, he forgave his debtors as he had been forgiven. A remarkable man.

"T" is for *triumph* over temptation. "Lead us not into temptation," says Jesus. In your prayers you can ask God not to lead you into temptation—all and any kind of temptation. You can say, "Lord, I don't want to fail You any more than I have to. I want to be your person. Thank You for forgiving my sins, but try to keep me from sinning so often."

The first promise I ever claimed after I said yes to Jesus Christ was the one in 1 Corinthians 10:13. At the end of the war, I was stationed for a year in Germany, and the sins of the flesh were all around and within. I said, "Lord, I am Your person now. I don't want to be a part of this scene any more, but I'm weak. First Corinthians 10:13 reads: 'No temptation has overtaken you except such as is common to man; but God is faithful, who will not allow you to be tempted beyond what you are able, but with the temptation will also make the way of escape, that you may be able to bear it.'" I said, "Lord, I claim that," and it worked.

But the temptations of the flesh are minor compared to the temptations of the spirit. The Holy Spirit calls us to some high-risk involvement at home and abroad for friends or strangers, and we are tempted to say "No." We are afraid to fail. We are timid. We do not trust God. Those are some of the temptations of the spirit. Jesus tells us to pray that God will not lead us into the temptations of the flesh or the spirit. Rather, we can claim boldly what He would have us be and do for the world.

I have had a few occasions to speak at the Crystal Cathedral in Garden Grove, California—a gorgeous, 3000-seat amphitheater and a part of an enormous campus of impressive buildings which house a thriving ministry. At lunch one day, Robert Schuller, the visionary responsible for all this, told me how it all began. "Twenty-five years ago I had a little church in a borrowed drive-in theater. On a visit to New York, I stopped in to see Norman Vincent Peale in his office. I was wrestling with whether or not I should launch out and start something new on a larger scale, when my eye caught this sign on Norman's wall: "I would rather attempt to do something great and fail than to attempt nothing and succeed."

Don't be tempted by the spirit of timidity and lack of trust. The Lord's Prayer reminds us we can triumph over temptation of the spirit as well as of the flesh.

Prayer is at the very heart of the life of faith. Prayer is simply talking and listening to the ultimate Being in the universe. It's like falling in love. Suddenly your life takes on a whole new meaning. You've got a new center, a relationship with a person that gives you excitement and joy. You are talking to the person you love, and you can talk to him or her all through the day, driving, showering, walking down the aisles of the supermarket, going to sleep, waking up. Think of C-H-R-I-S-T, the six elements of the conversation you can have with the Ultimate Person.

We find the bottom line in verse 13: *"If you then, being evil, know how to give good gifts to your children, how much more will your heavenly Father give the Holy Spirit to those who ask Him!"* As parents we can give our children a good many things. We can underwrite their education, bail them out of jail, pay their hospital bills, buy them a house. We can give them every conceivable gift, whether they want it or not. If our kids are too proud to receive help, we can even find ways to get around that. But the one thing we cannot give our children, unless they want to receive it, is our friendship. Friendship must be won. We can offer it, but there is no friendship, unless they accept it.

In the Holy Spirit we partake of God's friendship. Through His Spirit, God comes to be in us and with us, to talk to us and listen to us, and we to Him. It is a sign of His friendship. God gives His Spirit to us if we ask, and then the dialogue begins. We can forget about prayer, and just talk to our Father.

CHAPTER TWENTY-SEVEN—THE HOLY INVASION AND THE ADVERSARIES

LUKE 11:14–54

Scripture Outline

The Spiritually Blind (11:14–26)

The Sentimentalists (11:27–36)

The Legalists (11:37–44)

The Stumbling Block (11:45–54)

THE SPIRITUALLY BLIND

14 And He was casting out a demon, and it was mute. So it was, when the demon had gone out, that the mute spoke; and the multitudes marveled.

15 But some of them said, "He casts out demons by Beelzebub, the ruler of the demons."

16 Others, testing Him, sought from Him a sign from heaven. 17 But He, knowing their thoughts, said to them: "Every kingdom divided against itself is brought to desolation, and a house divided against a house falls. 18 If Satan also is divided against himself, how will his kingdom stand? Because you say I cast out demons by Beelzebub. 19 And if I cast out demons by Beelzebub, by whom do your sons cast them out? Therefore they will be your judges. 20 But if I cast out demons with the finger of God, surely the kingdom of God has come upon you. 21 When a strong man, fully armed, guards his own palace, his goods are in peace. 22 But when a stronger than he comes upon him and overcomes him, he takes from him all his armor in which he trusted, and divides his spoils. 23 He who is not with Me is against Me, and he who does not gather with Me scatters.

24 "When an unclean spirit goes out of a man, he goes through dry places, seeking rest; and finding none, he says, 'I will return to my house from which I came.' 25 And when he comes, he finds it swept and put in order. 26 Then he goes and

takes with him seven other spirits more wicked than himself, and they enter and dwell there; and the last state of that man is worse than the first."

—*Luke 11:14–26*

Those of us who lived through World War II will never forget the excitement we all felt as the Allied Armies geared up for an invasion of Europe, then occupied and controlled by the Nazi forces. Rumors of the invasion and its timing were rampant, and we all looked forward eagerly to that time when the free forces of the world would establish a beachhead on the European continent. Day by day we speculated, "When will it happen and how? Will it succeed? What are the back-up plans?"

I was thinking about those long-ago events as I read these verses. I was aware anew that God, in the person of His Son Jesus, came into the world as a Holy Invader to establish a beachhead in your life and mine. Any such invasion presupposes resistance by enemy forces. In these verses Jesus deals in some of His harshest language with those who represent the forces opposing this holy invasion.

First of all, there are the spiritually blind, and we can almost assume this blindness is a matter of choice. The early church fathers considered willing ignorance the essence of sin. We find the crowd watching as Jesus casts out a demon from a mute. When the man speaks, they decide he has been healed by the power of Satan. But Satan is not the author of healing and wholeness. Rather, it is Satan who blinds and deafens and cripples and distorts and destroys. To believe that God is the author of illness and Satan a liberator is the ultimate perversion.

The Bible warns repeatedly that by calling evil good and good evil, we endanger our very souls. There is a tendency today, especially in parts of the entertainment world, to glorify all that is seamy and degrading in life. We live in a violent, sex-obsessed society, and we can't stick our heads in the sand. But it is one thing to produce a thought-provoking story about these problems and quite another to be suggesting, ever so subtly, that this is a viable lifestyle. "Get with it. This is how the beautiful people live."—That's one kind of willing ignorance.

In this Scripture Jesus reminds us that neutrality is not an option. He says, *"He who is not with Me is against Me"* (v. 23). Further, when evil forces have been cast out—demons, mental or emotional illness, or whatever—a positive force must replace them. If the cure is not followed by an indwelling of God's power, the final state of the one healed may be seven times worse. If there is no new allegiance to God and His purposes, the enemy will claim us again.

THE SENTIMENTALISTS

27 And it happened, as He spoke these things, that a certain woman from the crowd raised her voice and said to Him, "Blessed is the womb that bore You, and the breasts which nursed You!"

28 But He said, "More than that, blessed are those who hear the word of God and keep it!"

29 And while the crowds were thickly gathered together, He began to say, "This is an evil generation. It seeks a sign, and no sign will be given to it except the sign of Jonah the prophet. 30 For as Jonah became a sign to the Ninevites, so also the Son of Man will be to this generation. 31 The queen of the South will rise up in the judgment with the men of this generation and condemn them, for she came from the ends of the earth to hear the wisdom of Solomon; and indeed a greater than Solomon is here. 32 The men of Nineveh will rise up in the judgment with this generation and condemn it, for they repented at the preaching of Jonah; and indeed a greater than Jonah is here.

33 "No one, when he has lit a lamp, puts it in a secret place or under a basket, but on a lampstand, that those who come in may see the light. 34 The lamp of the body is the eye. Therefore, when your eye is good, your whole body also is full of light. But when your eye is bad, your body also is full of darkness. 35 Therefore take heed that the light which is in you is not darkness. 36 If then your whole body is full of light, having no part dark, the whole body will be full of light, as when the bright shining of a lamp gives you light."

—*Luke 11:27–36*

The second group of adversaries to this holy invasion are the sentimentalists, those who would romanticize the mighty acts of God. In the midst of His healing and teaching and the ensuing confrontation with the authorities, Jesus is hailed by a woman in the crowd with a paeon of praise for His mother. In short, she is saying, "What a marvelous person *she* must have been. How wonderful to have been Your mother." Jesus' reply puts an end to such sentimental rhetoric. He tells us it is better to belong to Him spiritually than biologically. His hearers, then and now, have the opportunity to be a part of a holy invasion by doing the will of Jesus and His father. In doing so, we are His mother, father, sisters or brothers, even more than His biological kinfolk.

The sentimentalists usually manage to confuse the issue. They like to romanticize finding God in the great out-of-doors—in the mountains, the fields, and the oceans. Certainly God made all the beauty of the world. But, if you really want to see God, look around you and see His children—those marvelous, perverse, and wonderful creations made in His image. This is where we see the wonder of God. Yes, God the Creator is revealed among the pine trees and lakes. But He is most of all revealed in the family of brothers and sisters who hear His word and do it.

Jesus had harsh words for those romantic, spiritualizing, sentimentalists who wanted a sign. They would be given a sign, like the sign of Jonah. Nineveh repented when God delivered Jonah after three days of virtual death in the belly of the whale. Jesus tells them that they will see a greater sign than that.

THE LEGALISTS

37 And as He spoke, a certain Pharisee asked Him to dine with him. So He went in and sat down to eat. 38 When the Pharisee saw it, he marveled that He had not first washed before dinner.

39 Then the Lord said to him, "Now you Pharisees make the outside of the cup and dish clean, but your inward part is full of greed and wickedness. 40 Foolish ones! Did not He who made the outside make the inside also? 41 But rather give alms of such things as you have; then indeed all things are clean to you.

42 "But woe to you Pharisees! For you tithe mint and rue and all manner of herbs, and pass by justice and the love of God. These you ought to have done, without leaving the others undone. 43 Woe to you Pharisees! For you love the best seats in the synagogues and greetings in the marketplaces.
44 Woe to you, scribes and Pharisees, hypocrites! For you are like graves which are not seen, and the men who walk over them are not aware of them."

—Luke 11:37–44

And then there are those formidable adversaries—the legalists. Jesus is called to task by the scribes and the Pharisees for sitting down to eat without the ritual washing. In fact, ritual washing was not part of the law at that time. Rather, it was an oral tradition that the scribes, Pharisees, and lawyers observed in order to make themselves feel more righteous than ordinary people. In using the wonderful analogy of the cup (v. 39), Jesus is scathing in His remarks about their legalism. They are more concerned about form than substance, about appearance than reality.

He is outraged by the legalistic burdens the scribes and Pharisees have laid upon the Jews. For example, it was taught that on the Sabbath a man may not carry a burden in his right hand or left hand, in his bosom or on his shoulder. But, he may carry it on the back of his hand or with his foot, or with his mouth, or with his elbow, or in his ear, or in his hair, or in his wallet, if it is carried mouth-downward or between his wallet and shirt or in the hem of his shirt or in his shoe or sandal. That's only one of a thousand laws that faithful Jews were to follow. To paraphrase Jesus' reactions somewhat, He is saying, "What do you think you are doing? You have taken the joy of living as God's chosen people and made it a burden. Because of your laws, you have made worship burdensome. Instead of sharing with joy the material blessings God has given you, you've made it a ridiculous game—counting every little herb in your garden. You are so concerned with tithing the fruits of your garden that you have neglected justice and the love of God."

THE STUMBLING BLOCK

45 Then one of the lawyers answered and said to Him, "Teacher, by saying these things You reproach us also."

46 And He said, "Woe to you also, lawyers! For you load men with burdens hard to bear, and you yourselves do not touch the burdens with one of your fingers. 47 Woe to you! For you build the tombs of the prophets, and your fathers killed them. 48 In fact, you bear witness that you approve the deeds of your fathers; for they indeed killed them, and you build their tombs. 49 Therefore the wisdom of God also said, 'I will send them prophets and apostles, and some of them they will kill and persecute,' 50 that the blood of all the prophets which was shed from the foundation of the world may be required of this generation, 51 from the blood of Abel to the blood of Zechariah who perished between the altar and the temple. Yes, I say to you, it shall be required of this generation.

52 "Woe to you lawyers! For you have taken away the key of knowledge. You did not enter in yourselves, and those who were entering in you hindered."

53 And as He said these things to them, the scribes and the Pharisees began to assail Him vehemently, and to cross-examine Him about many things, 54 lying in wait for Him, and seeking to catch Him in something He might say, that they might accuse Him.

—*Luke 17:45–54*

At this point, a lawyer interrupts, offended by what Jesus has said. I think he may have later regretted that interruption, for Jesus seems to have the harshest words of all for those lawyers in the crowd. He says they have taken away the key of knowledge: *"You did not enter in yourselves, and those who were entering in you hindered"* (v. 52). I think there is still a special judgment on those people who have made no genuine commitment to Christ themselves, and who are a stumbling block for others who would do so. They have devoted their lives to religious legalism and have missed the meaning of the holy invasion.

Self-righteousness becomes a way to self-justification. Tom Wolfe's "Jogger's Prayer" wonderfully satirizes this kind of Phariseeism.

> Almighty God, as we sail with pure aerobic grace and striped orthotic feet past the blind portals of our fellow citizens, past their chuck-roast lives and their necrotic cardio-vascular systems and rusting hips and slipped discs and desiccated lungs, past their implacable inertia and inability to persevere and rise above the fully pensioned world they live in and to push themselves to the limits of their capacity and achieve the White Moment of slipping through the Wall, borne aloft on one's Third Wind, past their Cruisomatic cars and upholstered lawn mowers and their gummy-sweet children already at work like little fat factories producing arterial plaque, the more quickly to join their parents in their joyless, bucketseat landau ride toward the grave—help us, dear Lord, we beseech Thee, as we sail past this cold-lard desolation, to be big about it.

We find so many ways to say, "I thank God I am not like my neighbors." We have our own standards of legalism. We have many reasons to support our judgements. We become single-issue people. The issues vary: Which version of the Bible do you read? Are you a pacifist? Do you drink? Do you believe in prophecy (if so, which kind)? Have you demonstrated for civil rights, for no-nukes, for peace, for the ERA? Do you speak in tongues? Are you a tither, and what kind—before or after taxes, gross or net? Are foreign missions the focus of your faith? Are you Republican—or part of the Moral Majority? Are you a vegetarian, and if so, what about eggs and fish? These single-issue people are the legalists of today.

I was on a call-in radio show recently, talking about the spiritual dimensions of health, when someone called in to ask, "How do you stand on secular humanism?" The question had nothing at all to do with what had been said. It was one more example of single-issue focus, which is our present-day legalism.

One of the great dangers of this single-issue legalism is that it is a way of externalizing evil. The good news is that the King has come to invade not just the world, but your life and mine, and to deal with the evil inside us. The Holy Invader has made a beachhead in us, and we can become a part of extending that beachhead throughout the world.

CHAPTER TWENTY-EIGHT—RULES FOR DISCIPLESHIP

LUKE 12:1—13:5

Scripture Outline

No Secrets (12:1–12)

The Tyranny of Things (12:13–34)

Being Prepared (12:35–48)

No False Peace (12:49–56)

Reconcilers (12:57–59)

Life's Inequities (13:1–5)

I sometimes feel guilty when I think of all the couples I have married without preparing them properly for what is coming in terms of decisions that involve family holidays. For instance, where will you spend Christmas? With his parents or hers? How much do you want to spend on gifts for each other? If you have different ethnic backgrounds, what do you eat—turkey or lutefisk (if you happen to be Scandinavian)? I am Swedish, and we always opened our presents on Christmas Eve, as Scandinavians do. My wife balked. "No way! We are Americans. We will open presents on Christmas morning."

Which set of parents get preferential treatment? I heard about a lovely woman who walked into a suburban home to find a four-year-old boy playing with his train on the floor of the family room. "Dear," she explained, "you don't know me, but I am your grandmother on your father's side." Without looking up he said, "Well, I'll tell you something, ma'am. You've chosen the wrong side."

There is no way to help brides and grooms get ready for these conflicts over family loyalties. You can't hand out rules for living that will cover every situation and decision. There is no such pat rule book in the Christian life either. But certain rules are implicit throughout the Bible that apply to the genuine life of discipleship. In this chapter, Jesus is teaching some of them to His disciples. I found six different explicit rules about life in the kingdom in these next verses.

NO SECRETS

12:1 In the meantime, when an innumerable multitude of people had gathered together, so that they trampled one another, He began to say to His disciples first of all, "Beware of the leaven of the Pharisees, which is hypocrisy. 2 For there is nothing covered that will not be revealed, nor hidden that will not be known. 3 Therefore whatever you have spoken in the dark will be heard in the light, and what you have spoken in the ear in inner rooms will be proclaimed on the housetops.

4 "And I say to you, My friends, do not be afraid of those who kill the body, and after that have no more that they can do. 5 But I will show you whom you should fear: Fear Him who, after He has killed, has power to cast into hell; yes, I say to you, fear Him!

6 "Are not five sparrows sold for two copper coins? And not one of them is forgotten before God. 7 But the very hairs of your head are all numbered. Do not fear therefore; you are of more value than many sparrows.

8 "Also I say to you, whoever confesses Me before men, him the Son of Man also will confess before the angels of God. 9 But he who denies Me before men will be denied before the angels of God.

10 "And anyone who speaks a word against the Son of Man, it will be forgiven him; but to him who blasphemes against the Holy Spirit, it will not be forgiven.

11 "Now when they bring you to the synagogues and magistrates and authorities, do not worry about how or what you should answer, or what you should say. 12 For the Holy Spirit will teach you in that very hour what you ought to say."
—*Luke 12:1–12*

First of all, there are no secrets. You and I have to get used to the fact that nothing we do is hidden. It might have been hard for us, thirty or forty years ago, to understand that. We pictured God sitting in the heavens, writing everything we do in a big book. However, in this enlightened, computerized age, it's easier to understand how God could keep track of all our thoughts and deeds. A tiny silicone chip can hold one hundred thousand or more pieces of information, and your brain is a computer which holds the equivalent of thousands of silicone chips. That means that everything you have ever done or said is recorded, and it's conceivable that by plugging into some celestial terminal your entire life could be re-enacted on a large screen.

You may find that terrifying—to think that everything you have said and done will someday be revealed. Perhaps the terror is that you will be found less than perfect. It shouldn't be. God knows that we are not perfect. One piece of advice I give to young pastors (when asked) is, "Be sure to tell your congregation your faults before they discover them. You will strip them of all of their ammunition."

God's word to us is to walk in the light. When we translate that into living without pretense, it is scary. Think, for instance, about two young people on their very first date. The guy arrives in a beautiful BMW to pick up the girl. He's dressed in a three-piece suit. To impress her, they go to the best restaurant in town. As for her, she is dressed in understated elegance and sporting a marvelous hair-do that looks ever-so-casual. There they are, spending the perfect evening. But the fact is, he borrowed the car and the suit, and he spent a week's wages on the dinner; she had her face in a mud pack for two hours before she went out, and her hair-do cost a fortune. Even if somehow a real relationship is established that first time, they have got to eventually unmask and be who they really are.

Jesus is saying here that the danger is not in failing—we all fail—but in hypocrisy. Life in the kingdom means you need not pretend you are better than you are. You are loved and forgiven, and you don't have to hide and pretend.

THE TYRANNY OF THINGS

13 Then one from the crowd said to Him, "Teacher, tell my brother to divide the inheritance with me."

14 But He said to him, "Man, who made Me a judge or an arbitrator over you?" 15 And He said to them, "Take heed and beware of covetousness, for one's life does not consist in the abundance of the things he possesses."

16 Then He spoke a parable to them, saying: "The ground of a certain rich man yielded plentifully. 17 And he thought within himself, saying, 'What shall I do, since I have no room to store my crops?' 18 So he said, 'I will do this: I will pull down my barns and build greater, and there I will store all my

crops and my goods. ¹⁹ And I will say to my soul, "Soul, you have many goods laid up for many years; take your ease; eat, drink, and be merry."' ²⁰ But God said to him, 'Fool! This night your soul will be required of you; then whose will those things be which you have provided?'

²¹ "So is he who lays up treasure for himself, and is not rich toward God."

²² Then He said to His disciples, "Therefore I say to you, do not worry about your life, what you will eat; nor about the body, what you will put on. ²³ Life is more than food, and the body is more than clothing. ²⁴ Consider the ravens, for they neither sow nor reap, which have neither storehouse nor barn; and God feeds them. Of how much more value are you than the birds? ²⁵ And which of you by worrying can add one cubit to his stature? ²⁶ If you then are not able to do the least, why are you anxious for the rest? ²⁷ Consider the lilies, how they grow: they neither toil nor spin; and yet I say to you, even Solomon in all his glory was not arrayed like one of these. ²⁸ If then God so clothes the grass, which today is in the field and tomorrow is thrown into the oven, how much more will He clothe you, O you of little faith?

²⁹ "And do not seek what you should eat or what you should drink, nor have an anxious mind. ³⁰ For all these things the nations of the world seek after, and your Father knows that you need these things. ³¹ But seek the kingdom of God, and all these things shall be added to you.

³² "Do not fear, little flock, for it is your Father's good pleasure to give you the kingdom. ³³ Sell what you have and give alms; provide yourselves money bags which do not grow old, a treasure in the heavens that does not fail, where no thief approaches nor moth destroys. ³⁴ For where your treasure is, there your heart will be also."

—Luke 12:13–34

The second rule for the life of discipleship is to avoid the tyranny of things. In the middle of Jesus' teachings about life in the kingdom, someone interrupts with a request: *"Teacher, tell my brother to divide the inheritance with me."* And Jesus says, *"Who made Me a judge or an arbitrator over you?"* He came to reconcile us to God and to each other, and not to reapportion the wealth. This man wasn't even asking Jesus for a judicial opinion; he simply wanted

Jesus to tell his brother to give him a share. Jesus reminds us that possessions do not give life its meaning. Possessions can become a tyranny in our life so that we are full of greed.

Then there's reverse greed. We abhor possessions, as if they were evil in themselves. We want to be pure and above all that. Some of you may remember Gert Behanna, author of *The Late Liz*, and an evangelist of the late fifties and sixties. She was converted late in life and at the time felt led to give away her sizable fortune. She later regretted that decision. I heard her say often how much she would have enjoyed having that money for the people and the causes that she cared about in later life. Certainly God took care of her, but she missed the fun of being a steward. I think Jesus is saying here we need not be afraid of possessions. If they come, it's a great privilege to use them in God's causes.

Those people who suffer from "reverse greed" have difficulty believing that Jesus wore what was in His time a Brooks Brothers suit. He had only one garment, but a seamless one—the finest garment made then. On that occasion when expensive ointment was poured over His feet, ointment worth three hundred days' wages for a laborer, He rebuked those who complained that this should have been used to feed the poor. He said, "For you have the poor with you always, but Me you do not have always" (Matt. 26:11). There's a time for the extravagant gesture, as well as a time for practical considerations. There's a time to paint the walls, fix the roof, feed the poor; but there's also a time to celebrate. You are under the tyranny of things if you can't have them, or if you must have them. The message here is to go through life as a steward of all that God chooses to give you.

BEING PREPARED

35 "Let your waist be girded and your lamps burning; 36 and you yourselves be like men who wait for their master, when he will return from the wedding, that when he comes and knocks they may open to him immediately. 37 Blessed are those servants whom the master, when he comes, will find watching. Assuredly, I say to you that he will gird himself and have them sit down to eat, and will come and serve them. 38 And if he should come in the second watch, or come in the third watch, and find them so, blessed are those servants. 39 But know this, that if the master of the house had known what hour the thief would come, he would have watched and not allowed his house to be broken

into. ⁴⁰ Therefore you also be ready, for the Son of Man is coming at an hour you do not expect."

⁴¹ Then Peter said to Him, "Lord, do You speak this parable only to us, or to all people?"

⁴² And the Lord said, "Who then is that faithful and wise steward, whom his master will make ruler over his household, to give them their portion of food in due season? ⁴³ Blessed is that servant whom his master will find so doing when he comes. ⁴⁴ Truly, I say to you that he will make him ruler over all that he has. ⁴⁵ But if that servant says in his heart, 'My master is delaying his coming,' and begins to beat the male and female servants, and to eat and drink and be drunk, ⁴⁶ the master of that servant will come on a day when he is not looking for him, and at an hour when he is not aware, and will cut him in two and appoint him his portion with the unbelievers. ⁴⁷ And that servant who knew his master's will, and did not prepare himself or do according to his will, shall be beaten with many stripes. ⁴⁸ But he who did not know, yet committed things deserving of stripes, shall be beaten with few. For everyone to whom much is given, from him much will be required; and to whom much has been committed, of him they will ask the more.

—Luke 12:35–48

Jesus moves on to the third rule for discipleship: be ready. Avoid the tyranny of time. Jesus is saying, don't be frantic and don't be lazy. Don't be like the house steward who gets lazy while his master is gone. When the owner finally comes home he's not ready. Jesus condemns this person, not for evil done, but for good undone. There are things we know we should be doing, and we are not to be lulled into inactivity by the fact that the Lord has delayed His coming. Every day is eternity. Eternity is now. We are to do the things we would do if this were the last day—but not frantically or desperately.

I met with a group of men some time ago, and one commented, "I hope I don't die suddenly. I want to have time to straighten out some relationships." A second man promptly spoke up, "Well, why don't you do it anyway? If it's worth doing, do it now." The point is, if there are things you need to straighten out, do it now in a leisurely fashion. Don't wait until the doctor tells you you've got three weeks to live. One day while St. Francis was hoeing his garden, he was asked, "What would you do if you knew you only had one day to live?" "I would keep on hoeing my garden," was the reply. Our longevity ought not to determine our day-to-day agenda. We are simply to do those things which seem right, diligently and without panic.

NO FALSE PEACE

49 "I came to send fire on the earth, and how I wish it were already kindled! 50 But I have a baptism to be baptized with, and how distressed I am till it is accomplished! 51 Do you suppose that I came to give peace on earth? I tell you, not at all, but rather division. 52 For from now on five in one house will be divided: three against two, and two against three. 53 Father will be divided against son and son against father, mother against daughter and daughter against mother, mother-in-law against her daughter-in-law and daughter-in-law against her mother-in-law."

54 Then He also said to the multitudes, "Whenever you see a cloud rising out of the west, immediately you say, 'A shower is coming'; and so it is. 55 And when you see the south wind blow, you say, 'There will be hot weather'; and there is. 56 Hypocrites! You can discern the face of the sky and of the earth, but how is it you do not discern this time?"

—*Luke 12:49–56*

The fourth rule is that we are not to settle for false peace. In verse 51 Jesus says He didn't come to bring peace, meaning peace at any price or settling for the status quo in order not to make waves. If you lived in a house where sanitation was not practiced, where spoiled food was prepared in dirty pots and pans, you would demand changes. There are situations we would refuse to put up with if they endangered our health. How much more that is applicable if our very life and soul are at stake. In dramatic language, Jesus says He came to cast fire on the earth. Fire does two things: fire destroys the temporary, while it hardens or refines the durable. Too often our lives are devoted to the temporary, those things which the fire will erase. But His fire will make that which is of worth in you and me—our identity and our soul—endure forever.

RECONCILERS

57 "Yes, and why, even of yourselves, do you not judge what is right? 58 When you go with your adversary to the magistrate,

make every effort along the way to settle with him, lest he drag you to the judge, the judge deliver you to the officer, and the officer throw you into prison. [59] I tell you, you shall not depart from there till you have paid the very last mite."

—*Luke 12:57–59*

Jesus is advocating reconciliation. Be reconciled to your brother, He says. If you have a dispute with someone, don't let him bring you to court. Even lawyers these days are advising us to avoid litigation at all costs. A newly formed organization called the Christian Conciliation Society is providing an alternative to lengthy litigation in a number of states across the nation. Its members have discovered that most people never consider forgiveness an option. We Christians preach forgiveness and believe in it, but when it comes to a divorce, the division of property, or a grievance of any sort, no one seriously considers forgiveness. You may win if you go to court and press your case, but can you afford to win? The stress involved in winning your case may cost you your health, your peace of mind, and your life. It's an empty victory. Jesus' words here form the foundation for this new organization which is attempting to settle disputes between Christians without recourse to the courts.

LIFE'S INEQUITIES

13:1 There were present at that season some who told Him about the Galileans whose blood Pilate had mingled with their sacrifices. 2 And Jesus answered and said to them, "Do you suppose that these Galileans were worse sinners than all *other* Galileans, because they suffered such things? 3 I tell you, no; but unless you repent you will all likewise perish. 4 Or those eighteen on whom the tower in Siloam fell and killed them, do you think that they were worse sinners than all *other* men who dwelt in Jerusalem? 5 I tell you, no; but unless you repent you will all likewise perish."

—*Luke 13:1–5*

Life in the kingdom is not fair. Jesus puts to rest here once and for all the notion that sin causes suffering. That was an old Jewish belief—that misfortunes were the result of your wrong-doing. You remember at one point the disciples asked Jesus about the man born blind, "Rabbi, who sinned, this man or his parents, that he was born blind?" (John 9:2). Jesus' reply indicated that that was not the issue. God never sends suffering. Suffering comes as a result of living in a broken, fallen world. Life is not fair. Nobody ever said it was. If you understand that, you don't whine when hard things come and you're not smug if it's all going your way. One of my favorite Bible verses is Ecclesiastes 9:11, "The race is not to the swift, nor the battle to the strong, nor bread to the wise, nor riches to men of understanding, nor favor to men of skill; but time and chance happen to them all." We will all get our just desserts some day, but not in this life. In this life, evil may often prosper while the good may suffer. Jesus speaks to that in these verses.

I read something recently that John Travolta, the film actor, said: "The richer I get and the more famous I become, the more ordinary I realize I am, and that my only real talent is luck." What a gracious thing to say. Here he is, an admired, adored movie star, and he can't explain how it happened. Mostly, he says he was in the right place at the right time with the right gifts. Most of us are stewards of a lot of things we didn't deserve—education, health, nationality. In the world's eyes all of us are rich just by virtue of being European or American. We didn't deserve that. We can say, "Lord, thank You." Not smugly, but as stewards. On the other hand, if you are suffering in some measure far beyond those around you, God is not the author of that suffering. But He loves you and will be with you in it.

While reams have been written on the meaning of suffering, Jesus' words seem clear in these verses. He speaks of a group of Galileans who were murdered and of the eighteen people on whom a tower fell. His explanation is that they were no more sinful than anyone else. In other words, that's just the way life is.

That's why we need grace. That's why we need a Saviour. If the IRS singles you out for an audit and not your neighbor, just say, "Well, that's life." Mr. Nixon can protest that he was punished for doing what most other presidents had done. Well, that's the way life is. It doesn't all even out. But God is there with us, and He calls us to a kingdom where there is ultimate justice.

CHAPTER TWENTY-NINE—THE TEACHINGS OF JESUS
LUKE 13:6–35

Scripture Outline

The Compassionate Teacher (13:6–17)

The Central Message (13:18–30)

Inner Direction (13:31–35)

In chapter 13 we see Jesus as the unequalled teacher. Reflecting on our school years, most of us have strong feelings about our teachers, both negative and positive. I heard about a teacher who was being sentenced for going through a red light. "Teacher, I've been looking forward to this moment for a long time," said the judge. "Will you sit down over there and write five hundred times, 'I will not go through a red light again.'"

Jesus is considered by almost everybody one of the world's great teachers. We Christians believe He is much more than that. He is God incarnate, born to us in human form. But He is also the world's greatest teacher. His teachings, however, seem to give a good deal of offense. I heard it said once that if someone makes us think we're thinking, we love him. If he really makes us think we don't like him at all. Sometimes the teachers we don't like are the ones who really made us think. We can't appreciate them until much later in life.

This particular chapter in Luke gives us an opportunity to examine Jesus' teaching methods. They seem to exemplify the three marks of a great teacher. First of all, a great teacher teaches what is relevant. A great teacher communicates truths that are applicable to our lives and that can change the way we live. Genuine truth is universal, as over against esoteric facts that have application and relevance only for some groups of academicians.

The academic world is sometimes a little contemptuous of the popular and pragmatic. The great teachers know better.

In medicine right now there's a revolutionary new trend. Doctors are no longer treating diseases that happen to be in people. They are treating people who happen to have diseases. In the same way, great teachers are not teaching subjects, they are teaching students. As Jesus is teaching, He is interrupted by a woman with a problem. He stops His teaching to deal with her need. He demonstrates that people come before subject matter.

THE COMPASSIONATE TEACHER

6 He also spoke this parable: "A certain man had a fig tree planted in his vineyard, and he came seeking fruit on it and found none. 7 Then he said to the keeper of his vineyard, 'Look, for three years I have come seeking fruit on this fig tree and find none. Cut it down; why does it use up the ground?' 8 But he answered and said to him, 'Sir, let it alone this year also, until I dig around it and fertilize it. 9 And if it bears fruit, well. But if not, after that you can cut it down.'"

10 Now He was teaching in one of the synagogues on the Sabbath. 11 And behold, there was a woman who had a spirit of infirmity eighteen years, and was bent over and could in no way raise herself up. 12 But when Jesus saw her, He called her to Him and said to her, "Woman, you are loosed from your infirmity." 13 And He laid His hands on her, and immediately she was made straight, and glorified God.

14 But the ruler of the synagogue answered with indignation, because Jesus had healed on the Sabbath; and he said to the crowd, "There are six days on which men ought to work; therefore come and be healed on them, and not on the Sabbath day."

15 The Lord then answered him and said, "Hypocrite! Does not each one of you on the Sabbath loose his ox or donkey from the stall, and lead it away to water it? 16 So ought not this woman, being a daughter of Abraham, whom Satan has bound—think of it—for eighteen years, be loosed from this bond on the Sabbath?" 17 And when He said these things, all His adversaries were put to shame; and all the multitude rejoiced for all the glorious things that were done by Him.

—Luke 13:6–17

The leader of the synagogue, offended by this healing, protests. However, he does not dare directly criticize what Jesus has done. His remark is directed to the crowd. He complains that *they* ought not to come, expecting to be healed on the Sabbath. His anger at Jesus is taken out on the crowd. Jesus' rebuke deals with the real issue in question—the propriety of healing on the Sabbath. Jesus was not simply teaching about fruitful living. His exchange with the woman who had been ill eighteen years is a living parable. All great teachers understand the need to put their teaching into action.

I heard about an unmarried man who had been traveling all around the country giving a lecture on "Ten Commandments for Parents," when he fell in love and got married. After the arrival of his first baby, he changed the title of his talk to "Ten Suggestions for Parents." With the second baby his talk was called "Ten Helpful Hints for Parents." When a third child came, he stopped giving the talk altogether. Sometimes it's difficult to live out those principles we are talking about. You and I have the same problem applying what we believe and teach and preach to our daily attitudes and behavior.

THE CENTRAL MESSAGE

18 Then He said, "What is the kingdom of God like? And to what shall I compare it? 19 It is like a mustard seed, which a . man took and put in his garden; and it grew and became a large tree, and the birds of the air nested in its branches."

20 And again He said, "To what shall I liken the kingdom of God? 21 It is like leaven, which a woman took and hid in three measures of meal till it was all leavened."

22 And He went through the cities and villages, teaching, and journeying toward Jerusalem. 23 Then one said to Him, "Lord, are there few who are saved?"

And He said to them, 24 "Strive to enter through the narrow gate, for many, I say to you, will seek to enter and will not be able. 25 When once the Master of the house has risen up and shut the door, and you begin to stand outside and knock at the door, saying, 'Lord, Lord, open for us,' and He will answer and say to you, 'I do not know you, where you are from,' 26 then you will begin to say, 'We ate and drank in Your presence, and You taught in our streets.' 27 But He will say, 'I tell you I do not know you, where you are from. Depart from Me, all you workers of iniquity.' 28 There will be weeping and gnashing of teeth, when you see Abraham and Isaac and Jacob and all the prophets in the kingdom of God, and yourselves thrust out. 29 They will come from the east and the west, from the north and the south, and sit down in the kingdom of God. 30 And indeed there are last who will be first, and there are first who will be last."

—Luke 13:18–30

Every great teacher communicates one central truth. Whether he/she is teaching geography, history or mathematics, there is invariably some underlying principle or message that keeps surfacing, verbally and nonverbally. As varied as Jesus' teachings are, the central message is always there. He keeps underscoring that He came to establish a kingdom, the kingdom of God. In that kingdom, there is a new way to live in relationship with God. He compares that kingdom to any number of things. It's like a grain of mustard seed. That tiniest of seeds can become a tree, ten to twelve feet tall. The kingdom He is establishing is like leaven in a loaf of bread. Though hidden, it permeates everything. He tells us the kingdom is full of surprises. You will not know exactly who is and who is not in the kingdom until you move beyond this life into the next. We are going to be amazed to see who is in the kingdom. It won't be just the old church crowd. We'll see people we never expected to see. That's the whole thrust of verse 30: *"There are last who will be first, and there are first who will be last."*

There is much resistance in us to the whole idea of a narrow gate. We think that's too restrictive. But there is a narrow gate to anything worthwhile in life. If you want to be a great musician, you've got to go through the narrow gate of discipline, hard work, and denial. A first-rate athlete has had to pass through the narrow gate of careful diet, exercise, and countless hours of practice. There is a narrow gate to academic or business success. To enter the kingdom of God, you've got to put the things of God first. Jesus tells us to put the kingdom first and we'll be in it. Nevertheless, we're going to be amazed at some of the people who are also in it.

INNER DIRECTION

31 On that very day some Pharisees came, saying to Him, "Get out and depart from here, for Herod wants to kill You."

32 And He said to them, "Go, tell that fox, 'Behold, I cast out demons and perform cures today and tomorrow, and the third day I shall be perfected.' 33 Nevertheless I must journey today, tomorrow, and the day following; for it cannot be that a prophet should perish outside of Jerusalem.

34 "O Jerusalem, Jerusalem, the one who kills the prophets and stones those who are sent to her! How often I wanted to gather your children together, as a hen gathers her brood under her wings, but you were not willing! 35 See! Your house is left to you desolate; and assuredly, I say to you, you shall not see Me until the time comes when you say, 'Blessed is He who comes in the name of the LORD!'"

—Luke 13:31–35

Finally, the great teacher enables the student to find inner direction. A great teacher helps you find your own goal. Your goals are no longer determined by those around you. You begin to march to a different drummer. You find a whole new direction from God. So many of us are guilty of radar living. Our radar is out picking up moods. We're other-directed. We try to fit in, make it, be right with the crowd. How rare are those people in our lives who help us begin to be inner-directed.

Jesus refused to be other-directed. When He is warned that King Herod is out to get Him, He replies that that sly fox is not going to set His agenda. He is going to continue to minister for the next three days and beyond, with no change of plan. It seems to me there are two ways that those who are other-directed can be trapped. They can be trapped in trying to please others, or they can be trapped by a stubborn determination to rebel against any and all suggestions or directions. To be inner-directed means that our agenda is dictated by the inner voice, the "still, small voice" of which the Bible speaks (1 Kin. 19:12).

Robert Louis Stevenson wrote: "To know what you prefer instead of humbly saying, 'Amen' to what the world tells you you ought to prefer, is to have kept your soul alive." That's what Jesus demonstrates for us here. We have kept our soul alive when we are inner-directed through the voice of the Holy Spirit Himself.

The chapter ends with a poignant lamentation. Jesus must accept, though with sadness, the fact that there are people who will not accept the kingdom. His agony over Jerusalem and its hardness of heart is the same agony He has now for the hardness of heart of those of us in the New Jerusalem. Jesus, then and now, is in anguish over those who cannot accept the life He is offering, who have hardened their hearts to the plea of God to come into His kingdom.

CHAPTER THIRTY—EXCUSES! EXCUSES!
LUKE 14:1–35

Scripture Outline

EXCUSES AND SELF-JUSTIFICATION

14:1 Now it happened, as He went into the house of one of the rulers of the Pharisees to eat bread on the Sabbath, that they watched Him closely. 2 And behold, there was a certain man before Him who had dropsy. 3 And Jesus, answering, spoke to the lawyers and Pharisees, saying, "Is it lawful to heal on the Sabbath?"

4 But they kept silent. And He took him and healed him, and let him go. 5 Then He answered them, saying, "Which of you, having a donkey or an ox that has fallen into a pit, will not immediately pull him out on the Sabbath day?" 6 And they could not answer Him regarding these things.

7 So He told a parable to those who were invited, when He noted how they chose the best places, saying to them: 8 "When you are invited by anyone to a wedding feast, do not sit down in the best place, lest one more honorable than you be invited by him; 9 and he who invited you and him come and say to you, 'Give place to this man,' and then you begin with shame to take the lowest place. 10 But when you are invited, go and sit down in the lowest place, so that when he who invited you comes he may say to you, 'Friend, go up higher.' Then you will have glory in the presence of those who sit at the table with you. 11 For whoever exalts himself will be humbled, and he who humbles himself will be exalted."

12 Then He also said to him who invited Him, "When you give a dinner or a supper, do not ask your friends, your brothers, your relatives, nor rich neighbors, lest they also invite you back, and you be repaid. 13 But when you give a

feast, invite the poor, the maimed, the lame, the blind. [14] And you will be blessed, because they cannot repay you; for you shall be repaid at the resurrection of the just."

—Luke 14:1–14

In this chapter, Jesus seems to be changing all the usual rules of behavior. He is suggesting that the rule of life is love, not law. The lawyers and Pharisees here are concerned above all about keeping the law. Jesus reminds them that they would not hesitate to help a suffering donkey or an ox on the Sabbath. A child of God is of much greater value. According to the Jewish rules, you could help someone on the Sabbath only if his life was threatened. Obviously, someone with dropsy was not in mortal danger. But Jesus was teaching that rules are secondary to the well-being of God's children.

We all have certain religious rules we live by. One of yours may be that whenever possible you attend worship on Sunday. On the Sabbath, you try to be in your place, in your church, celebrating the grace of God, worshiping and singing praises to Him. That's a good rule to keep. But suppose in keeping that rule, you feel superior to your neighbor. You say, "He or she seldom goes to church. I always go." We are in trouble if we keep the rules to justify ourselves and to feel more righteous than others. In the Christian life, we are not striving for success in keeping the rules. We are to love our neighbors and put their interests first.

Beginning with verse 7, Jesus is reversing the usual rules governing social situations. He seems to be saying that humility is more important than being esteemed. When you go to a party, take the less prestigious seat and let your host elevate you. This is a shocking turnaround for most of us, who aspire to some kind of place of honor. He suggests we invite those people to our parties who are unable to invite us back. There is to be no thought of reciprocity. We are to do the magnanimous thing without any quid-pro-quo attitudes. The usual law of life is to use our invitations and our social clout to acquire friends and prestige. We want to put in our debt those who can enhance our social and business status.

[15] Now when one of those who sat at the table with Him heard these things, he said to Him, "Blessed is he who shall eat bread in the kingdom of God!"

[16] Then He said to him, "A certain man gave a great supper and invited many, [17] and sent his servant at supper time to

say to those who were invited, 'Come, for all things are now ready.' [18] But they all with one accord began to make excuses. The first said to him, 'I have bought a piece of ground, and I must go and see it. I ask you to have me excused.' [19] And another said, 'I have bought five yoke of oxen, and I am going to test them. I ask you to have me excused.' [20] Still another said, 'I have married a wife, and therefore I cannot come.' [21] So that servant came and reported these things to his master. Then the master of the house, being angry, said to his servant, 'Go out quickly into the streets and lanes of the city, and bring in here the poor and the maimed and the lame and the blind.' [22] And the servant said, 'Master, it is done as you commanded, and still there is room.' [23] Then the master said to the servant, 'Go out into the highways and hedges, and compel them to come in, that my house may be filled. [24] For I say to you that none of those men who were invited shall taste my supper.'"

—Luke 14:15–24

Jesus talks about the kingdom of God as a great banquet, a party. He says that the King is throwing an elaborate and festive banquet to which He invites guests. God invites us to enjoy His presence forever and ever, feasting and celebrating, but there are many who will make excuses for not responding. The Bible is the ultimate psychology book. In it God's own word illuminates the human heart.

Jesus is dealing here with something that depth psychologists did not begin to plumb until nineteen hundred years later—that life breaks down as a result of our defense mechanisms.

In analysis, you pay a great price and lie on someone's couch for many months to get rid of your defense mechanisms—those devices you use to shield yourself from truth. Defense mechanisms or excuses are all a part of self-justification, and self-justification is simply a form of self-worship. You think that you're special and that the rules don't apply to you. That's what sin is all about, whether you approach it psychoanalytically or biblically.

I think some of the most deadly words in the English language are "All I said was—", as in "All I said was, is your mother coming to visit again?" "All I said was—" can be translated to mean, "I'm innocent. My motives are pure. I made a simple statement and that touchy person got hostile." When we preface our remarks with, "All I said was—" or "All I did was—", we are saying, "There's nothing wrong with me. The problem is with all those people around me."

Those of us who have this problem (and I include myself) waste time in trying to figure who was wrong, time that could be used more creatively. Instead of saying, "Well, I made a mistake," we say, "Why, it really wasn't my fault. Somebody handed me the wrong memo at the wrong time." If we admit our errors, we can turn our mistakes and failures into fertilizer or compost in which something good will grow.

There's a story I love about one of President Franklin Roosevelt's election campaigns. His campaign manager was about to print three million copies of his acceptance speech with an accompanying photograph. At that point, it was discovered that the photographer had never given his permission for the use of this photograph. According to the copyright laws, you can be fined a dollar per copy for publishing unauthorized photographs, and that's roughly three million dollars. The campaign manager was in a panic. But instead of wasting time finding out who slipped up, he shouldered the blame and began to think creatively. He immediately cabled the photographer and said, "I have a plan that could mean great publicity for you. What's it worth to you if I use your photo on this campaign material?" The photographer cabled back, "I can't afford more than two hundred and fifty dollars." It was a deal.

In marriage, we waste a lot of time deciding who's right. I can't think of a single time over the long years of marriage when love hasn't blossomed when one of us in a tight situation was able to say, "It's my fault and I'm sorry." I love to forgive my wife. She loves to forgive me. It enhances our relationship. Most of the fighting takes place over who was wrong. We all enjoy the role of forgiver. But to say "I'm wrong" takes some degree of maturity.

This "no excuse" kind of living has physical benefits. The medical establishment tells us that one serious threat to good health is stress. There is almost nothing more stressful than having to go through life proving you are right in every situation. The energy that you and I expend trying to justify ourselves is an enormous strain on the body. If you don't have to justify yourself, you can relax. You're not afraid of failing or being caught off base.

In His story, Jesus is rebuking those people who are making excuses. Instead of simply admitting they don't want to come, they have to justify their lack of response. Most excuses are phony. The excuses Jesus describes here are no exception. In those days, when giving a banquet, it was the custom to send out the servants twice. The first time, in advance of the party, the guests were told the date. "Save Thursday, January 18." When January 18 came, the servants went out again announcing the time. In this parable, when the householders sent out the servants setting the date, all of the guests accepted. When the day actually came, they declined—all with elaborate excuses. One was tied up with a real estate investment. Another had a business deal and a third was newly married. All three were occupied with legitimate concerns, but unfortunately they gave those concerns priority over God and His kingdom.

The excuses are so obviously weak. The man who bought the field couldn't come because he was going to see it. Who checks out a real estate investment after it is purchased? Similarly, you wouldn't buy a pair of used oxen (or a used car) unless you had already examined them. Neither of those excuses had any credibility. As for the third man, there was a rule in those days that if you were newly married you were exempted from military service for one year. You were given time to be a good husband. But, marriage did not exempt you from all other responsibilities. All three excuses were very feeble.

For years I had a good excuse for not having a more regular quiet time, a time for Bible reading and prayer. In my prayers, I would say, "Lord, I'm so busy. Help me to simplify my schedule so I can put You first." One day He seemed to say, "Larson, you haven't missed a meal in years. You get enough sleep most of the time. You find time for the things that are important to you. I'm not that important to you. I can handle that. Can you handle it?" It was a moment of truth. Do you believe that God's love is big enough to handle our lack of love for Him? If not, we must make excuses. The kingdom of God is a banquet that some people have found so dull they'd rather spend their time with business matters, property deals, or family concerns. Do we dare tell God, "Serving You is dull business"? God can deal with that as long as we don't give Him some phony excuse.

It says elsewhere in the Bible, "Let your yes be yes; let your no be no." Eric Berne, one of our classic psychologists, said, "Healthy people are those who can say 'yes'—or 'no.'" When you need to qualify that, when you say "yes, but—," or "no, but—" you're less healthy psychologically.

Martin Luther once said that sin does not hurt us as much as our own righteousness. Excuses are an attempt to be righteous and innocent before God. God's gift to us in Jesus Christ on the Cross is not innocence, but responsible guilt. I can be responsibly guilty and confess my failure, and I can be forgiven. When I am responsibly guilty there is a chance to move on. To live without excuses is to accept our humanity and fallibility, which is what real humility is all about. I can confess my failure because I have the security of being loved and forgiven by the ultimate Person.

COUNTING THE COST

25 Now great multitudes went with Him. And He turned and said to them, 26 "If anyone comes to Me and does not hate his father and mother, wife and children, brothers and sisters, yes, and his own life also, he cannot be My disciple. 27 And whoever does not bear his cross and come after Me cannot be My disciple. 28 For which of you, intending to build a tower, does not sit down first and count the cost, whether he has enough to finish it— 29 lest, after he has laid the foundation, and is not able to finish, all who see it begin to mock him, 30 saying, 'This man began to build and was not able to finish.' 31 Or what king, going to make war against another king, does not sit down first and consider whether he is able with ten thousand to meet him who comes against him with twenty thousand? 32 Or else, while the other is still a great way off, he sends a delegation and asks conditions of peace. 33 So likewise, whoever of you does not forsake all that he has cannot be My disciple.

34 "Salt is good; but if the salt has lost its flavor, how shall it be seasoned? 35 It is neither fit for the land nor for the dunghill, but men throw it out. He who has ears to hear, let him hear!"

—Luke 14:25–35

The chapter ends with a warning. Jesus says we must count the cost. We must hate mother, father, sisters, brothers, spouse, and children, even our own life, for His sake. It seems a strange message. But the Aramaic word used for "hate" really means "to love a great deal less." I think Jesus means that if God and His kingdom are of all-consuming importance, then all other loves are far less by comparison. The great banquet is open to us when we no longer have to hide behind defense mechanisms or excuses. We no longer have to pretend we are good, because we know that we're not. Our message to the world is that we are loved and forgiven.

Jesus calls us salt. Salt has two peculiar properties. It flavors life and it preserves from corruption. When you and I live without excuses as those loved and forgiven, we flavor life everywhere—at the office, at home, or in the church. We become the preserving element, those who stand for justice and righteousness despite the world's corruption.

We've all heard the phrase, "Today is the first day of the rest of your life." The reverse is also true. "Today can be the last day of your past." Today can be the day when we resolve, with God's help, to live the next year making no excuses.

Life is now in session. Are you present?

CHAPTER THIRTY-ONE—LOST AND FOUND

LUKE 15:1–32

Scripture Outline

In the Far Country (15:1–10)

Coming Home (15:11–32)

Do you remember your first experience of being lost? I can remember going downtown with my mother to Marshall Fields department store as a preschooler and getting lost. A floor-walker eventually found me and brought me to a room for lost children. I thought I'd never see my mother again. But, lo and behold, she found me. I still remember the joy and relief of that reunion.

I'm sure you have similar memories. Perhaps you've been hopelessly lost as an adult. I have. On one occasion we were crossing Lake Ontario in a little single-engine houseboat. We were out of sight of land; visibility was zero because of fog; the compass didn't work; and there was no radio. Gas was low and the currents uncertain. Suddenly and miraculously, the headland appeared. We sighted the lights of the harbor and pulled in safe and sound.

We've all lived through those traumatic experiences of being lost and being found. It is in those terms that Jesus talks about the kingdom of God. It is the best explanation Jesus can give us to help us understand something of what coming into the kingdom is. We must experience being lost and being found.

It is an experience we all know in various degrees. It happened to a forty-five-year-old woman I know. She was told that she suffered a terminal illness and had a year at most to live. My friend quit her job and settled her affairs and then was mysteriously healed. Three years have passed and she is still with us. She was prepared for a premature death and received life. It's a dramatic example of being lost and found.

We can feel lost about a failed marriage and be full of guilt and remorse about a divorce. All hope of happiness is gone when someone comes along and makes a second chance possible. This second love may seem to be the person you were meant to belong to. Again, the lost is found. But, contrary to a popular song lyric, love is *not* always better the second time around. I heard about a gal whose friend appeared at her door dressed entirely in black. She said, "Millie, what happened? You are in mourning. Did your husband die?" "My husband didn't die," replied her friend, "but he's been behaving so badly lately, I'm going back into mourning for my first husband."

We can experience lostness when we are caught in some dishonesty. That's what happened to Charles Colson, who was convicted and sentenced to jail. It seemed all was lost. Yet God found him in prison and gave him a whole new direction and an exciting ministry. We can be lost in immorality. If somehow those secret sins come to light and we are forgiven and accepted, it's like being found once again. Depression and mental illness can be forms of lostness. J. C. Penney, the famous storekeeper, was seriously depressed as a young man. He tells of being confined in a mental hospital suffering such severe depression that the doctors had given up on him. One morning, on hearing a commotion down the hall, he put on his bathrobe and found his way to the chapel where some people were singing about putting your trust in the Lord. Penney was the son of a Baptist preacher. He knew all about Jesus and decided once again to trust Him. His whole life changed, and from that point until He died at ninety-five, the Lord was the center of his life. Lost and found.

IN THE FAR COUNTRY

15:1 Then all the tax collectors and the sinners drew near to Him to hear Him. 2 And the Pharisees and scribes complained, saying, "This Man receives sinners and eats with them." 3 So He spoke this parable to them, saying:

4 "What man of you, having a hundred sheep, if he loses one of them, does not leave the ninety-nine in the wilderness, and go after the one which is lost until he finds it? 5 And when he has found it, he lays it on his shoulders, rejoicing. 6 And when he comes home, he calls together his friends and neighbors, saying to them, 'Rejoice with me, for I have found my sheep which was lost!' 7 I say to you that likewise there will

be more joy in heaven over one sinner who repents than over ninety-nine just persons who need no repentance.

8 "Or what woman, having ten silver coins, if she loses one coin, does not light a lamp, sweep the house, and search carefully until she finds it? 9 And when she has found it, she calls her friends and neighbors together, saying, 'Rejoice with me, for I have found the piece which I lost!' 10 Likewise, I say to you, there is joy in the presence of the angels of God over one sinner who repents."

—Luke 15:1–10

In this chapter, Jesus describes three kinds of lostness. We can be lost like the sheep. A shepherd once explained to me how sheep get lost. They nibble their way into lostness. They move from one tuft of green grass to the next. They keep moving along from tuft to tuft, sometimes right through a hole in the fence. When they're done nibbling they can't find the hole and they're lost. Some of us know what that is—to nibble ourselves bit by bit into the far country.

Or, there is the lost coin. It is lost through carelessness. You choose the wrong friends, hang out in the wrong places, make the wrong choices. Somehow you get lost through sheer indifference or negligence.

COMING HOME

11 Then He said: "A certain man had two sons. 12 And the younger of them said to his father, 'Father, give me the portion of goods that falls to me.' So he divided to them his livelihood. 13 And not many days after, the younger son gathered all together, journeyed to a far country, and there wasted his possessions with prodigal living. 14 But when he had spent all, there arose a severe famine in that land, and he began to be in want. 15 Then he went and joined himself to a citizen of that country, and he sent him into his fields to feed swine. 16 And he would gladly have filled his stomach with the pods that the swine ate, and no one gave him anything.

17 "But when he came to himself, he said, 'How many of my father's hired servants have bread enough and to spare, and I perish with hunger! 18 I will arise and go to my father, and will say to him, "Father, I have sinned against heaven and before you, 19 and I am no longer worthy to be called your son. Make me like one of your hired servants."

20 "And he arose and came to his father. But when he was still a great way off, his father saw him and had compassion, and ran and fell on his neck and kissed him. 21 And the son said to him, 'Father, I have sinned against heaven and in your sight, and am no longer worthy to be called your son.'

22 "But the father said to his servants, 'Bring out the best robe and put it on him, and put a ring on his hand and sandals on his feet. 23 And bring the fatted calf here and kill it, and let us eat and be merry; 24 for this my son was dead and is alive again; he was lost and is found.' And they began to be merry.

25 "Now his older son was in the field. And as he came and drew near to the house, he heard music and dancing. 26 So he called one of the servants and asked what these things meant. 27 And he said to him, 'Your brother has come, and because he has received him safe and sound, your father has killed the fatted calf.'

28 "But he was angry and would not go in. Therefore his father came out and pleaded with him. 29 So he answered and said to his father, 'Lo, these many years I have been serving you; I never transgressed your commandment at any time; and yet you never gave me a young goat, that I might make merry with my friends. 30 But as soon as this son of yours came, who has devoured your livelihood with harlots, you killed the fatted calf for him.'

31 "And he said to him, 'Son, you are always with me, and all that I have is yours. 32 It was right that we should make merry and be glad, for your brother was dead and is alive again, and was lost and is found.'"

—Luke 15:11–32

The third kind of lostness Jesus describes is a chosen state. You know exactly what you are doing. You thumb your nose at God and parents and society. Like the prodigal, you go to a far country because you choose to.

How is this lost young man found? The Scripture suggests it is not the result of some great spiritual revelation. Being found does not require getting your act cleaned up and changing your life style. Remember, God cleans the fish *after* He catches them. The turning point comes when this willfully lost young man "comes to himself," which simply suggests that he makes a wise choice. He says, "This is stupid. I don't need to live like this. I have a home and a father. Maybe he will take me back as a servant." No mystic experience.

There are two truths in the story that are very reassuring. The first is that somehow you and I have a home in God. When we're lost, it's because we have strayed from the place we were meant to be. Each of us has in us a God-shaped blank, and nothing else will fill that blank—not marriage, children, job, or success. The story of Adam and Eve in Genesis 3 is our story. When we left the garden, we left the presence of God and we have been homesick ever since. We were made for life at home with God.

But the second exciting lesson here is that Jesus is aggressively looking for us. You find the symbol of the shepherd in many other world religions, but only in the Gospels is the shepherd pictured as one who is actively looking for the lost sheep. It's an extraordinary and powerful image.

In His ministry Jesus sought the lost in all sorts of unlikely places. He offended the religious leaders by eating with the lost—those who were not righteous, not clean, not good. Jesus is the Great Physician, and a physician does not set a broken arm from across the street; he goes where the patient is. Jesus seeks us out in our lostness. Being found is simply coming home, finding our roots once again, or for the first time.

I had some clothes altered recently, in the course of which I met a Jewish-American tailor. He told me about making a trip to Israel several years ago. He said, "It's a strange thing, pastor; I've never been there before. I'm not a religious man. I don't go to the synagogue. But when I got off that plane in Israel, I said to my wife, 'We have come home. We were meant to live in this place.' Ever since then, I've been making plans to sell out and go there. I know I won't live as well. I can't make as much money and have as many comforts. But somehow, that's home."

We must have some sense of our true home in order to be aware of being lost. If you know you are lost, have been lost, and will be lost in the future, it's a gift. That awareness is a prerequisite for coming home. I love the story of the little boy who used to play in the park every day under a statue of General Grant on horseback. In time, his family decided to move from the city, and he went out to say good-by to all his playmates in the park. In a last gesture of farewell, he stood under the statue he loved and said very tearfully, "Good-by, General Grant and whoever that is on your back. I will miss you." He was already homesick. Your homesickness, your longing to be where God is, is God's good gift to you.

In our Scripture there are four lost items—a sheep, a coin, a prodigal son, and his elder brother. The first three are obviously lost. The fourth is lost and doesn't know it. He is the tragic one. He does not have any awareness of lostness. He never strayed or broke the rules, and yet he missed out on the gift of the father's extravagant love.

Shakespeare said that the wise man knows himself to be a fool. The fool thinks he is a wise man. Let me rephrase that and say, "The wise person knows when he is lost, understands the source of his homesickness, and returns to a father who loves him."

P. T. Forsyth, the great English preacher, said, "The only way to the Father is through the far country." Must the far country be moral dissolution? It may be that. But the far country is the place where you become disillusioned with who you are. You are in the far country at the point where you are disappointed with the world and say, "Is this all there is?" And the Father says, "Of course not. Come home."

CHAPTER THIRTY-TWO—HOW TO MAKE YOUR MONEY WORK FOR YOU

LUKE 16:1–31

Scripture Outline

Lasting Purchases (16:1–18)

Planning for the Future (16:19–31)

A friend in Montana told me about a sheepherder who discovered oil on his land and became enormously rich. One of the first things he bought was a Rolls Royce limousine, the kind usually driven by a chauffeur who sits in front of a glass partition. When the sheepherder brought this splendid car in for service, the mechanic was properly impressed. "What a marvelous machine," he said. "What do you like best about it?" "Well," said the sheepherder, "I can take my sheep to market now without having them lick my neck."

The sheepherder was thoroughly enjoying his money, and, however much or little we have, that's important. You may have all your money invested in just staying alive, or you may have more than you need. I can't give any investment advice, and I don't plan to explore Christian theories of economics. That's a complicated and controversial subject. Rather, I'd like to discuss how we can enjoy our money—money we have now or may have in the future.

In the past year my wife and I went with some parishioners to visit our missionaries to the Masai in Kenya, Jeanne and Denny Grindall. In a few short years these two lay people from Seattle have changed the way these primitive stone-age people live. In addition to the gospel, the Grindalls have brought water to arid valleys and taught these nomads to settle down and grow vegetables. Traditionally, the Masai have lived in huts of dung and twigs, with no light or ventilation. Because the animals live in and around the huts, it's not unusual to see babies almost entirely covered with flies. Each hut has an open fire of coals on the floor, and infants are constantly falling into this pit and being horribly burned.

The model village the Grindalls have constructed is a stark contrast. Each family has a clean, concrete hut—ventilated, bug- and rodent-free, and with a raised fire pit. But each such house is worth the price of a good steer, and the Masai measure their wealth by the size of their herd. Most remain unconvinced that they should part with a single steer to improve the way their families live. We would say those are strange values, but each of us has our own set of values, and some of them would seem strange indeed to someone else.

LASTING PURCHASES

16:1 He also said to His disciples: "There was a certain rich man who had a steward, and an accusation was brought to him that this man was wasting his goods. 2 So he called him and said to him, 'What is this I hear about you? Give an account of your stewardship, for you can no longer be steward.'

3 "Then the steward said within himself, 'What shall I do? For my master is taking the stewardship away from me. I cannot dig; I am ashamed to beg. 4 I have resolved what to do, that when I am put out of the stewardship, they may receive me into their houses.'

5 "So he called every one of his master's debtors to him, and said to the first, 'How much do you owe my master?' 6 And he said, 'A hundred measures of oil.' So he said to him, 'Take your bill, and sit down quickly and write fifty.' 7 Then he said to another, 'And how much do you owe?' So he said, 'A hundred measures of wheat.' And he said to him, 'Take your bill, and write eighty.' 8 So the master commended the unjust steward because he had dealt shrewdly. For the sons of this world are more shrewd in their generation than the sons of light.

9 "And I say to you, make friends for yourselves by unrighteous mammon, that when you fail, they may receive you into an everlasting home. 10 He who is faithful in what is least is faithful also in much; and he who is unjust in what is least is unjust also in much. 11 Therefore if you have not been

faithful in the unrighteous mammon, who will commit to your trust the true riches? 12 And if you have not been faithful in what is another man's, who will give you what is your own?

13 "No servant can serve two masters; for either he will hate the one and love the other, or else he will be loyal to the one and despise the other. You cannot serve God and mammon."

14 Now the Pharisees, who were lovers of money, also heard all these things, and they derided Him. 15 And He said to them, "You are those who justify yourselves before men, but God knows your hearts. For what is highly esteemed among men is an abomination in the sight of God.

16 "The law and the prophets were until John. Since that time the kingdom of God has been preached, and everyone is pressing into it. 17 And it is easier for heaven and earth to pass away than for one tittle of the law to fail.

18 "Whoever divorces his wife and marries another commits adultery; and whoever marries her who is divorced from her husband commits adultery.

—Luke 16:1–18

Jesus tells here two parables about money. The first one deals with the purpose of money. Some have said that this story of the unrighteous steward is the most difficult of all the parables. Incompetence and dishonesty seem to be rewarded. That's not the message of this parable. In verse 9, Jesus talks about *"unrighteous mammon."* Unrighteous mammon was interest money, profit from usury. The Jews were forbidden to lend money at interest, but they got around this by lending out commodities, oil, corn, or wheat, and charging interest. Since you could dilute the oil, the interest on that was 100 percent. On wheat, interest was perhaps 20 percent. This man, through his steward, was charging his neighbors interest, and this illegal interest was the unrighteous mammon to which Jesus refers.

When the steward finds that he is going to be fired, he tells all those who owe his master money to forget about the interest. They can return just exactly what they borrowed and no more. He bought friends and favor for the future when he would be unemployed. Not dumb! He was not punished for this because by doing it he bought favor for the master as well. The steward's dishonesty made his master look pious. It's an interesting story. George Buttrick has said, "This rogue acted with foresight." He bought friends with money. Jesus is suggesting we act with the same kind of foresight and use our money for that which is lasting.

We cannot put our security in money. Bank accounts, bonds, stocks, real estate, or gold have fluctuating worth. Those who lived through the crash of 1929 are well aware of that. In Germany after World War I, people traded wheelbarrows full of money for a loaf of bread. In our own time, the bond market has bottomed out and gold has dropped to one-half of what it was worth just a few short years ago. Oil may become a glut on the market. There is a story about a starving man who said, upon greedily tearing open a box, "Oh, it's only gold." In our time there are the survivalists who are trading their money for a camp in the woods with guns and food. If they are right, God forbid, our money will be useless. The future is uncertain and we dare not put our hope in things.

Money is meant to be a source of blessing. It is to be used to bless you, your neighbors, and the world. Having grown up with a minimum of this world's goods, I sometimes let things become too important to me. When we bought our first house, I think I was inclined to behave as if the family existed to maintain the house—to keep it clean and in good condition. Fortunately, my family never bought that idea. They helped me to see that the house is supposed to serve the needs of the family. It's a good lesson. Things are to serve people; not people, things.

My stepfather left a great impression on my life. In the years that I knew him he never attended any church. He was not wealthy, but comfortable. He donated a lot of his money to Christian work and individual seminary students. From time to time I would learn about some incident of my stepfather's secret generosity and remark on it. His answer always went something like this, "Bruce, I am the most selfish person in the world. I'm so selfish I want to see the smile on people's faces while I'm living. I can't enjoy it when I'm dead."

We have such hangups about our money, who earns it, who spends it. Did you know that Socrates was trained to be a stonecutter and yet he never spent a day in his life cutting stone? His wife worked to support him and their three children, while he gave free lessons to students. He was not hung up on having to make a living, and I trust that it was a happy arrangement for the rest of the family as well. A steady and adequate income is a great plus in life, but it is not the prime thing. Someone has said, "Money is foreign currency to the person whose citizenship is in heaven." The real question is: do you own your money, or does it own you?

PLANNING FOR THE FUTURE

[19] "There was a certain rich man who was clothed in purple and fine linen and fared sumptuously every day. [20] But there was a certain beggar named Lazarus, full of sores, who was laid at his gate, [21] desiring to be fed with the crumbs which fell from the rich man's table. Moreover the dogs came and licked his sores. [22] So it was that the beggar died, and was carried by the angels to Abraham's bosom. The rich man also died and was buried. [23] And being in torments in Hades, he lifted up his eyes and saw Abraham afar off, and Lazarus in his bosom.

[24] "Then he cried and said, 'Father Abraham, have mercy on me, and send Lazarus that he may dip the tip of his finger in water and cool my tongue; for I am tormented in this flame.' [25] But Abraham said, 'Son, remember that in your lifetime you received your good things, and likewise Lazarus evil things; but now he is comforted and you are tormented. [26] And besides all this, between us and you there is a great gulf fixed, so that those who want to pass from here to you cannot, nor can those from there pass to us.'

[27] "Then he said, 'I beg you therefore, father, that you would send him to my father's house, [28] for I have five brothers, that he may testify to them, lest they also come to this place of torment.' [29] Abraham said to him, 'They have Moses and the prophets; let them hear them.' [30] And he said, 'No, father Abraham; but if one goes to them from the dead, they will repent.' [31] But he said to him, 'If they do not hear Moses and the prophets, neither will they be persuaded though one rise from the dead.'"

—Luke 16:19–31

The second parable raises the whole question of stewardship versus entitlement. We are in a time right now where we all think we are entitled. We believe what we have is really ours. Charles W. Bray Ill, Deputy Director of the U.S. Internal Communication Agency, wrote something brilliant about all this in *Quote* magazine (Jan. 15, 1981). "We have come to a time where we say, 'You deserve a break today.' Too many of us believe that. If we're poor, we deserve welfare; if we're rich, we deserve a tax break; if we are workers, we deserve better fringe benefits; if we own Chrysler, we deserve a bail-out; if we are a special interest, we deserve a special hearing."

The Pharisees thought they were entitled. They had the strange idea that money was deserved. Money was a sign that they were blessed by God, and poverty was the result of God's curse. Jesus repudiates that whole idea. All of us are stewards of what we have, and we are to use it to bless others, to bring life, to bring health and hope and joy.

In the parable of the rich man and Lazarus, bear in mind that Jesus is not condemning all the rich while suggesting that the poor will all go to heaven. Each parable teaches only one point. Jesus doesn't question how the rich man got his money or that he has it. The rich man isn't even necessarily a bad man. The rich man may have been a deeply caring person dismayed by unemployment and inflation figures, or he may have been a generous donor to charitable causes. But whatever else he was, in this story he is blind to the person in need who is sitting outside his gate. He is damned for his casual indifference to the person right at his door.

His is not an isolated case. It's easy to have great compassion for the human race while we ignore somebody next door, down the street, or in the office. I learned this in my first parish. We were living in a tiny apartment over the parish house of a church in Binghamton, New York. In addition to parish duties, I was involved in fund raising for a gospel mission to help the destitute and alcoholic. One snowy day, a stranger appeared at the parish house door wanting help. He turned out to be the son of parishioners and a prodigal many times over. His parents had already killed about twenty fatted calves for him and had finally given up. I had a busy day ahead of me and I was feeling put-upon and not especially charitable. I remember complaining to the Lord, "I can't take in every drunken beggar in Binghamton." In response, a voice seemed to say very clearly, "I didn't ask you to take in every drunk—just this one." And, of course, I did.

The verses here suggest that if you have the resources to help and choose not to, you are judged. And the poor are judged as well. The poor are to be stewards of what they have as much as the rich or middle class. The secret is to understand that what you have is not yours; it is loaned to you for a time. Nobody really owns anything. There's an old saying, "There are no pockets in a shroud." You take nothing with you. I heard of one man who said, "If I can't take it with me I'm not going!" Well, he is going. The steward was dismissed by his master. We need to bear in mind that one day all of us will be dismissed. That's what death is. Are you planning for that time? You are if you are a steward of your things, large or few, and are using them to bless those around you and across the world.

Incidentally, Albert Schweitzer was persuaded by this parable. He believed Africa was the poor beggar at the gate of Europe. He left the academic world of Europe where he had earned five Ph.D. degrees and went to care for his poor brothers and sisters "at the gate" in Lambarene.

This parable points to the fact that arrogance often accompanies wealth. The rich man, sometimes called Dives, is as arrogant in the afterlife as he had been in this life. Seeing the poor man in heaven *("Abraham's bosom,"* v. 22) while he himself is in need and dying of thirst, he cries out, *"Father Abraham, . . . send Lazarus that he may dip the tip of his finger in water and cool my tongue"* (v. 24). He still assumes he can summon service. Perhaps that's part of his sin. The poor man does not complain about his state in this world, and he does not gloat when he has it made in heaven. He simply accepts whatever comes as from God's hand. In the case of the rich man, his arrogance persists after the grave.

The rich man, however, does express some concern for his brothers. He asks Father Abraham to send someone back to warn them that their choices in this life have consequences in the next. Jesus says that there is no hope for the brothers. Anyone familiar with the Old Testament has missed the message if he is not prompted to care for a beggar at the gate. It really seems that the rich man's concern about his brothers is a form of self-justification. We assume he is saying, "If I had had more light, I would have acted differently." Jesus makes it clear he had enough light and yet missed the obvious truth.

Finally, Jesus is talking about a strange paradox. Ultimately unselfishness is true selfishness. The saints that we honor, historically and in the present, are those who are able to share their resources with no sense of sacrifice. St. Francis left millions to become a wandering monk for Jesus. Does anyone feel sorry for St. Francis? Mother Teresa could have lived in a nice, comfortable apartment in Yugoslavia, playing checkers with her grandchildren. We wouldn't dream of feeling sorry for her—stuck in Calcutta. The great missionary David Livingstone walked all over the continent of Africa, sharing the good news of Jesus Christ. He walked through a thousand villages in the years he was there caring for people and loving them. Years later a missionary was talking to a native tribe about Jesus when an old woman interrupted him. "Oh, wait a minute. That man was here. He visited our village some years ago." To her, David Livingstone was Jesus. Certainly he is an extraordinary example of someone who understood that resources are to be given away. He invested his in treasures that "neither moth nor rust destroys" (Matt. 6:20).

CHAPTER THIRTY-THREE—THREE LEVELS OF LIFE: FORGIVENESS, GRATITUDE, PRAISE

LUKE 17:1–19

Scripture Outline

The Survival Level (17:1–10)

Wholeness and Power (17:11–19)

A psychiatrist received a postcard from one of his vacationing patients. It read, "Having a wonderful time. Why?" A lot of us feel guilty if we're having a good time. But what kind of time do you think God wants us to have—today, this week, next week? Is life a vale of tears? Are we worms put here to struggle and toil endlessly? I think our theological, ecclesiastical ancestors who wrote the Westminster Confession of Faith had real insight into God's will for us. The first catechism question is, "What is the chief end of man?" The answer is, "To glorify God and enjoy Him forever." That is exactly the kind of time we're supposed to have, glorifying God and enjoying Him.

It seems to me that Jesus is giving us here a prescription for doing that on three separate levels. We are to begin on the level of *forgiveness.*

THE SURVIVAL LEVEL

17:1 Then He said to the disciples, "It is impossible that no offenses should come, but woe to him through whom they do come! 2 It would be better for him if a millstone were hung around his neck, and he were thrown into the sea, than that he should offend one of these little ones. 3 Take heed to yourselves. If your brother sins against you, rebuke him; and if he repents, forgive him. 4 And if he sins against you seven times in a day, and seven times in a day returns to you, saying, 'I repent,' you shall forgive him."

—Luke 17:1–4

Jesus says offenses and temptation to sin will come to us, and they will. Unless you lock your doors and don't answer the telephone, you will have plenty of cause for offense. Life is like that. If you are the offender, you would be better off with a millstone hanging around your neck. We are to rebuke the person who sins. Sin is never a private thing. Any time you and I transgress against ourselves or our neighbors, we are committing a public offense. All sin is public and hurts the entire human race and the body of Christ.

We read that if somebody comes to you seven times asking for forgiveness you are to give it. We all know people like that who seem to have the knack of offending us seven times in the same day. We are to forgive them seven times, if they say they are sorry.

5 And the apostles said to the Lord, "Increase our faith."
6 So the Lord said, "If you have faith as a mustard seed, you can say to this mulberry tree, 'Be pulled up by the roots and be planted in the sea,' and it would obey you. 7 And which of you, having a servant plowing or tending sheep, will say to him when he has come in from the field, 'Come at once and sit down to eat'? 8 But will he not rather say to him, 'Prepare something for my supper, and gird yourself and serve me till I have eaten and drunk, and afterward you will eat and drink'? 9 Does he thank that servant because he did the things that were commanded him? I think not. 10 So likewise you, when you have done all those things which you are commanded, say, 'We are unprofitable servants. We have done what was our duty to do.'"

—Luke 17:5–10

When the disciples heard what Jesus said about forgiveness, they asked Him to increase their faith because it sounded so impossible. He corrected them and said that if they had a faith as large as a grain of mustard seed they could move a sycamine tree. A sycamine tree is a kind of mulberry, with a root system so intricate that it would take six hundred years to untangle it, according to the rabbis.

In verses 7–10 Jesus reminds the disciples that they are servants, and as such they have certain duties. In those days a master owned his servants. There are times when it is essential to pull rank. You are out in a boat for the first time with young children and you say, "Wear your life jacket." They may protest, but the parent doesn't mind being dictatorial if the child's life is at stake. "Listen," you say, "I'm your mother [father]. Wear your life jacket." Jesus is giving this kind of a command in the matter of forgiveness.

Your capacity to forgive the same person seven times every day is the key to your spiritual survival. But if you don't forgive, you are also going to suffer physically. You may even die prematurely. Medical people tell us that there is concrete evidence that grudges and resentments cause much of our illness: cancers, cardiovascular diseases, arthritis, migraines. Our health is directly related to our ability to forgive. The sincerity of the person asking forgiveness has nothing to do with our response. Jesus says to forgive for our own sake.

The great Swiss psychiatrist, Carl Jung, spoke about our need to forgive our worst enemy—ourselves. "What if I should discover that the most impudent of all the offenders, the very enemy itself—these are within me . . . that I am the enemy who must be loved? What then?" Someone has said that when we learn to love ourselves, humanity has lost another problem and the world has discovered a new friend. So, forgive everybody, including your worst enemy, who may be within.

We must then, first of all, live on the level of forgiveness for basic survival. Next, we need to live on the level of *gratitude.*

WHOLENESS AND POWER

11 Now it happened as He went to Jerusalem that He passed through the midst of Samaria and Galilee. 12 Then as He entered a certain village, there met Him ten men who were lepers, who stood afar off. 13 And they lifted up their voices and said, "Jesus, Master, have mercy on us!"

14 So when He saw them, He said to them, "Go, show yourselves to the priests." And so it was that as they went, they were cleansed.

15 And one of them, when he saw that he was healed, returned, and with a loud voice glorified God, 16 and fell down on his face at His feet, giving Him thanks. And he was a Samaritan.

17 So Jesus answered and said, "Were there not ten cleansed? But where are the nine? 18 Were there not any found who returned to give glory to God except this foreigner?" 19 And He said to him, "Arise, go your way. Your faith has made you well."

—Luke 17:11–19

In the healing of the ten lepers, Jesus does not reach out and touch them. He doesn't say, "Be healed." He tells them to show themselves to the priest. He was telling them to *act as if* they were healed, and they were healed. In faith they started out, and they were healed on the way.

The ten who acted in faith were healed, but just one came back and praised God and was grateful. Jesus asks him, *"Where are the nine?"* (v. 17). We could assume that He felt hurt because nobody thanked Him. But I think He was disappointed for another reason. He tells the leper who came back, *"Your faith has made you well"* (v. 19). Ten were healed, but only one was made well, and that's far more important than being healed. The point made here, I think, is that unless gratitude is a part of our nature, we can't be whole people. The other nine were merely healed. If ingratitude is more deadly than leprosy, they were in worse shape than before. Only one came back and was made whole.

You may have heard the story of the man who was betrayed by a friend. He went to him and asked, "How could you do this to me? Who picked you up out of the gutter? Who gave you your first job? Who lent you money and bailed you out of jail?" The reply was, "You did, that's true. But what have you done for me lately?"

On the other hand, there are those people who go through life with a great sense of wonder and gratitude for every circumstance. I love the story of the immigrant shopkeeper whose son came to see him one day complaining, "Dad, I don't understand how you run this store. You keep your accounts payable in a cigar box. Your accounts receivable are on a spindle. All your cash is in the register. You never know what your profits are." "Son, let me tell you something," answered his dad. "When I arrived in this land all I owned was the pants I was wearing. Now your sister is an art teacher. Your brother is a doctor. You are a CPA. Your mother and I own a house and a car and this little store. Add that all up and subtract the pants and there is your profit." A well person has a sense of gratitude for any and all good fortune.

The psychiatry Freud introduced is a mixed blessing, but the whole purpose of psychoanalysis is very sound. You spend all those long years on a couch so that you can come to the place where you forgive all those from your past who have hurt you, especially your parents. The sum and substance of successful analysis is that you forgive those who have wounded you. You can avoid years of analysis by following Jesus' teaching here. Whether your parents deserted you, abused you, drank too much, tried to possess and control you—whatever their sin, forgive them. Whether they loved you wisely or unwisely, it doesn't matter. Whatever they were, forgive them and bless them for your own sake. That's the point of what Jesus is saying to us here.

The one commandment given with a promise is, "Honor your parents—so that your days may be long in the land which the Lord your God gives you." If you can't forgive and bless your parents, your days are going to be shortened. You forgive them simply for selfish reasons. Think of all you have learned from your parents, good or bad. They have taught you a great deal about life and you are wiser and better able to cope.

I'd say the same thing to you about all the people in your life who have hurt you, your spouse, your boss, your friend. Bless them and be grateful for all you have learned from them. If they could have acted more lovingly, they would have. Bless them and let the resentments go. That's living on the level of gratitude.

The third level is one that's new to me. It is the level of *praise*. This leper came back praising God and yet he still had enormous problems. His leprosy was healed, but he had been living as an outcast with no family and no job. He had no home and no village. Yet he is praising God even in the midst of his unsolved problems. There is much evidence about why and how we are to praise God in our problems. Ephesians 5:20 says, "Giving thanks for all things to God the Father in the name of our Lord Jesus Christ." In 1 Thessalonians 5:16–18 we read, "Rejoice always, pray without ceasing, in everything give thanks; for this is the will of God in Christ Jesus for you." Romans 8:28 tells us, "And we know that all things work together for good to those who love God, to those who are the called according to His purpose."

Each of us has a problem right now. Nobody still living is problem-free. Let's think about how we can praise God in that present problem. First of all, we do not say with the Christian Scientists that there is no problem, no pain, no illness, and no sin. We Christians believe sin abounds. We hurt people. We are hurt.

There is pain and illness. Second, we can't pretend it's fun to have a painful problem. That's masochism. If you enjoy your problem, you're weird. Third, remember that God is not the source of your problem. He doesn't send illness and pain.

Focus, rather, on the belief that God is bigger than the problem and is present right now in the middle of this painful thing you're caught up in. Say, "God, I praise you. You are bigger than the mess I am in." This way of living is new for me, but it is an old spiritual discipline. William Law, eighteenth-century English theologian and clergyman, said, "If anyone can tell you the shortest, surest way to all happiness and perfection, he must tell you to make it a rule to yourself to thank and praise God for everything that happens to you, for it is certain that whatever seeming calamity happens to you, if you thank and praise God for it, you turn it into a blessing." Helen Keller, blind and deaf saint, wrote, "I thank God for my handicaps. Through them I have found myself, my work and my God." John Wesley, the evangelist and founder of the Methodist Church, wrote, "Thanksgiving is inseparable from true prayer. It is almost essentially connected with it. He that always prays is ever giving praise, whether in ease or pain, both for prosperity and for the greatest adversity." Paul writes, "For I have learned in whatever state I am, to be content" (Phil. 4:11).

Our son Peter's favorite story is about a balloonist of a hundred years ago who was going to take a trip over the Alps. He had the whole itinerary planned carefully, but each day when he'd start off in his hot air balloon for Town A, the wind blew him to Town B. The next day it was C instead of D and then E instead of F. Invariably, each time he landed, he said, "I didn't know about this place. Had I known, I would have planned to land here." Instead of being disappointed, each day was a delightful surprise. If you plan on going from A to B and you end up in C, rejoice anyway and then ask God what He has for you there.

In whatever state you are, you can learn to praise God. The point is nobody has it all. If you are single, you have certain privileges. You may doubt that, but it's true. You are in control of your life. You eat and sleep on your timetable. You're free to travel where you like. Being married is a great blessing, but there are problems. The point is, you can choose to focus on the negative or the positive of every situation. You can say, "Whatever circumstances I am in right now—married, single, married to the wrong person, whatever—I praise You, Lord, because You are bigger than the mess I'm in right now."

God wants us to live on all three of these levels. The first level of forgiveness is simply for survival. The second is the level of gratitude for wholeness beyond health. But it's at the level of praise where I suspect God's power can break through in the most dramatic ways.

Chapter Thirty-Four—The Kingdom: Where and When?

Luke 17:20–37

20 Now when He was asked by the Pharisees when the kingdom of God would come, He answered them and said, "The kingdom of God does not come with observation; 21 nor will they say, 'See here!' or 'See there!' For indeed, the kingdom of God is within you."

22 Then He said to the disciples, "The days will come when you will desire to see one of the days of the Son of Man, and you will not see it. 23 And they will say to you, 'Look here!' or 'Look there!' Do not go after them or follow them. 24 For as the lightning that flashes out of one part under heaven shines to the other part under heaven, so also the Son of Man will be in His day. 25 But first He must suffer many things and be rejected by this generation. 26 And as it was in the days of Noah, so it will be also in the days of the Son of Man: 27 They ate, they drank, they married wives, they were given in marriage, until the day that Noah entered the ark, and the flood came and destroyed them all. 28 Likewise as it was also in the days of Lot: They ate, they drank, they bought, they sold, they planted, they built; 29 but on the day that Lot went out of Sodom it rained fire and brimstone from heaven and destroyed them all. 30 Even so will it be in the day when the Son of Man is revealed.

31 "In that day, he who is on the housetop, and his goods are in the house, let him not come down to take them away. And likewise the one who is in the field, let him not turn back. 32 Remember Lot's wife. 33 Whoever seeks to save his life will lose it, and whoever loses his life will preserve it. 34 I tell you, in that night there will be two men in one bed: the one will be taken and the other will be left. 35 Two women will be grinding together: the one will be taken and the other left. 36 Two men will be in the field: the one will be taken and the other left."

37 And they answered and said to Him, "Where, Lord?"

So He said to them, "Wherever the body is, there the eagles will be gathered together."

—*Luke 17:20–37*

Eschatology, which is the science of last things, was a difficult and fascinating subject in New Testament times and it still is. The popularity of Hal Lindsey's *The Late Great Planet Earth* is indicative of our continued interest in these matters. Ultimately, you and I have to come up with our own theory of eschatology—the last days. We are in trouble if we define our life only in terms of the last days, but, on the other hand, there will be a final curtain, and we cannot ignore that.

A few years ago an interesting book entitled *The Boys of Summer* was written by Roger Kahn about the old Brooklyn Dodgers baseball team. The author tracked down many of the greats of that team to see what they were doing twenty years later. Some were living full and rewarding lives, while others were like figures in some Greek tragedy, wailing over what life had done to them. One story is about Clem Levine, the great relief pitcher. The book tells us he lived for the team. He was their heart, soul, and inspiration. He was the first to arrive at every game and the last to leave. He took no time for his family, particularly his young son. Now that he is retired, he says, "My son has no time for me." He is a disillusioned and unhappy man.

Another member of the team was Carl Erskine, the pitcher. Baseball did not dominate his life in the same way. He had a retarded son who needed him, and so his time was geared for that second responsibiity. Now, long past those great years of baseball, Carl is a fulfilled person. It's a pointed lesson. Even in the middle of great days, we still need to have an eye on the future and build accordingly.

When we consider the kingdom—where or when?—we need to differentiate the kingdom from the last days. The kingdom is here now, and it will be here forever. It's a very present event. Jesus was asked then, as we ask now, when the kingdom of God would come. He said, *"The kingdom of God does not come with observation; . . . the kingdom of God is within you"* (vv. 20, 21). The kingdom is not a place you can go to. Either you live in it or you don't. Romans 14:17 says, "For the kingdom of God is not food and drink, but righteousness and peace and joy in the Holy Spirit."

One of the great luminary theologians of the twentieth century was Emil Brunner. His book *The Misunderstanding of the Church* is a particular favorite of mine. In it, he says those Christians in the Reformed tradition believe that there are two churches. The first is the church visible, made up of all the members on all the rolls of all churches. Then there's the church invisible, which is comprised of all true believers. We have concrete records and counts on the church visible. Brunner says the church invisible is just as visible. Those in that spiritual Mafia, the Christian underground, know the others in it. The church invisible is the kingdom of God, and it is real and tangible.

The kingdom of God is a colony in the midst of a secular world, where we can demonstrate an alternative lifestyle. I don't believe we are called to establish a theocracy, whereby the few who claim to know God's will get to legislate morality for the rest of society. Nations have tried that. Our job is to live out the fact that we belong to a King, to each other, and to the world. Our lives provide a choice for others. They can live as the world lives, or as this minority culture lives. Those in the kingdom are a minority group. We are not seeking to impose our will on the world but to love the world and to serve it.

In this context then, what about the last days? Jesus calls them *"the days of the Son of Man"* (v. 22). What does that mean? The king tells us that some day He is coming in visible power. We needn't wonder about that. We will all see it. When the last curtain is closed and the kingdom comes, it will be something like lightning across the summer sky at night. Someone told me a while back that "when Mrs. Hutton speaks, E. F. listens." Similarly, we'll all be listening and watching when the king decides to come in power. You needn't wonder if it has already occurred in some dark corner and you've missed it.

Jesus tells us in these verses that we are not to trust anyone who says, "I know *when* the kingdom is coming. I know *when* the last days will be." Many years ago Billy Graham, a dedicated man of God, was predicting we had only ten years left. He was wrong. He doesn't make those predictions any more. The apostle Paul made the same mistake. In spite of Jesus' warning, he was sure the end was coming soon. Some twenty and thirty years later, the disciples changed their strategy. Two thousand years later, we are still uncertain about the timing of that last curtain, and Jesus tells us not to believe those who say they know.

And yet there are those who persist in saying they know and who would give us a timetable. There are some obvious reasons for this. Some of these self-styled prophets are simply self-centered. They think they are the center of the universe and God's purpose is to serve and bless them. As these one-dimensional people get older and haven't long to live, they become convinced the end is near. "If I'm gone, what's the purpose of keeping the world around? The last days must be coming." There's a lot of last-days theology in retirement homes. (Jesus must be coming any day now if I'm going out.)

Another group of people who have great certainty about the last days are the depressed. I talked to one woman whose life has been very sorrowful recently. She was convinced the Second Coming is near. I said, "That's because you have no hope for the present. How can life go on when you are so desolate?" Then there are the irresponsible people. They don't worry about conservation or world hunger because the Lord is going to come any day now. They don't believe in missions or sacrificial giving because the end is at hand and none of that will matter. The Lord gives us a clear warning here that we are not to heed those who want to escape responsibility by claiming they know God's timetable.

We might wonder just what difference this day of the Son of Man will make. Jesus says that of two people in the same bed, or grinding at the same mill, or working in the same field, one will go and one will stay. But that rift is already here. Right now, as we said, you are in the kingdom or out, and in one sense the last days won't change anything. Our identity and allegiance will simply be revealed at that time. Perhaps that's why the Bible cautions against marriage between a believer and an unbeliever. If you become one body, mind, and soul with someone who is not in the kingdom, you will be separated on that Judgment Day. Actually, you live in two different worlds already. It seems a hard word, but it is not. If you love someone and become part of that person's life, how can you bear that ultimate separation if he or she never becomes part of the kingdom? So, we are constrained to live all of our days with one eye on that final curtain.

We all have our personal eschatology. If you are practicing some secret sin, having an affair, or cheating on your taxes, it may all be revealed and you will reap the consequences of your actions. Eschatology, the last days, does not just refer to the ultimate time when God brings down the curtain on the world. We must live in the light of our individual and corporate eschatology all the time. Jesus speaks about Noah and Lot's wife. Noah, with his family, built an ark to escape the coming disaster. Why were his neighbors so hard to convince? They were not evil necessarily. They were just too busy eating and drinking, marrying and burying, conducting business. They were too busy to think about the catastrophe. They were caught up in the details of the present.

The sin of Lot's wife was that she couldn't give up the past. Instead of looking ahead to what God had for her and her family, she looked backward and turned into a pillar of salt. I heard about two children who studied this story in Sunday school and were discussing it. "Do you believe that story about Lot's wife turning into a pillar of salt?" asked one. "Sure, I believe it," said the other. "My mother went out driving the other day and she looked back and turned into a telephone pole." Tragedy overtook Lot's wife because she was not future-looking. She was tied to the past.

We can think of many examples of personal and social eschatology. Hiroshima is one. Suddenly life ended for tens of thousands of people. The Jewish people in Germany during the time of the Nazis could not believe that a mass destruction was coming—a sudden eschatology. The town of Coventry, England, experienced eschatology when, in a matter of moments, bombers leveled the town and destroyed its people, its factories, and its great cathedral. The *Titanic* was considered the world's safest liner—iceberg-proof and sink-proof. Yet passengers having martinis on the deck were caught up in an unexpected moment of eschatology.

On a day when your physician says those dreaded words, "I think you have cancer," you are plunged into an eschatological moment. If we live only for the now, we are not prepared. Some years ago I was on a plane about to land in Newark, New Jersey, when the pilot announced that our landing gear would not go down. All sorts of emergency measures were taken. We flew out over the Atlantic and dumped our gasoline. The runway was sprayed with foam, and fire trucks were lined up on the field to meet us. As you may have guessed, we did make it, without any mishap. They did get the landing gear down. But that was an eschatological moment for me. I thought, "Am I ready? I've lived a great life, but am I prepared for this moment?" That moment may come to all of us many times along the way.

That's one of the major thrusts of evangelism. We have the urgency to make sure that our neighbors and friends are ready. We could liken it to yelling "Fire!" in a burning building. On such an occasion, we wouldn't say, "May I suggest that at your convenience you amble over to the telephone and put a call in to the fire department?" We Christians have a sense of urgency about the kingdom of God so that those ultimate last days, personal or social, will not find us unprepared. Søren Kierkegaard, the great Danish theologian, said, "You can't sew unless you put a knot in your thread." Life is like that. The knot in our thread is the knowledge that someday it will be over for all of us and we must be ready for that day. That's what gives us perspective for the living of all of our life.

Having said all that, we can't deny that many Christians are absorbed by prophecy. They consider the Bible the basis for all this prophecy. But biblically, prophecy is not future-telling. It is forth-telling about the mighty acts of God. A prophet, in the biblical sense, is what we call a witness. You bear witness to your neighbors, friends, and colleagues about the Lord, about what He has done in your life, about what He is doing in your church or in the world. We speak forth about the mighty acts of God.

Any other kind of prophecy is some sort of cosmic guessing game: "The world will end in the year 2010." Who cares? It will end someday—tomorrow or in ten thousand years. Jesus tells us the time is not important. I am reminded of the story of two Indians who were watching a lighthouse being built on a coast near their village. It was finally finished and they couldn't wait to see how it worked. After observing a while, one turned to the other and said, "Look! Lights flash, horns honk, bells ring, and still the fog comes in." So much of present-day prophecy is like that—a lot of commotion that in no way affects the timetables of eternity.

We get ready for the last days by living in the kingdom now, and by loving the King and His world. We get ready for Him today, tomorrow, and ten thousand years from now, by doing His will as best we understand it, by spending time with Him. We are living in the kingdom when we trust the King. Ultimately, Christian faith is not having to worry about whether or not we have enough faith when the last days come. None of us has enough faith now, and we won't have enough when that time comes. Real faith means trusting God to supply what's missing.

No matter how stormy life gets for us, we need not panic because we have read the last chapter. God in Christ loves us, and we are now and will be forever in His kingdom. Sir William Osler, the great pioneer Christian doctor, once said, "If we throw all of our energy, intelligence, and enthusiasm into doing superb work today, there will be nothing to fear tomorrow."

Our Lord says in verse 37 that the body will draw the eagles. Some scholars have concluded that the eagles are symbolic of the Roman soldiers. Others assume this is a mistranslation for "vultures." At any rate, carrion birds, which eagles are not, come where the body is. This life will end and decomposition will take place. But you and I have read the last chapter. We can enter the kingdom now and live in it forever more by saying "yes" to the King.

CHAPTER THIRTY-FIVE—AN OFFER YOU CAN'T REFUSE

LUKE 18:1–30

Scripture Outline

Practicing Constancy (18:1–8)

Learning Humility (18:9–14)

Coveting Childlikeness (18:15–17)

Seeking Single-Mindedness (18:18–23)

A Marvelous Offer (18:24–30)

In the last years of my mother's life, she frequently asked, "Someday, son, would you preach on 'The Goodness of God'?" I was not very receptive. I'd say, "Mother, that's redundant. Everybody knows God is good. He wouldn't be God if He weren't." But she herself was overwhelmed with the goodness of God and thought more people ought to hear about it. I am beginning to think she may have been right.

I remember some years ago riding the New York City subway and reading something on the wall that shocked me. I was shocked almost every day riding the subway, but this time it was a pleasant shock. I looked up and saw an advertising card from the New York Bible Society quoting a single verse from the Psalms: "I have been young and now I am old, yet I have not seen the righteous forsaken or his children begging bread." It seemed a bizarre message in that city of abysmal slums and desperate poverty. But this outrageous claim is the other side of the coin of Christian sacrifice. Jesus said, "He that would save his life will lose it, and he that would lose his life will find it." Nevertheless, as you give up your right and your due, He gives you back not only eternal life, but the things of this life. In this chapter, we have the remarkable promise that we will receive manyfold more family and houses than we gave up, and in the age to come, everlasting life. It's an offer we can't refuse and the kind of promise my mother believed in so strongly.

These verses seem to indicate that God pays great wages. It's a little embarrassing, isn't it? I would like to think I'm working for nothing, and somehow putting God in my debt. But God stands in no one's debt. St. Francis left millions as a prince of the land in Spain and became poor for Christ's sake. He served the lepers, loved the poor, traveled in the holds of slave ships to preach about Jesus, but he was called the "Joculator Domine"—the hilarious saint. And God blessed him abundantly with houses and lands and friends all over the world.

PRACTICING CONSTANCY

18:1 Then He spoke a parable to them, that men always ought to pray and not lose heart, 2 saying: "There was in a certain city a judge who did not fear God nor regard man. 3 Now there was a widow in that city; and she came to him, saying, 'Get justice for me from my adversary.' 4 And he would not for a while; but afterward he said within himself, 'Though I do not fear God nor regard man, 5 yet because this widow troubles me I will avenge her, lest by her continual coming she weary me.'"
6 Then the Lord said, "Hear what the unjust judge said. 7 And shall God not avenge His own elect who cry out day and night to Him, though He bears long with them? 8 I tell you that He will avenge them speedily. Nevertheless, when the Son of Man comes, will He really find faith on the earth?"
—*Luke 18:1–8*

In these verses from chapter 18, Jesus talks about some of the positive qualities we need to have to be recipients of the abundant blessings He has for us. The first one is *constancy.* Don't give up. Hang in there. The parable of the unrighteous judge and the widow teaches just one point. The point is not to describe the woman or the nature of God. The single point is that if an unrighteous, secular judge will finally hear your appeals, how much more will your appeals be heard by your heavenly Father, who loves you and cares about you supremely. If you say, "Father, help," He will hear. Believe that God is on your side—always. You may ask if that isn't Norman Vincent Peale's positive thinking or Bob Schuller's possibility thinking. The answer is yes. It's also the apostle Paul's belief that Christ will *"always* lead us in triumph" (2 Cor. 2:14).

Lloyd Ogilvie, my longtime friend and pastor of Hollywood Presbyterian Church, led a retreat for our church's elders a while back. He told us a story about one of the elders in his church, a man with extravagant faith, who believes God can do all things. Asked to consider any new idea, he listens, asks questions, and then invariably says, "Why not? If this is for God and His kingdom—why not?" The other elders once conspired to test him, and they all approached him one day with all sorts of outrageous ideas for expanding the kingdom in some way. Each time he listened and gave the expected answer: "Why not?" He really believes that Christ will always lead us in triumph. It's not a bad modus operandi.

In his Institute for Successful Churchmanship, Bob Schuller warns that there is something wrong with every great idea. It doesn't take any faith to point out the flaws. Instead of saying, "We can't afford that," or "That would never work," try saying, "Why not? Let's see if we can't find a way to do it." The psychologist William James said, "Be not afraid of life. Believe that life is worth living and your belief will create that fact." Believe that all things are possible, like the woman in this parable. Practice constancy. Don't give up.

LEARNING HUMILITY

9 Also He spoke this parable to some who trusted in themselves that they were righteous, and despised others:
10 "Two men went up to the temple to pray, one a Pharisee and the other a tax collector. 11 The Pharisee stood and prayed thus with himself, 'God, I thank You that I am not like other men—extortioners, unjust, adulterers, or even as this tax collector. 12 I fast twice a week; I give tithes of all that I possess.'
13 And the tax collector, standing afar off, would not so much as raise his eyes to heaven, but beat his breast, saying, 'God, be merciful to me a sinner!' 14 I tell you, this man went down to his house justified rather than the other; for everyone who exalts himself will be humbled, and he who humbles himself will be exalted."

—Luke 18:9–14

The second Christian virtue we read about here is *humility*. Jesus tells the story of the Pharisee and the tax collector. Both were sincere and devout. As a matter of fact, one kept the law scrupulously, or thought he did. The other was in a profession in which extortion and dishonesty were expected. It's very unfair that the man of such exemplary behavior is not acceptable, while the one with the questionable vocation is. The Pharisee had everything, except the one essential thing. The publican had nothing but the one essential quality—which is a sense of his own unworthiness and his need for God's grace.

Our opinion of ourselves reflects who we think God is. The man who said, "I am not like other men; I fast; I give tithes" seemed to see God as a big corporation in which he owned a large block of stock. I'm sure he felt he would one day have enough stock to be a director in the corporation. The publican saw God as unmerited grace, burning love, and endless forgiveness. He was awed by the God he knew.

Being a new being in Christ means reversing our natural tendencies. Someone once said to me, "Larson, do you know what's wrong with you? You judge other people by their actions and yourself by your intentions. If you could reverse that, it would change your life." Since then I've been trying to judge others not by what they do, but by what they meant to do. Try judging yourself not by what you meant, but by what you did—which is how people perceive you. That's a giant step on the way to humility.

COVETING CHILDLIKENESS

15 Then they also brought infants to Him that He might touch them; but when the disciples saw it, they rebuked them. 16 But Jesus called them to Him and said, "Let the little children come to Me, and do not forbid them; for of such is the kingdom of God. 17 Assuredly, I say to you, whoever does not receive the kingdom of God as a little child will by no means enter it."

—*Luke 18:15–17*

The third quality Jesus recommends here is *childlikeness.* This does not mean childishness, or even innocence. Children are not more virtuous than adults. They're as selfish and self-centered as the rest of us. But they are usually guileless and uncomplicated. You ask a child, "Do you want an ice cream cone?" and he/she says, "Sure." I was called this last year to join an interfaith delegation to Taiwan, as a guest of the Taiwanese government. My reaction was wary. I said to the congressman who called me, "Wait a minute, Congressman. My mother taught me a long time ago that there's no such thing as a free lunch. What's the bottom line?

What will I be expected to sign?" He assured me there was no catch, but I am so sophisticated I don't trust anybody who wants to give me something for nothing. Children aren't like that. That's why Jesus intervened when the disciples tried to keep the children away. He said, "Of such is the kingdom of heaven" (Matt. 19:14).

My roommate in college died of cancer at age twenty-nine. Wally was my best friend, a Methodist minister's son. He was tall and handsome and a first-string basketball player. He sang like an angel and earned his way through school singing at weddings and funerals. Wally was one of the most childlike people I have ever known. He didn't pay much attention to girls, but he was greatly sought after by them. As Wally's roommate, I found the girls were very kind to me as an entree to Wally.

In an effort to court Wally, a number of these girls would invite him along on family outings to the opera or the symphony or out to expensive restaurants. He was delighted. After a certain length of time, I invariably got a call from some girl's mother asking, "Are Wally's intentions honorable? We've spent all this time and money on him. Just what are his feelings about our daughter?" I would try to explain, "He just thought you liked him." Being childlike is great protection in life. People can't take advantage of you. Wally walked through life unscathed, impervious to the designs and schemes of others. Being childlike means we can receive God's unconditional love and say, "Thank you." We are not suspicious and doubtful. That's the kind of childlikeness Jesus is commending here.

I heard about a minister who was offered a glass of homemade cherry brandy in a parishioner's home. He refused at first, but when the couple he was visiting insisted, he took a glass and liked it so well that he downed a second glass and even a third. At the end of the evening, the parishioner said, "I see you really like my cherry brandy. I'll be glad to give you a case of it if you will acknowledge the gift in church, publicly." The minister agreed. The next week his case of cherry brandy was delivered. The gift was acknowledged in the bulletin the following Sunday. "The minister wants to thank Mr. Smith for his gift of cherries and the spirit in which they were delivered." His thank you was either an example of childlikeness or the epitome of guile. All the same, if you really have no hidden agenda, you can go through life receiving in the childlike manner God would have us acquire.

The Roman Catholic novelist Romano Guardini wrote that worship is rather like play. It is the most nonutilitarian of all human activities. He says: "It [worship] is in the highest sense the life of a child, in which everything is picture, melody, and song. It is a kind of holy play in which the soul, with utter abandon, learns how to waste time for the sake of God." You can come to worship to do something, to learn something, to take some notes. Or, you can come as a child to celebrate the God who loves you and wants to make you a partner with Him in redeeming the world.

SEEKING SINGLE-MINDEDNESS

18 Now a certain ruler asked Him, saying, "Good Teacher, what shall I do to inherit eternal life?"

19 So Jesus said to him, "Why do you call Me good? No one is good but One, that is, God. 20 You know the command-ments: 'Do not commit adultery,' 'Do not murder,' 'Do not steal,' 'Do not bear false witness,' 'Honor your father and your mother.'"

21 And he said, "All these things I have kept from my youth."

22 So when Jesus heard these things, He said to him, "You still lack one thing. Sell all that you have and distribute to the poor, and you will have treasure in heaven; and come, follow Me."

23 But when he heard this, he became very sorrowful, for he was very rich.

—Luke 18:18–23

The fourth quality that Jesus advocates here is *single-mindedness.* In the story of the rich young ruler, the Gospel writers have given us a composite picture of this young man. Mark says he is rich, Matthew says he is young, and Luke says he is a ruler. He starts by greeting Jesus with *"Good Teacher."* Nobody used that adjective in addressing a rabbi. Good was reserved for God. Jesus probes for his motive. Is this flattery, or does he really believe that Jesus is God? Jesus tells the young man to "seek first the kingdom of God above all else." The young man declares he has kept all the rules and Jesus brings up his wealth. Can he give it away to the poor? He could not, and went away sorrowful. Jesus is not saying here that you cannot have money and be a disciple. Rather, He indicates that if anything—in this case, wealth—is more important than the kingdom, you can't enter. If you really want the kingdom, not sec-ond or also, but first and only, then you have it.

A MARVELOUS OFFER

24 And when Jesus saw that he became very sorrowful, He said, "How hard it is for those who have riches to enter the kingdom of God! 25 For it is easier for a camel to go through the eye of a needle than for a rich man to enter the kingdom of God."

26 And those who heard it said, "Who then can be saved?"

27 But He said, "The things which are impossible with men are possible with God."

28 Then Peter said, "See, we have left all and followed You."

29 So He said to them, "Assuredly, I say to you, there is no one who has left house or parents or brothers or wife or children, for the sake of the kingdom of God, 30 who shall not receive many times more in this present time, and in the age to come eternal life."

—Luke 18:24–30

Jesus goes on to say that it is harder for a rich man to enter the kingdom than for a camel to go through a needle's eye. For the Jew, money was a sign of blessing. The disciples are puzzled and ask who, then, can be saved? Peter wants to know, "What about us?" It's a valid concern. By way of response, Jesus makes this marvelous offer, an offer you can't refuse. He says, *"Assuredly, I say to you, there is no one who has left house or parents or brothers or wife or children, for the sake of the kingdom of God, who shall not receive many times more in this present time, and in the age to come eternal life"* (vv. 29, 30).

I think we have too often spiritualized this text. I have read so many commentaries that indicate that Jesus, of course, does not mean material blessings, but spiritual blessings. I happen to believe He means what He says. He is talking about the things of this world and the material blessings to come. Sometimes it's hard to prosper and remain faithful. The Israelites wandered for forty years in the wilderness with only a bit of manna and water. They were lean and hard and conquered the land. They were God's people. Once God gave them the land, they became lazy and indulgent. God wants to bless us, but when we are blessed with things, there's only one way to keep our blessings from sinking us—by giving them away. The more we give away, the more we get.

Among other things, I believe He wants to give us the four qualities Jesus holds before us in this chapter—constancy, humility, childlikeness, and single-mindedness. H. P. Hunt, the Texas millionaire, said, "If you know how rich you are, you're not very rich." The really rich have no idea how rich they are. I don't believe we who are God's children have any idea how rich we are. I hope we'll never plumb the depths of how rich we are, but go to our Father in Jesus' name and receive all He wants to give.

Chapter Thirty-Six—The Beginning of the End: Facing Death

Luke 18:31–43

Scripture Outline

> The Laws of Life (18:31–34)
>
> Existential Moment (18:35–43)

A Roman Catholic priest in France insists this actually happened to him. Late one night he was walking down a side street in Paris when a man approached with a gun and muttered, "This is a stickup." When the priest opened his overcoat to get his wallet, the robber noted his clerical collar. "Oh, Father," he said, "I would never rob a priest. Forgive me." Greatly relieved, the priest took out a pack of cigarettes and offered one to the robber. "No, thank you," said the robber. "I've given them up for Lent." The story makes us laugh because it's such a contradiction of belief and practice. If your faith does not somehow affect your daily life, it is phony faith. Faith and works are inseparable.

THE LAWS OF LIFE

³¹ Then He took the twelve aside and said to them, "Behold, we are going up to Jerusalem, and all things that are written by the prophets concerning the Son of Man will be accomplished. ³² For He will be delivered to the Gentiles and will be mocked and insulted and spit upon. ³³ They will scourge Him and kill Him. And the third day He will rise again."

³⁴ But they understood none of these things; this saying was hidden from them, and they did not know the things which were spoken.

—*Luke 18:31–34*

These verses remind us that life and death are inseparable and our faith must speak to both conditions. Some years ago, in a visit to the University of Massachusetts School of Education, I found a class on death education being offered. Future teachers were being prepared to teach this subject in the public schools. The premise was that children are not prepared for dealing with death. They seldom see death and they rarely even hear it discussed. They are unprepared for the death of a family member or friend.

One hundred years ago citizens had the good fortune to die at home. Now, most die in hospitals—a terrible place to have to die, surrounded by strangers and at the mercy of routine, often impersonal care. I hope that when my time comes I'll have the good fortune to be in my own home, surrounded by my noisy grandchildren and the smell of home cooking. The hospital is a good place to convalesce, but a poor place to die.

In these verses Jesus looks at death squarely, and I think we need to deal with the subject just as realistically. It's like handling a thistle. If you hold it gently it will prick your whole hand, but if you grab it boldly, you will break its spine and destroy its capacity to hurt you. We Christians need to look at death the same way—to examine it boldly and deal with it rationally.

There are some very apparent observations we can make about death. The first is that it is inevitable. That seems all too obvious, and yet I am always struck by how surprised people are by the death of somebody they love. They are unprepared for it and can't believe it could have happened. But it *will* happen. It is inevitable—for you, for your loved ones, for me, for all of us. The beginning of the end is right now, today. You are on your way to death, no matter how young you are, or how healthy you are. The irrevocable process has begun.

We should be aware in reading these verses that this is the third time that Jesus tells His disciples about His impending death. On the third day He will be raised, but for the time being He is facing a painful, humiliating death. The disciples cannot face such a possibility. Incidentally, Luke records that Jesus predicts His death on seven different occasions. The manner of His death was foreordained, and His death was inevitable.

A doctor I know told me that on his first day as an intern in the emergency room he watched four people die. That afternoon he called his wife and said, "Honey, I don't think I'm going to make it in this profession." Somehow, to come to grips with the ultimate end of any human being is terrifying, and yet, in accepting death, the doorway to life is opened. I think that is why Jesus repeatedly discussed His end with His disciples. Only as they began to accept His death could they understand the meaning of His life.

One of my secular heroes of the last decades was Saul Alinsky, a prophet to the poor. He spoke all over the country, helping the underprivileged in ghettos and slums to get the rights they deserved as citizens. Asked once about the secret of his life, Alinsky said, "A few years ago I came face to face with the fact of my own death—that someday I would die. When I accepted that and didn't hide it, life opened up for me. I could begin to live between now and then." Accepting the inevitability of death is part of God's strategy for living now to the full.

The second observation seems as obvious as the first. Death is necessary. It is the law of life. In the life created by God here on earth, there is the absolute certainty of death and resurrection. One form of life must die that another form may be born. Life is given that new life may come. One of the great tragedies of organizations, particularly church-related ones, is that we can't ever let them die a natural death. Groups come together for valid purposes—missions, study, prayer. For a time they flourish. A generation later that may not be so. The organization has served its purpose, but we feel the need to keep it going. We plead for people to serve as officers, or we may browbeat others to attend or contribute money. We seem unable to let anything die. And yet the great law of life is death and resurrection. If we let some organizations die to the glory of God, something new can be raised from the rubble.

Most parents understand this law of death and resurrection. They have invested a good part of themselves in their children. They have given up time, privacy, and considerable money. They do all that willingly that the child's life may prosper. We can think of all sorts of dramatic and touching examples of a life given that others might live. Many of us watched the national TV news report of the crash of Flight 90 at the Washington, D.C., National Airport in the spring of '82. The plane flew just a few hundred yards and crashed into the Potomac. The cameras caught some moving moments and some heroic actions. One mystery figure was a bald man with a glorious moustache who was situated in the tail of the plane. Every time the helicopter lowered a ring he would grab it and pass it on to somebody else. He passed five people on to life before he himself slipped under the water and was drowned. He gave his own life that five others might live.

The apostle Paul says, "For I could wish that I myself were accursed from Christ for my brethren . . ." (Rom. 9:3). He understood that somehow at the heart of the nature of God a costly sacrifice is required that life might come. Jesus' death was necessary, but it had a unique purpose, unlike your death and mine. He had to die that you and I might conquer death and live. There have been volumes written on the Atonement, advancing endless theories of what it means and why it was necessary. I don't think any of us really understand the Atonement. But it is enough to know that God Himself willingly gave His life through His Son, Jesus, and because of that voluntary death you and I have access to abundant and eternal life.

Your death and mine are necessary in a different way. We have to die to inherit what God has for us. The Scripture tells us our mortality shall put on immortality, our corruptible flesh must put on incorruptibility. Somehow, the hidden gift is that we might become what God had in mind for us forever and ever.

John Wesley once said, "Thank God our people die well." Death is partly a horror, but it is also a blessing we can face unafraid. One of the privileges of the pastorate is to be on hand when God's saints are dying. The death of a believer is often a touchingly beautiful event, when the moment anticipated for so long becomes a reality.

EXISTENTIAL MOMENT

35 Then it happened, as He was coming near Jericho, that a certain blind man sat by the road begging. 36 And hearing a multitude passing by, he asked what it meant. 37 So they told him that Jesus of Nazareth was passing by. 38 And he cried out, saying, "Jesus, Son of David, have mercy on me!"

39 Then those who went before warned him that he should be quiet; but he cried out all the more, "Son of David, have mercy on me!"

40 So Jesus stood still and commanded him to be brought to Him. And when he had come near, He asked him, 41 saying, "What do you want Me to do for you?"

He said, "Lord, that I may receive my sight."

42 Then Jesus said to him, "Receive your sight; your faith has made you well." 43 And immediately he received his sight, and followed Him, glorifying God. And all the people, when they saw it, gave praise to God.

—*Luke 18:35–43*

The blind man in this account has something important to teach all of us. He was in despair and heard a commotion. He asked, "What is it?" He was told that Jesus of Nazareth was passing by, and he must have heard of Him and known who He was. He knew it was the *"kairos,"* the moment of opportunity, and he cried out, *Jesus, Son of David, have mercy on me.* He refused to be hushed, and Jesus heard him. One man broke the rules of polite society and created a scene. Apparently that touched Jesus, and He asked the man what it was He wanted. "My sight," is the reply. Jesus tells Him his faith has saved him.

The blind man seized the moment. Jesus is passing by right now in our lives. This is the moment. If we don't seize it, we miss something extraordinary. Our spiritual blindness continues. The disciples had their physical sight, and they were blind to understanding. The man without physical sight understood the importance of the moment and acted.

Jesus modeled something significant for us at His own death, certainly an untimely one at age thirty-three. His last words on the Cross were, "It is finished." Would that you and I were able to say those words as we come to our last moment, suddenly or slowly, today or tomorrow or in three score years and ten. If you can say, "It is finished, and I have become the person God meant me to be," death loses much of its horror.

Those people who have a great deal of unfinished business fear death most. Their lives are strewn with unhealed and unrewarding relationships. So much has been left unsaid. "I love you." "I need you." "Thank you." "I'm sorry." Somehow the right moment for the reconciling word never came. That's unfinished business. In the death of a marriage partner, I believe grief is lessened by the memory of a fulfilling relationship. Grief goes on and on for those who have had a provisional relationship, who have been waiting for some breakthrough of love and intimacy.

Most of us have all sorts of unfinished business. Some of it is the garbage we pick up in life. Today, when someone enters the army at a place like Fort Dix, New Jersey, there is a great box at the entrance with a big hole in the top. The rule is that you may drop into that box with impunity any illegal substance you have with you—drugs, alcohol, knives, guns, whatever. No questions are asked. You drop those items into the box and begin a new life in the army. However, if you keep them and are caught, you are held accountable.

God has provided us with the great garbage disposal of the universe. Jesus says we can leave our garbage with Him and move on and claim a new life now and forever. Leave your resentments, your jealousies, your hatreds, your angers. Leave all those ugly thoughts. Leave all those things and there'll be no questions asked. If you insist on carrying them with you, you'll pay a great price.

Another item of unfinished business concerns God's agenda for our lives. Review constantly what you think that is for yours, so that when the time comes, suddenly or in full course, you can say, "It is finished." I heard about two men who were standing in the rain in New York arguing over a taxi. Finally one surrendered the cab to the other and walked over to where his wife was huddled in a doorway out of the rain. "Why did you give him that cab?" she demanded. "Well, dear, he needed the cab more than I did," was the explanation. "He was late for his karate lesson." You may think you need a cab until you meet someone who changes your agenda. The point is that as we get new insight our agenda needs to be reexamined and revised. We need to ask, "God, what is it You're hoping I can be and do?" If we can be and do that in the time left, then we can say, "It is finished."

I often wonder what eventually became of the blind man. He may have had some regrets in later years. Perhaps he said to himself, "I stood in the presence of the Son of God, the Messiah, and all I asked for was my sight. Think of the things I might have asked for. I might have asked for wisdom, for faith. I might have asked for the ability to love all the difficult people in my life."

On one occasion James and John asked for political power: "May we sit on your right and left hand in the kingdom?" (Mark 10:37) They must have realized later what a stupid request that was. But that's who they were at the time. As we grow spiritually, we understand a little more what God has in mind for us, and so we keep reviewing the agenda. Perhaps the blind man was haunted by the memory of that encounter. We have each day the opportunity of such an encounter. Jesus is passing by. He says, "What do you really want from Me?" Being who He is, He will probably give you what you ask for.

I heard about three survivors of a shipwreck who were adrift on the ocean in a lifeboat for many days. One day, a bottle floated by. When they grabbed it and uncorked it, a genie appeared. "You have liberated me," said the genie. "For that, I will give each of you one wish." One man said, "I wish I was back home with my sweetheart in New York"—and he was gone. The second man said, "I wish I could return to my family in Los Angeles." With that he was gone. The third man said, "Oh, I'm so lonely. I wish my friends were back again." The good news is that we believe that with God we all have more than one wish. But He is passing by, and like the blind man, we must seize the moment. Ask Him to deal with your unfinished business. If you have made a foolish wish earlier, revise it.

Life is not measured in length. The most tragic people are those who live provisionally for a long, long time. You see them sometimes in nursing homes, men and women of great years, haunted and unfulfilled. Jesus never promised us long life. He promised us an abundant life—pressed down, heaped up, and running over, one which will be endless. The apostle Paul said, "Whether I live or whether I die, I am the Lord's." That's the good news. To be the Lord's is to have no unfinished business.

When Paul traveled to Jerusalem for the last time, headed for trial and imprisonment, his Christian brothers and sisters begged him not to go. He was resolute. He said, "I go bound in the spirit to Jerusalem, not knowing the things that will happen to me there" (Acts 20:22). You don't know what will happen to you or your loved ones today. Death is waiting somewhere ahead for all of us, but we go bound in the Spirit and trusting in the One in whom we have believed.

Chapter Thirty-Seven—What About Sudden Conversion?

Luke 19:1–10

19:1 Then Jesus entered and passed through Jericho.
² Now behold, there was a man named Zacchaeus who was a chief tax collector, and he was rich. ³ And he sought to see who Jesus was, but could not because of the crowd, for he was of short stature. ⁴ So he ran ahead and climbed up into a sycamore tree to see Him, for He was going to pass that way. ⁵ And when Jesus came to the place, He looked up and saw him, and said to him, "Zacchaeus, make haste and come down, for today I must stay at your house." ⁶ So he made haste and came down, and received Him joyfully. ⁷ But when they saw it, they all complained, saying, "He has gone to be a guest with a man who is a sinner."

⁸ Then Zacchaeus stood and said to the Lord, "Look, Lord, I give half of my goods to the poor; and if I have taken anything from anyone by false accusation, I restore fourfold."

⁹ And Jesus said to him, "Today salvation has come to this house, because he also is a son of Abraham; ¹⁰ for the Son of Man has come to seek and to save that which was lost."

—Luke 19:1–10

The possibility of conversion, or sudden change, is one of the most relevant topics in almost every area of human endeavor. Present-day psychologists, psychiatrists, and psychotherapists believe, contrary to Freud, that you *can* transcend your childhood; you need not be what your parents have made you. That's good news.

The medical world is examining the possibility of change. Recently, cardiovascular researchers separated all of us into two types, type A and type B. Type As are hard-working, over-achievers who are prone to die of heart attacks. Type Bs go through life smelling the daisies, having fun, and enjoying the world, and they live longer. Now instead of concentrating solely on methods of treatment for Type As, doctors are asking if there is a chance that Type A can be changed into Type B.

Some educators are now suggesting that I.Q. is changeable. That score you achieved in the primary grades may not be fixed at all. There are indications that I.Q. scores can be raised, that radical changes are possible. I am told that in the Soviet Union over the last few years, the number one graduate study subject is conversion, and not from a Christian or spiritual point of view. The Russians understand the political significance of this whole field. The nation able to change its citizens' values, motivations, goals, and lifestyles has the ultimate power beyond nuclear weapons.

Conversion is at the very center of the biblical message. Throughout the Old and New Testament, the message is that it's never too late to change. You need not be locked into what you have always been and done. You are not a prisoner of your track record. For too long, we in the church thought sudden conversion, the Billy Graham kind of conversion, was for fundamentalists, for weird charismatics, for gospel missions, or tent meetings. But the possibility of sudden conversion is God's gift to everybody, liberal or conservative, high church or low. Whatever your political, theological stance, it is never too late to repent and turn to God (the essence of conversion) suddenly or gradually.

History abounds with examples of sudden and surprising conversions. John Wesley—son of an Anglican priest and missionary to America—had one. This great theological giant returned to England, discouraged and defeated. One day, sitting in a chapel in Aldersgate, he found "his heart strangely warmed." John Wesley was converted and became the great fountain of life for the Methodists and for all of England.

St. Augustine had a dramatic conversion. The same monk who had such struggles with the temptations of the flesh, who prayed, "O Lord, make me pure, but not yet," became the great saint we revere today. William Booth was an unlikely convert. This rough-cut man, appalled that the poor and the homeless had nowhere to turn, founded the Salvation Army. One day he prayed, "Lord, I give you everything there is in this man, William Booth. Do with me what you will." With that one man's conversion, a movement started that changed hundreds of thousands of lives. Frank Laubach, founder of the Christian Literacy Campaign, was converted at age forty-five, after his career had taken a disappointing turn. He subsequently invented a reading system that has enabled millions of the world's illiterates to read.

In terms of the conversion experience, the story of Zacchaeus is an important case study. Jesus was coming to visit Jericho, a town far below sea level, by the Jordan River. It was then a very important center of commerce, the hub of all the trade routes from Jerusalem. King Herod had a palace there. It was a historic city. Mark Antony once gave Jericho to Cleopatra as a present. Joshua and his trumpeters had brought down its walls.

Jesus was passing through this important city, and crowds had come out to see Him—this strange, holy man, who might be the Messiah. Zacchaeus, a wealthy tax collector, was a part of that crowd. But, being a short man, he was unable to see, so he climbed a tree. Even today the very rich often have little regard for propriety. They are free to behave eccentrically, dress carelessly, and drive strange old cars. When you're rich you have nothing to prove. Zacchaeus, being a rich man, was free to do something ridiculous—climb a tree.

The parade finally arrives. Jesus passes by and in spite of the crowd on both sides of the road He notices Zacchaeus. He summons him to come down and feed His disciples and Himself. Immediately, Zacchaeus scrambles down and scurries home to get the servants going on the lunch menu. I've always wondered why, out of the entire city of Jericho, Jesus zeroed in on Zacchaeus. I used to think it was because the conversion of a corrupt tax collector would be such a telling demonstration of the power of God. I don't think that any more. Rather, I think Jesus went through that town looking for the most ready and open person there. Though Zacchaeus seemed the least pious and the least religious, he was the most hungry for the new life God had for him.

Luke gives us a condensed story of the encounter. They go home; they sit and eat, probably a sumptuous luncheon banquet. If you were a novelist, how would you write the dialogue? Who would do most of the talking? Did Jesus tell Zacchaeus all about God, conversion, prayer, and Christian ethics? Was Jesus the great, inexhaustible fountain of wisdom and Zacchaeus the audience? Or, is it possible that when you are in the presence of God, He asks about *you?* In Zacchaeus' case, things like, "Tell me about your life. How did you get so rich? Do you have any friends? Do you and your wife get along? Tell me about your children." We don't have any record of what actually happened, but I have the feeling that when you sit in the presence of Ultimate Love, *you* are the agenda.

Zacchaeus was an immediate convert and his faith was put into practice instantly. He says, "Guess what? I'm going to pay back everything I've defrauded fourfold." That was not generous. According to Roman law, if you defrauded somebody you were to repay them fourfold. He met the law's requirements, but beyond that he proposed to give away half of his goods. That was entirely voluntary.

Jesus says, "Today salvation has come to this house." Salvation has come not just to Zacchaeus, but to his entire household. When the head of the household commits his or her life to the Lord, the whole house is blessed. Salvation had come that very moment to Zacchaeus' house. Zacchaeus went cold turkey, like an addict who gives up drugs or alcohol, with no gradual withdrawal. In an instant, he gave up his money and his old lifestyle, and salvation was pronounced.

Conversion has been defined by William James in his *Varieties of Religious Experience:* "To be converted is a process, gradual or sudden, by which a self, hitherto divided and consciously wrong, inferior and unhappy, becomes unified and consciously right, superior and happy in consequence of its firmer hold upon religious realities." This conversion need not be sudden. It can be a long time coming. The physical birth process in its final stages takes just minutes or even seconds, but that baby has been coming for nine months. Sometimes conversion looks sudden, but the struggle may have been going on for a long time. The Hound of Heaven, to use the phrase from Francis Thompson's wonderful poem, has pursued you down the labyrinth of years. One day you stop running and He overtakes you.

The good news here and all through Scripture, is that it is never too late; you can begin again. Who are the converted, according to the biblical record? Abraham the liar. Jacob the cheat. David the adulterer. Rahab the harlot. Peter the coward. Nicodemus the proud religious leader. All unlikely converts.

I read about a man who retired after forty years in a job that required catching the 7:30 bus every morning. On the first morning of his retirement, he commented on the breakfast his wife had fixed. "Honey, I don't like eggs this way." "But, I've been serving you eggs over lightly for forty years," she exclaimed. "Why didn't you tell me before?" "I never had time," was the reply. It's a poor excuse—for him and for us. When is the time to consider conversion? Today is the accepted hour. Today salvation can come to your house and mine.

Chapter Thirty-Eight—Stewards of the Mysteries of God

Luke 19:11–27

A story is told about President Franklin D. Roosevelt, a remarkable and charismatic man who sometimes wearied of those long receiving lines at the White House. He complained that no one really paid any attention to what was said. One day, during a reception, he decided to try an experiment. To each person who passed down the line and shook his hand he murmured, "I murdered my grandmother this morning." The guests responded with phrases like: "Marvelous! Keep up the good work." "We are proud of you." "God bless you, sir." It was not until the end of the line, while greeting the ambassador from Bolivia, that his words were actually heard. Nonplussed, the ambassador leaned over and whispered, "I'm sure she had it coming." I suggest that most of us are like the other guests. We think we know what's going to be said, so we don't bother to listen.

11 Now as they heard these things, He spoke another parable, because He was near Jerusalem and because they thought the kingdom of God would appear immediately. 12 Therefore He said: "A certain nobleman went into a far country to receive for himself a kingdom and to return. 13 So he called ten of his servants, delivered to them ten minas, and said to them, 'Do business till I come.' 14 But his citizens hated him, and sent a delegation after him, saying, 'We will not have this man to reign over us.'

15 "And so it was that when he returned, having received the kingdom, he then commanded these servants, to whom he had given the money, to be called to him, that he might know how much every man had gained by trading. 16 Then came the first, saying, 'Master, your mina has earned ten minas.' 17 And he said to him, 'Well done, good servant; because you were

faithful in a very little, have authority over ten cities.' [18] And the second came, saying, 'Master, your mina has earned five minas.' [19] Likewise he said to him, 'You also be over five cities.'

[20] "Then another came, saying, 'Master, here is your mina, which I have kept put away in a handkerchief. [21] For I feared you, because you are an austere man. You collect what you did not deposit, and reap what you did not sow.' [22] And he said to him, 'Out of your own mouth I will judge you, you wicked servant. You knew that I was an austere man, collecting what I did not deposit and reaping what I did not sow. [23] Why then did you not put my money in the bank, that at my coming I might have collected it with interest?'

[24] "And he said to those who stood by, 'Take the mina from him, and give it to him who has ten minas.' [25] (But they said to him, 'Master, he has ten minas.') [26] 'For I say to you, that to everyone who has will be given; and from him who does not have, even what he has will be taken away from him. [27] But bring here those enemies of mine, who did not want me to reign over them, and slay them before me.'"

—Luke 19:11–27

This Scripture is so familiar to all of us. Any believer has read it over one hundred or perhaps even one thousand times. But read it again and forget what you think it says, and see if God does not have a fresh insight for living. It is Jesus' last teaching before His final week in Jerusalem, and so it must be important. In this story of the nobleman, his citizens, and his servants, Jesus presents three very distinctive lifestyles.

First, there are the people who say, "I want it my way. I'm going to get all I can." This is the attitude of the citizens who are to be the subjects of the future king. They don't want him. They have their own plans. They represent all those who insist on life on their own terms. They often succeed because of their very determination to get what they want. But, having it all on your own terms is a mixed blessing. Unfortunately, enough is never enough. That's how we're made. We can have it all, and yet somehow the hunger for power and wealth is not assuaged. Bertrand Russell once said, "It is preoccupation with possession more than anything else that prevents man from living freely and nobly." If the object of your life is a great getting—of prestige, wealth, power—you are the victim of an ever-increasing appetite which can never be satisfied.

The *Wall Street Journal* did a survey in October 1981 in conjunction with a Gallup Poll, of some of the country's top executives, all making salaries in six figures (anywhere from $100,000 to $999,000). One survey question was, "What is your greatest fear?" The reply, almost without exception, was, "I fear I will not have enough in this time of inflation." These successful men and women who have made it by most standards are still worried that they won't have enough. One man volunteered, "I still eat fish and chips at Arthur Treacher's." It takes a certain wisdom to know when enough is enough, and to be able then to move on to the existential questions of life, questions that ought to plague everybody: Who am I? Why am I here? What's the purpose of life?

If we were no longer plagued by economic concerns, "Can I get the right job? Can I keep my job? Can I make enough to pay my bills?"—we could move on to the whole question of the meaning of life. There's no way to come to grips with that apart from an eschatalogical theology—a "last times" answer. Wherever we are in this drama we're living out, how is it going to end?

The parable Jesus tells here is a timely one. King Herod had just died and his son had journeyed to Rome to press his claims for the kingdom. Meantime, his subjects were sending delegations to Caesar saying, "This man is not acceptable as our king." Jesus is telling a contemporary story in veiled terms. In the parable, the nobleman was given the kingdom and he returned to slay those who didn't want him in power. As Christians, we believe that Jesus is the King and that in the last days He will return to His kingdom. Whether you are an atheist, a skeptic, or one who practices any brand of non-Christian religion doesn't change that reality. Jesus tells us through this parable, "Right now you are free to debate and argue, but when the final curtain is closed, I am Lord!"

The story of the servant who kept his *mina* safe in a handkerchief presents us with a second way to live—cautiously and conservatively. These are the people who want to go through life hurting no one, breaking no rules, and making no enemies. Their aim is to get through life being good old boys, or good old girls. They're determined not to consume, but to leave everything the way they found it. They see life as a picnic area. Their aim is to pick up all the paper and garbage, leaving the place just as it was. It seems commendable until we take into account that someone planted the trees, provided the tables, the fireplaces, the restrooms, and trash cans. Simply picking up after yourself is not enough. You are a parasite on those who plant and build and go and do.

Beyond that, it's impossible to go through life disturbing nothing. You cannot live without breaking some rules, making some enemies, creating a few waves. Thomas Carlyle said, "No man lives without jostling and being jostled. In all ways he has to elbow himself through the world, giving and receiving offense."

Some years ago I interviewed the administrative head of a psychiatric research hospital near Baltimore. He told me that a great number of his patients couldn't handle the fact that to live in this world you must do violence to others and to the world, inadvertently or deliberately. If you get a job, someone else doesn't get it. If you're the valedictorian of your class, someone else has not made it. Vegetarians abhor the slaughter of animals for food, but they eat plants or destroy trees for firewood. To live you must prey upon the world. This doctor was not a believer, but he had a real appreciation for the Christian concept of a Saviour who can forgive the violence we have all done to someone or something.

To think we can live in the world using nothing and hurting no one is contrary to what we read in the Scriptures. The truth is you only have what you use. A friend of mine had been keeping notes on sermons for many years. He had notes from scores of preachers, famous and otherwise—a huge box of them. He told me, "One day I asked myself exactly what good those sermon notes were. Anything that was of any use is now part of my life." He took his box of notes and burned it. He realized the futility of storing up truths that had not been applied to his life.

The third lifestyle we are presented with in this particular Scripture is that of the faithful steward. In this story of the nobleman who goes to the far country, Jesus is actually describing His kingdom, of which He is, of course, the King. Ten servants are given one *mina* each (a *mina* is a pound; a pound is one hundred drachmas). One drachma was the wage then for one day's work, so one hundred days' wages were given to each of these ten servants, to be invested while the nobleman was gone. We are told only what three of the servants did with their money, and of those three, only the one who increased his investment ten times was praised. The one who made five pounds was rewarded with five cities, but only the most fruitful servant was commended. The servant who simply saved his original pound displeased his master to such an extent that his one pound was taken away.

Jesus seems to be saying that there are only two classes of people—the fruitful and the unfruitful. The fruitful are alive and reproducing. It is a powerful injunction that we are to leave more behind than we found. If we don't, we have missed the message.

We are stewards of our lives and of all we have. The apostle Paul says in 1 Corinthians 4:1: "Let a man so consider us [those of us who are Christians], as servants of Christ and stewards of the mysteries of God." As a Christian you are more than a steward of your life. You are a steward of the mysteries of God. We believe that God loves us, that Jesus died for us, and that His spirit is now available to us. Those are some of the mysteries of which we are stewards.

Another one is *you*. If you are a Christian, you are someone in whom God lives. You may look frail and imperfect, but somehow in that earthen vessel is a treasure. We read in Scripture that all of creation, every known form of life in heaven and earth and the cosmos, is standing on tiptoe to see if you and I, God's most extraordinary creations, will find our inheritance. Will we become those unique miracles that God had in mind at our creation and redemption?

As stewards of our own lives, are we increasing? We may be fearful, like the spies Moses sent from Israel who came back saying, "We can't conquer that land. There are giants there." Because of their fear, the Israelites wandered for forty more years. They did not claim their inheritance. Later God said to the Israelites: "Every place that the sole of your foot will tread upon, I have given you" (Josh. 1:3). We can claim the day. The Spirit of the living God is in us. To be fruitful, we invest our lives, our jobs, our money, our reputations, our security. Otherwise, we decrease and die.

We are also stewards of the mysteries of the church, the body of Christ. We are the family of God. Jesus says, "These are my brothers and my sisters, my mother and my father." We say to the world, "Come in in God's name." But every part of the body, every congregation, must face whether or not it is increasing or decreasing. It is not enough to preserve what is. As stewards of the mysteries of the body of Christ, we need to be investing for the future so that there will be more loving, caring, support, mission, and involvement for the next generation.

Finally, we are stewards of the world, one of God's mysteries. God made the world, and so loved the world that Christ died for the world. The world is ours because we are His and the world is His. Will there be more justice, more equality, more compassion, more liberty, more opportunity, more peace in the world because we have lived? If we are fruitful, we will be more tomorrow than we are today, personally, as members of the body of Christ, and as servants of the world. May our aim be to hear those words of commendation from verse 17, *"Well done, good servant."*

CHAPTER THIRTY-NINE—WHEN THE PARADE PASSES BY

LUKE 19:28–44

28 When He had said this, He went on ahead, going up to Jerusalem. 29 And it came to pass, when He drew near to Bethphage and Bethany, at the mountain called Olivet, that He sent two of His disciples, 30 saying, "Go into the village opposite you, where as you enter you will find a colt tied, on which no one has ever sat. Loose it and bring it here. 31 And if anyone asks you, 'Why are you loosing it?'thus you shall say to him, 'Because the Lord has need of it.'"

32 So those who were sent went their way and found it just as He had said to them. 33 But as they were loosing the colt, the owners of it said to them, "Why are you loosing the colt?"

34 And they said, "The Lord has need of him." 35 Then they brought him to Jesus. And they threw their own clothes on the colt, and they set Jesus on him. 36 And as He went, many spread their clothes on the road.

37 Then, as He was now drawing near the descent of the Mount of Olives, the whole multitude of the disciples began to rejoice and praise God with a loud voice for all the mighty works they had seen, 38 saying:

" 'Blessed is the King who comes in the name of the LORD!'

Peace in heaven and glory in the highest!"

39 And some of the Pharisees called to Him from the crowd, "Teacher, rebuke Your disciples."

40 But He answered and said to them, "I tell you that if these should keep silent, the stones would immediately cry out."

41 Now as He drew near, He saw the city and wept over it, 42 saying, "If you had known, even you, especially in this your day, the things that make for your peace! But now they are hidden from your eyes. 43 For days will come upon you when your enemies will build an embankment around you, surround

you and close you in on every side, 44 and level you, and your children within you, to the ground; and they will not leave in you one stone upon another, because you did not know the time of your visitation."

—Luke 19:28–44

Pretend for a moment that you are standing in Jerusalem about 2,000 years ago, a part of that first Palm Sunday parade. You might cheer or weep or simply watch silently. Parades are usually stirring. They are a means of honoring heroes or celebrities, sometimes all too transitory. The poignant thing is that some parades are for people who don't deserve them, while the deserving often go unrecognized.

A parade, or the absence of one, can have a profound effect on one's life. Some years ago I heard about the homecoming of one of our great missionaries who had served more than forty years in a remote part of Africa. On the boat with him was a United Nations ambassador who had spent six weeks in Africa jaunting about here and there. As the ship came in to New York Harbor, fire boats appeared, spouting water festively. Tugboats tooted. Bands came alongside. There was a great tumult of praise and celebration for this returning ambassador. The missionary began to feel sorry for himself, saying, "Forty years for Jesus and nobody knows or cares that I'm coming home." At that moment he seemed to hear Jesus say, "Well done, good and faithful servant." Nevertheless, he later confessed that simply did not seem like *enough*. He was as human as the rest of us. We want to hear Jesus say, "Well done," but wouldn't it be nice if someone planned a parade for us just once?

Let's review some of the exciting and dramatic events of that first Palm Sunday. First of all, are you aware that Jesus planned His own parade? He didn't wait for His loyal friends to give Him a gold watch. Up to this point, He had maintained some degree of anonymity. He had been trying to keep a low profile, cautioning those who had been healed and helped, "Go and tell no one." But now the time had come for some recognition. I think He acted totally without conceit. He needed a parade and He knew that the world needed this particular parade. He planned His parade unashamedly for His own sake, as well as for the sake of His followers, then and now.

That's true humility, and I'm so far from that. Most of my life I have been so hungry for appreciation that if I received it, I somehow minimized it. For years I couldn't handle a simple compliment on a sermon. If someone made an appreciative comment, I'd say, "It was nothing." Or, I'd put the person on the defensive by asking, "What are you going to do about it?" Finally, my wife said, "Why can't you just say 'thank you' and let it go at that?" I'm learning to do just that. If God really was the author of the sermon and the Spirit gave me freedom and authority to deliver it, I should be able to enjoy it as much as my hearers.

Wives have a way of keeping us humble. I heard about a man who was receiving an honorary degree at some great university. In introducing him, the president said, "The man we are honoring today is a great man. You might say he's a very great man. I would even say he is a very, very great man." Driving home after the ceremony, the man turned to his wife and said, "Dear, how many very, very great men do you think there are in the world?" She said, "One less than you think there are, dear."

Jesus decided to have a parade to make a statement about His greatness. As a boy I was always amazed that He knew exactly where the donkey was. I used to think that somehow He had telepathic powers like Superman. Now I realize that He had walked up and down those streets daily. I'm sure He had often noticed this little donkey colt and decided to use it eventually for the parade. You might wonder about the symbolism of an unused donkey. Anything offered to God had to be pure and perfect. So Jesus chose an unused, unbroken animal. The donkey was a symbol of peace in those days. Horses were symbols of military might. Conquering generals came on horses. An ambassador coming on a peaceful mission rode a donkey. Jesus was an ambassador of peace from the ultimate kingdom.

He tells His disciples what to say to the owners of the colt: *"The Lord has need of it"* (v. 31). They must have known who Jesus was and therefore that explanation was enough. Many people were so poor that a single family could not afford a donkey. A group might chip in and corporately buy one to share. And yet when these owners are told that the Master needs their donkey, they do not even protest. They don't ask, "Where are you taking him and for how long? Will he be sacrificed?" They gave the colt gladly.

As I read these verses, I couldn't help wondering if I could give up something precious in my life simply because Jesus asked me to. Of course, if we know what that one thing is, we at least know where the growing edge is in our lives. Is it money, home, position, family? Could we give Him that one thing if we were not sure of getting it back again?

It's interesting that we in the church have always commemorated this parade on what is called Palm Sunday. Luke records no palms. I think we should speak of Parade Sunday. The parade is the central event. There may or may not have been palm branches. Palm branches were often used on such occasions, but Luke doesn't mention that. He tells us that the crowd spread their garments on the road, which was traditionally done for famous military or civic leaders, and they cheered. The religious leaders dared not prevent them from doing so. They complained to Jesus, and again, in true humility, He told them that if the crowd were silenced the very stones of the streets and the walls would cry out. He was not embarrassed by the cheers.

When He drew near to Jerusalem, He wept. There is a dramatic view of Jerusalem from the top of the Mount of Olives looking across the Kidron Valley. And Jesus, catching sight of that beautiful city, wept because He understood the real tragedy of the moment. In one sense, all parades are sad. Their heroes fade, their purposes are short-lived. I think Jesus understood that this moment of glory was not to last. Then He prophesied the fall of Jerusalem. He said, *"The days will come upon you when your enemies will build an embankment around you, surround you and close you in on every side"* (v. 43). Incredible as that must have sounded then, it's exactly what happened in the years that followed. That great walled city came under siege and was surrounded by a huge earthen ramp. The walls were scaled and those inside were destroyed.

Parades have both a joyful and a poignant quality. Crowds were cheering, and yet, what was there to cheer, actually? A few clothes in the road, a borrowed donkey, a King who would not live the week out. It makes me think of the final scenes in the *Wizard of Oz*, when the Wizard is exposed as all sound and fury with no substance. The parade was permanent in that we live with its effects, but within a week's time, it was as if the parade had never happened.

I think this particular parade had several important purposes. First of all, it fulfilled the prophecy of Zechariah 9:9 that the Messiah would come into Jerusalem riding on a donkey. Jesus fulfilled the prophecy, but He isn't locked into that prophecy. The prophecy was locked into the event. There's a difference. The parade had political and personal dimensions, which is usually true for most parades. Jesus was making His move, saying to the authorities, "Now is the time. Do what you will. This is the moment of opportunity." And for each person in that crowd and each one of us today there was a political dimension to this event.

It has something to say about our life, about our time. Jesus wept over Jerusalem because He knew the crowd would reject the King and His kingdom. It's like a parent who sees his or her child on a collision course and can do nothing to prevent it.

Some years ago I took that exact walk with my friend Lloyd Ogilvie. We were leading a tour of pilgrims, and one day we broke away from the group and took a taxi to Bethany, the home of Mary and Martha and Lazarus. We visited the tomb where Jesus had raised Lazarus from the dead. Then we started our walk following the steps of our Lord until we came to the top of the Mount of Olives where Jesus looked over the valley and wept.

Along the way, a few miles back, some little boys had joined us. We were delighted and thought there ought to be some children in this re-creation of that earlier parade. Just as we were standing there in awe, one little boy tugged on my coat, "Mister, would you like to have my sister? She lives right over there." We were aware how little had changed in two thousand years. In this place where God established a beachhead of love, people are still being bartered and degraded. We continued on our way with a new understanding of why Jesus might have wept.

Jerusalem is symbolic of all of our hometowns and cities. We could weep for all our neighbors who know not the things that make for peace, for the unredeemed loneliness which results in destructive patterns. If we were really aware of the heartbreak in any average town, we would weep more than we do.

Finally, why a parade? Because Jesus needed one. We all do. I hope that there will be at least one parade for you in this life, even if you have to plan it yourself. Thinking about all this, I asked a friend recently if there had been any parades in his life (meaning recognition and honors). "Yes," he said, "I've had parades. And mostly they helped me see beyond the parades." If you've never had a parade, a time of being honored, of course you want that. If the honors are withheld, we live with regrets and bitterness and "if onlys." Someone has said that one of the marks of our time is the desire for instant fame. It's everybody's ambition to appear just once in *People* magazine. The whole world reads about us and then promptly forgets us. But for one week we're famous.

Parades serve another important function. They are the prelude to being discarded. Jesus was soon to be discarded. Judas was already in the process of discarding Him. Peter was about to discard Him in a brief conversation with a servant girl. Even those beloved brothers, James and John, thought about discarding him.

The crowd, now cheering "Hosannah, Hosannah," would soon be yelling, "Barabbas, Barabbas," in Pilate's court. The parade has a way of letting you down. Often we are being eased out at the very same time that we are being honored. At retirement, a gold watch and a banquet prepare you for being discarded. Even the celebration of a golden wedding anniversary or an eightieth birthday has its somber side. Your family and friends realize you are about to move on, and the party is part of a group farewell.

But the parades are for those who watch as much as for the heroes. The original Palm Sunday parade was primarily for Jesus, but it was also for the disciples. It was for the crowd, offering them one more chance to respond to the King. The parade was for you and me because Jesus is still passing by in your life and mine, giving us one more chance to say, "Yes, I want what You offer." Or, "No, deal me out."

In that original crowd was Bartimaeus, who was once blind and now could see. There was Lazarus, once dead and now alive. The parade began in his home town of Bethany. Nicodemus was in the crowd, a secret disciple who ultimately stood up to be counted. We're all those people and many more. The parade, then and now, gives us one more chance to respond to the King.

CHAPTER FORTY—POWER POLITICS IN THE CHURCH

LUKE 19:45—21:4

Scripture Outline

THE OPPOSITION

45 Then He went into the temple and began to drive out those who bought and sold in it, 46 saying to them, "It is written, 'My house is a house of prayer,' but you have made it a 'den of thieves.'"

47 And He was teaching daily in the temple. But the chief priests, the scribes, and the leaders of the people sought to destroy Him, 48 and were unable to do anything; for all the people were very attentive to hear Him.

—Luke 19:45–48

Life is a game of power politics. There's no way to avoid it. In almost every relationship, a power struggle is going on, however unconsciously. Sometimes it's thinly disguised in humor. There is the wife who confronted her husband one evening as he was reading the paper. "Honey, put your paper down. What do you think of this hat?" He said, "That's the most ridiculous hat I ever saw. It doesn't do a thing for you. Take it back." "I can't do that," she parried. "This is my old hat. But since it offends you so much I'll go right down and buy a new one that will please you." This woman is a clever power politician.

You've probably encountered power politics on the job, whether that job is volunteer or paid, and especially if you have tried to make some changes in the system. Karl Marx once said, "If you want to understand the nature of a structure, try to change it." Suddenly all forces come together, even those formerly at enmity, to confront the radical change agent.

That's why meetings can be so infuriating. How often have you come home from a meeting, even one in the church, saying, "I'm through with meetings. No more committees." We tend to think that in these meetings truth and wisdom and light will of course prevail. Instead of that, we find that decisions are being made on the basis of emotion rather than logic. Furthermore, the task at hand does not seem to be the real agenda of the meeting. Power politics are erupting.

Jesus comes into the temple, the ultimate place of religious significance in all Jerusalem, and tries to bring radical change and renewal. In his book, *Self-Renewal,* John Gardner said that no organization in the church, business, or government can survive unless from time to time it reexamines its purpose for being and returns to that original agenda; otherwise it gets deflected into all sorts of side issues. The scribes and Pharisees had turned the true worship of God into legalism and the keeping of endless rules.

The Sadducees and the Pharisees represented two factions in the church at that time. The Sadducees were the aristocrats—the wealthy, the privileged, and the theologically conservative. Does that sound familiar? They were also pro-Rome, because the Romans insured the status quo in which the Sadducees had power. Then there were the Pharisees, very pious but liberal. They often brought fresh and helpful interpretations to God's Word, and Jesus sometimes quoted them positively.

Incidentally, though not mentioned here, the Zealots were a third group. Their concern was not about religion or God. Their number one goal was to free the nation from Roman rule. They were the "my country, right or wrong" group. There were other factions, but these were the three major ones. When Jesus began to call for change, all three groups joined forces to get rid of Him. Rather than pushing for any of their causes, He was insisting that true piety consists of loving God with your whole heart and your neighbor as yourself. He was an offense to all of them.

A while back Hazel and I had an unusual opportunity to understand the repressive climate of legalism into which Jesus came. On our trip to Taiwan as guests of that government, our small inter-faith group included three conservative rabbis and their wives. I was astonished to observe the number of rules which were mandatory for these six Jewish people. For example, they could eat almost none of the food at dinners hosted for us, since it wasn't kosher. On Friday, their Sabbath, they set out on foot for the one synagogue in Taipei, a considerable distance away. They couldn't take a cab, since that would be considered working.

Since it was the Sabbath, they were forbidden to push the elevator button in the hotel to go to and from their rooms, incidentally, on the ninth floor. Again, that would be work. The strategy there is to wait until somebody comes along to push the button. You go up with that person, get out on the floor selected and walk up or down the rest of the way. These sincerely religious and intelligent people are still living by the same kinds of rules that prevailed in Jesus' times. How audacious of Him to come into that scene and suggest that this kind of legalism was not what serving God was all about. What an affront Jesus was to those living by the rules. By their standards, He didn't keep the Sabbath laws or the thousands of dietary laws and, of course, they wanted to discredit Him.

> **20:1** Now it happened on one of those days, as He taught the people in the temple and preached the gospel, that the chief priests and the scribes, together with the elders, confronted Him ² and spoke to Him, saying, "Tell us, by what authority are You doing these things? Or who is he who gave You this authority?"
>
> ³ But He answered and said to them, "I also will ask you one thing, and answer Me: ⁴ The baptism of John—was it from heaven or from men?"
>
> ⁵ And they reasoned among themselves, saying, "If we say, 'From heaven,'He will say, 'Why then did you not believe him?' ⁶ But if we say, 'From men,' all the people will stone us, for they are persuaded that John was a prophet." ⁷ So they answered that they did not know where it was from.
>
> ⁸ And Jesus said to them, "Neither will I tell you by what authority I do these things."
>
> *—Luke 20:1–8*

In these verses, the attempts to discredit Jesus center in three separate questions. They are the kinds of questions we invent in every age to discredit an opponent. The first was, "By what authority do You do these things?" In other words, what are your credentials? What seminary ordained you? Was it liberal or fundamentalist, conservative or evangelical? Jesus avoids the trap by asking about John the Baptist's authority. His opponents realize that however they answer they will provoke the crowd. When they refuse to answer, Jesus claims the same privilege.

A QUESTION OF OWNERSHIP

9 Then He began to tell the people this parable: "A certain man planted a vineyard, leased it to vinedressers, and went into a far country for a long time. 10 Now at vintage-time he sent a servant to the vinedressers, that they might give him some of the fruit of the vineyard. But the vinedressers beat him and sent him away empty-handed. 11 Again he sent another servant; and they beat him also, treated him shamefully, and sent him away empty-handed. 12 And again he sent a third; and they wounded him also and cast him out.

13 "Then the owner of the vineyard said, 'What shall I do? I will send my beloved son. Probably they will respect him when they see him.' 14 But when the vinedressers saw him, they reasoned among themselves, saying, 'This is the heir. Come, let us kill him, that the inheritance may be ours.' 15 So they cast him out of the vineyard and killed him. Therefore what will the owner of the vineyard do to them? 16 He will come and destroy those vinedressers and give the vineyard to others."

And when they heard it they said, "Certainly not!"

17 Then He looked at them and said, "What then is this that is written:

'The stone which the builders rejected
Has become the chief cornerstone'?

18 Whoever falls on that stone will be broken; but on whomever it falls, it will grind him to powder."

19 And the chief priests and the scribes that very hour sought to lay hands on Him, but they feared the people—for they knew He had spoken this parable against them.

—Luke 20:9–19

The story of the wicked vinedressers is an analogy about Israel to whom God gave a land that they might go and bear fruit. God now wants the fruit, and they cannot produce it. Jesus is telling them that God requires fruits of righteousness and new life, of peace and joy. He reminds them they have killed all the prophets and servants sent to collect God's fruits and they may even kill His son and heir. Of course they were angry.

Jesus is speaking here about a basic problem in the church. To whom does the vineyard belong? Does it belong to the church with all its various buildings and laborers, be they church officers or bishops or even the Pope? No, the vineyard belongs to the one who planted it. We tend to forget that and act as if it belongs to us and to our particular faction.

A QUESTION OF PATRIOTISM

20 So they watched Him, and sent spies who pretended to be righteous, that they might seize on His words, in order to deliver Him to the power and the authority of the governor.

21 Then they asked Him, saying, "Teacher, we know that You say and teach rightly, and You do not show personal favoritism, but teach the way of God in truth: 22 Is it lawful for us to pay taxes to Caesar or not?"

23 But He perceived their craftiness, and said to them, "Why do you test Me? 24 Show Me a denarius. Whose image and inscription does it have?"

They answered and said, "Caesar's."

25 And He said to them, "Render therefore to Caesar the things that are Caesar's, and to God the things that are God's."

26 But they could not catch Him in His words in the presence of the people. And they marveled at His answer and kept silent.

—Luke 20:20–26

The second question, about giving tribute to Caesar, is really a question about patriotism, an old stand-by in discrediting your opponent. How do you feel about your country? Are we "America, love it or leave it" people, or are we in the ranks of those who protest national policies on war or nuclear armament? It's a timely question. Jesus says to make a choice is too simplistic, and He shows the two sides of the coin. We have to live in both worlds. We have a duty to our nation, however we interpret that, and we belong to God. We must live responsibly with both loyalties.

A QUESTION OF ORTHODOXY

27 Then some of the Sadducees, who deny that there is a resurrection, came to Him and asked Him, 28 saying: "Teacher,

Moses wrote to us that if a man's brother dies, having a wife, and he dies without children, his brother should take his wife and raise up offspring for his brother. 29 Now there were seven brothers. And the first took a wife, and died without children. 30 And the second took her as wife, and he died childless. 31 Then the third took her, and in like manner the seven also; and they left no children, and died. 32 Last of all the woman died also. 33 Therefore, in the resurrection, whose wife does she become? For all seven had her as wife."

34 Jesus answered and said to them, "The sons of this age marry and are given in marriage. 35 But those who are counted worthy to attain that age, and the resurrection from the dead, neither marry nor are given in marriage; 36 nor can they die anymore, for they are equal to the angels and are sons of God, being sons of the resurrection. 37 But even Moses showed in the burning bush passage that the dead are raised, when he called the Lord 'the God of Abraham, the God of Isaac, and the God of Jacob.' 38 For He is not the God of the dead but of the living, for all live to Him."

39 Then some of the scribes answered and said, "Teacher, You have spoken well." 40 But after that they dared not question Him anymore.

—Luke 20:27–40

The third question was the resurrection question, and it was posed to determine whether Jesus was conservative or liberal. The question of the seven men who died leaving one wife was a crafty question posed by crafty men. It's in a category with some of the questions we ask today. "Are you a pietist or are you for social action?" "Are you pre-mil or post-mil?" "Are you an evangelical?" "Do you speak in tongues?" "Are you a secular humanist?" "Do you believe in biblical inerrancy?" We all have certain questions we use to rate the other person's orthodoxy. On the basis of their answer, we dismiss or include them.

Years ago, one of the critical questions concerned the Virgin Birth. Emil Brunner, one of the leading European theologians, came to this country on a lecture tour during that time. On the morning before a speech in Chicago, some anonymous caller phoned to ask if he believed in the Virgin Birth. Brunner wanted to know what that had to do with anything. The caller explained, "I need your answer in order to decide whether I'll come to your lecture." "I can't believe you Americans," was Brunner's comment.

A QUESTION OF ANCESTRY

[41] And He said to them, "How can they say that the Christ is the Son of David? [42] Now David himself said in the Book of Psalms:

'The LORD said to my Lord,

" *Sit at My right hand,*

[43] *Till I make Your enemies Your footstool.'"*

[44] Therefore David calls Him *'Lord';* how is He then his Son?"

—Luke 20:41–44

In these verses Jesus discusses His lineage. He uses verses from the Psalms to emphasize that He is the Lord of David and all his descendants. That must have seemed an unforgivable affront to those who were attempting to challenge His power by means of those three shrewd and potentially explosive questions.

Whether we like it or not, power politics are a part of the life of most of our churches. The apostle Paul says: ". . . When you come together as a church, I hear that there are divisions among you . . ." (1 Cor. 11:18). We have the super patriots and those who abhor many of our nation's policies. There are the traditionalists and the antitraditionalists. There are pro and con factions on ERA, abortion, nuclear proliferation, and many other issues. In our congregation, we even have clapping and anticlapping factions. Some say clapping is irreverent. Others believe that to sit and do nothing when you are moved and thrilled is an abomination. We have music factions—those who want to hear nothing written after 1900, and others who say, "The gospel is contemporary. Can't the music reflect that?"

The problem comes when we believe only our faction is God's faction, when we assume that only we know what is best, and we run roughshod over all opposition.

TRUE PIETY

[45] Then, in the hearing of all the people, He said to His disciples, [46] "Beware of the scribes, who desire to go around in long robes, love greetings in the marketplaces, the best seats in the synagogues, and the best places at feasts, [47] who devour widows' houses, and for a pretense make long prayers. These will receive greater condemnation."

21And He looked up and saw the rich putting their gifts into the treasury, [2] and He saw also a certain poor widow putting in two mites. 3 So He said, "Truly I say to you that this poor widow has put in more than all; 4 for all these out of their abundance have put in offerings for God, but she out of her poverty put in all the livelihood that she had."

—Luke 20:45—21:4

In the final verses of chapter 20 and the first four of chapter 21, Jesus contrasts two lifestyles: that of the scribes, who are living a lie, making an elaborate show of their piety, and that of the penniless widow who is serving God with all she has. The latter is a model for us as we sort through all the confusing factions and seek to find God's will for our lives personally and corporately. I saw an ad in our Sunday newspaper which said, "Church of Christ—For Sale by Owner." I sometimes think God must feel like saying, "Earth—For Sale by Owner." But He hasn't yet. He is still the Chief Cornerstone.

Scripture Outline

> Living in an Impermanent World (21:5–6)
>
> Ways of Coping (21:7–19)
>
> Finding Security (21:20–38)

LIVING IN AN IMPERMANENT WORLD

⁵ Then, as some spoke of the temple, how it was adorned with beautiful stones and donations, He said, ⁶ "These things which you see—the days will come in which not one stone shall be left upon another that shall not be thrown down."
—Luke 21:5–6

The signs of the times are all around us. We read of floods, earthquakes, and hurricanes; of wars and rumors of wars. There are ominous signs of the earth's upheaval and of nations in chaos. Jesus discusses here the signs of the times in Jerusalem two thousand years ago. It's confusing because Jesus weaves together two contrasting strands, two different end times.

He prophesies the destruction of Jerusalem but He also speaks of the end of the world and the cosmos. He speaks of two temples. First, there is the magnificent temple in which He is teaching and the destruction of which He foretells. At the time Jesus spoke these words, the second restoration of the temple had been going on for forty-six years. It was A.D. 63 before it was actually completed. But that glorious building, planned by Solomon, was only one temple. If the temple is the place where God is dealing with His people, then truly and surely Jesus is the new temple.

The temple was the epitome of grandeur and security to the Jews at the time. It was four football fields wide and five football fields long, made of marble so pure it looked like a great mountain of snow from a distance. One wall was solid gold, a blinding sight in the sunshine. There were single columns of marble forty feet high and gifts of furniture from rulers of all the known world. Even Ptolemy had given a desk. Jesus predicted that this incredible building, full of treasures, would pass away. His hearers were baffled. But in A.D. 70, seven years after the restoration was completed, that temple of stone was destroyed and the other temple, the temple of Jesus' earthly body, was destroyed in less than a week.

Throughout all these warnings, Jesus' underlying message was that everything in life is impermanent apart from God and His kingdom: *"Heaven and earth will pass away, but my words will by no means pass away"* (v. 33). There are few things of permanence in our world. If you have lived a half century, as I have, you've seen enormous changes impossible to comprehend. When I was a boy, Britain was a great naval power. Her ships were everywhere preserving the peace—the Pax Britannica. I have just read that the British are selling off most of their navy. They are becoming a third-rate naval power. Our bitterest enemies from World War II, Germany and Japan, have become our best allies. America, which led the world in the industrial revolution, is presently exporting primarily agricultural products. Who could have predicted such a total reversal?

Christian morality is becoming a minority ethic. Our children understand that better than we do. If they want to live by God's rules, they are bucking the tide. The cultural and ethical climate of our land has changed in the space of a few years. Who would have guessed that the OPEC nations would ever be suffering economically, or that Detroit would lose its lead in the car market to Japan and Germany and other nations? Where is the Great Society of Lyndon Johnson? The liberalism of the sixties seems totally dead, and we're experiencing another swing to conservatism.

Let's say your security has been in a happy and fulfilling marriage. Almost certainly, one of you will outlive the other. One partner will lose his or her security. That shouldn't surprise us. If your security is in your children, they are certain to grow up and leave you. They may still love you, but they are going to leave you if they're healthy children. Puberty is that time when your children stop asking you where they have come from and won't tell you where they're going. But—they are going, be sure of that. We cannot even find a secure place to invest our money. Is it real estate, stocks, bonds, money market funds? Financial advisers have no clear word for us about investing our surplus, assuming we have any in the first place.

If we feel secure because of our military might there's a lesson to be learned in the great ape house of the New York Zoo. Between the cages housing the gorilla and the orangutan is the cage bearing the sign: The Most Dangerous Animal in the World. As you approach this cage, you find yourself staring at a mirror under which is this sign: "You are looking at the most dangerous animal in the world. It, alone, of all the animals that ever lived can exterminate—and has exterminated—entire species of animals. Now it has achieved the power to wipe out all life on earth, including its own." If your security is in your country—America, first, last and always—remember that Greece was once the world's greatest power. That power moved west to Rome, then west again to France, and once more to England and finally west to us. If you think this is the last stopping place, history will refute you.

WAYS OF COPING

7 So they asked Him, saying, "Teacher, but when will these things be? And what sign will there be when these things are about to take place?"

8 And He said: "Take heed that you not be deceived. For many will come in My name, saying, 'I am He,' and, 'The time has drawn near.' Therefore do not go after them. 9 But when you hear of wars and commotions, do not be terrified; for these things must come to pass first, but the end will not come immediately."

10 Then He said to them, "Nation will rise against nation, and kingdom against kingdom. 11 And there will be great earthquakes in various places, and famines and pestilences; and there will be fearful sights and great signs from heaven. 12 But before all these things, they will lay their hands on you and persecute you, delivering you up to the synagogues and prisons. You will be brought before kings and rulers for My name's sake. 13 But it will turn out for you as an occasion for testimony. 14 Therefore settle it in your hearts not to meditate beforehand on what you will answer; 15 for I will give you a mouth and wisdom which all your adversaries will not be able to contradict or resist. 16 You will be betrayed even by parents and brothers, relatives and friends; and they will put some of you to death. 17 And you will be hated by all for My name's sake. 18 But not a hair of your head shall be lost. 19 By your patience possess your souls.

—Luke 21:7–19

When Jesus speaks about the end of the world and the cosmos, He says that many false Messiahs will come insisting they know "when." We are not to listen to them. There has been no shortage of false Messiahs, from Joseph Smith to Mr. Moon of the Moonies to James Jones and his unfortunate followers in Guyana. In every generation there are false Messiahs claiming they know more than Jesus did.

I was on a flight from the Orient to San Francisco a while ago on the very night when the "Jupiter effect" was supposed to take place. You may remember that for the first time in one hundred years all the planets were in a line and there were to be cosmic consequences, so it was said. Some traveling companions were convinced that California would drop off into the sea, a victim of a shift in the great San Andreas fault, and we would have no place to land. The world is full of false prophets and misleading signs.

It seems to me there are three ways we can live in this world of impermanence. One is to be fearful, to go seeking for every sign and listening to every false Messiah. Jesus tells us here not to be led astray. When the time comes, it will be obvious to all of us. Second, we can adopt a "what the heck" attitude. We can try to escape the cares of the world in hedonism. Unfortunately, none of us can avoid those feelings of depression and discouragement, loneliness and betrayal. The tendency is to say, "Who cares?" and to sneak off into pleasure-seeking and self-fulfillment. It's easy to fall victim to the "what the heck" attitude.

Jesus tells us instead to "watch and pray." He is asking us to watch and pray, secure in our insecurities. Your friends may betray you, your spouse may leave you, your children may disappoint you, but, he says, *Not a hair of your head shall be lost* (v. 18). Our only permanent possession is our soul. You and I will sin and God has, at a tremendous price, forgiven us our sins. When you lose your soul you lose your only permanent possession. If you know who you are and whose you are, that is permanent.

Verse 14 has special meaning for me. I was in a small Bible study group some years ago in New York City where a discussion of the problem of noninvolvement came up. There had been any number of stories in the newspapers of crimes committed in full view of passersby who were afraid to get involved. As Christians, we felt we needed to decide in advance whether or not we would be willing to risk our lives for somebody else. With my usual humility, I was sure I would be willing.

The day after we had this discussion, as I was walking from the Port Authority Bus Terminal to my office, a very suspicious-looking man and woman carrying a black bag and glancing behind them, ran past me. I was sure they had committed some crime, robbed a bank, or mugged someone. I found myself trying to keep up with them, still uncertain of what might be required. You can't tackle somebody on the basis of vague suspicions—not in New York. I expected to hear someone yell, "Murder! Help! Thieves!" but I heard nothing. Just as all three of us got to the corner, a mounted policeman rushed by in pursuit. The couple ran down into the subway, but he leaped from his horse, followed and caught them. Was I ever relieved! Verse 14 was engraved on my heart. There is no way to plan ahead of time what we will do or say when the Lord requires something of us.

FINDING SECURITY

20 "But when you see Jerusalem surrounded by armies, then know that its desolation is near. 21 Then let those who are in Judea flee to the mountains, let those who are in the midst of her depart, and let not those who are in the country enter her. 22 For these are the days of vengeance, that all things which are written may be fulfilled. 23 But woe to those who are pregnant and to those who are nursing babies in those days! For there will be great distress in the land and wrath upon this people. 24 And they will fall by the edge of the sword, and be led away captive into all nations. And Jerusalem will be trampled by Gentiles until the times of the Gentiles are fulfilled.

25 "And there will be signs in the sun, in the moon, and in the stars; and on the earth distress of nations, with perplexity, the sea and the waves roaring; 26 men's hearts failing them from fear and the expectation of those things which are coming on the earth, for the powers of the heavens will be shaken. 27 Then they will see the Son of Man coming in a cloud with power and great glory. 28 Now when these things begin to happen, look up and lift up your heads, because your redemption draws near."

29 Then He spoke to them a parable: "Look at the fig tree, and all the trees. 30 When they are already budding, you see and know for yourselves that summer is now near. 31 So you also, when you see these things happening, know that the kingdom of God is near. 32 Assuredly, I say to you, this generation will by no

means pass away till all things take place. 33 Heaven and earth will pass away, but My words will by no means pass away.

34 "But take heed to yourselves, lest your hearts be weighed down with carousing, drunkenness, and cares of this life, and that Day come on you unexpectedly. 35 For it will come as a snare on all those who dwell on the face of the whole earth. 36 Watch therefore, and pray always that you may be counted worthy to escape all these things that will come to pass, and to stand before the Son of Man."

37 And in the daytime He was teaching in the temple, but at night He went out and stayed on the mountain called Olivet. 38 Then early in the morning all the people came to Him in the temple to hear Him.

—Luke 21:20–38

When heaven and earth pass away, only God's Word will be permanent. I feel that applies not just to the Living Word but the one that comes to us through Scripture as well. A friend of mine has told me that her Danish immigrant mother required her six children to memorize Bible verses. Each day they were asked to recite them for her. This devout woman gave something permanent to her children—the Word of God in their hearts.

Verse 37 gives us an unusual picture of Jesus as a commuter. It's comforting to think of that if you are or have ever been a commuter. He taught every day in the temple and traveled back to the Mount of Olives at night, most probably because He couldn't afford the high rent in Jerusalem. That's why most of us commute. Decent housing in the heart of the city is too expensive. I'm sure Jesus used His commuting time to be with God in meditation and prayer. It can be that kind of time for any present-day commuter—a time to go back to the Word of God, to Jesus, the Living Word, to be refreshed, feeding the only permanent part of your life.

To Catch an Angel, by Robert Russell, is the autobiography of a young blind man who lives alone on an island in the middle of a river. He goes rowing on the river almost every day by means of a fairly simple system. He attaches a bell to the end of the dock with a timer. The bell rings every thirty seconds. He can row up and down that river, and every thirty seconds judge his distance by the sound of the bell. When he has had enough, he finds his way home by means of the bell. In the young man's words, "The river lies before me, a constant invitation, a constant challenge, and my bell is the thread of sound along which I return to a quiet base."

Life is like a great river. God calls us to venture out on it where there is danger and excitement. But our security is in the bell, which is the Word of God, Jesus Himself. He is the Living Word, and you can hide His spoken words in your heart. That's permanent. When the river gets too wild or you get too weary, that security brings you home.

CHAPTER FORTY-TWO—THE TRAITOR AND THE FINAL DIALOGUE

LUKE 22:1–38

Scripture Outline

> The Betrayer Among Us (22:1–23)
> Explaining the Kingdom (22:24–30)
> A Prediction (22:31–34)
> Advice for the Future (22:35–38)

THE BETRAYER AMONG US

22:1 Now the Feast of Unleavened Bread drew near, which is called Passover. ² And the chief priests and the scribes sought how they might kill Him, for they feared the people.

³ Then Satan entered Judas, surnamed Iscariot, who was numbered among the twelve. ⁴ So he went his way and conferred with the chief priests and captains, how he might betray Him to them. ⁵ And they were glad, and agreed to give him money. ⁶ So he promised and sought opportunity to betray Him to them in the absence of the multitude.

⁷ Then came the Day of Unleavened Bread, when the Passover must be killed. ⁸ And He sent Peter and John, saying, "Go and prepare the Passover for us, that we may eat."

⁹ So they said to Him, "Where do You want us to prepare?"

¹⁰ And He said to them, "Behold, when you have entered the city, a man will meet you carrying a pitcher of water; follow him into the house which he enters. ¹¹ Then you shall say to the master of the house, 'The Teacher says to you, "Where is the guest room where I may eat the Passover with My disciples?"' ¹² Then he will show you a large, furnished upper room; there make ready."

¹³ So they went and found it just as He had said to them, and they prepared the Passover.

14 When the hour had come, He sat down, and the twelve apostles with Him. 15 Then He said to them, "With fervent desire I have desired to eat this Passover with you before I suffer; 16 for I say to you, I will no longer eat of it until it is fulfilled in the kingdom of God."

17 Then He took the cup, and gave thanks, and said, "Take this and divide it among yourselves; 18 for I say to you, I will not drink of the fruit of the vine until the kingdom of God comes."

19 And He took bread, gave thanks and broke it, and gave it to them, saying, "This is My body which is given for you; do this in remembrance of Me."

20 Likewise He also took the cup after supper, saying, "This cup is the new covenant in My blood, which is shed for you.

21 But behold, the hand of My betrayer is with Me on the table. 22 And truly the Son of Man goes as it has been determined, but woe to that man by whom He is betrayed!"

23 Then they began to question among themselves, which of them it was who would do this thing.

—Luke 22:1–23

Judas is the great question mark in history. Many books have been written about him, who he was, and why he did what he did. I think it's because we identify so much with Judas. Most of the books try to put him in the best possible light. They say he was loyal to Jesus, but in his concern that things were not moving fast enough, he wanted to force Jesus into revealing His power. He thought he understood more about the world and the kingdom than Jesus did. It is a rationale that harkens right back to Genesis 3 and man's first sin. Adam and Eve disobeyed in an attempt to be as wise as God. Most of us think we know better than God does. Some say that was Judas' problem.

There are many variations on this theory about poor, misguided Judas. I don't happen to believe any of them. I think Judas knew exactly what he was doing and he is judged, as we are judged, by his actions. We prefer to be judged by our intentions. That doesn't work in a court before a judge and jury. We can't explain a traffic violation, for instance, by claiming "I didn't mean to do it. I meant well." We must pay for our offense.

Last fall, a friend of mine drove into apple country with his wife. In passing a beautiful orchard, they saw a man filling a bushel basket with apples. My friend stopped and asked to buy some. "Just help yourself," he said. They climbed out of the car and got some paper bags and filled them with the choicest apples. On leaving, they asked again, "Are you sure we can't pay you?" "Oh, no," he said. "I'm stealing them too." Now, had the law or the orchard owner come along at that point, good intentions would be irrelevant. They were stealing apples.

We identify with Judas and try to build a case for him, missing the point that there is no case for him. He is guilty. He is a traitor. We can't even claim it was Satan's fault. Satan is working on all of us all the time, especially if you're an important part of God's kingdom as Judas was.

And yet, in one sense, Jesus was not trapped by Judas. Nobody knew where the Passover feast would be except Peter and John. They were given very mysterious directions for finding the room. Jesus kept the location a secret, probably because of Judas. He was determined that his arrest would take place at the time He had chosen, and not before. Peter and John were to enter the city and look for a man carrying a water jar. Only women carried water jars in those times; men carried waterskins. This unusual sight of a man doing women's work would be a sign. They were to follow that man and say certain words to him—words which are, in effect, passwords. Jesus has carefully arranged this intrigue. He knows His betrayal time is at hand, but He makes careful plans so that this important Passover feast will not be interrupted.

We can see in our minds this circle of men reclining as was the custom, heads into the table, eating. They have all been together for three years. Jesus has shared His kingdom with them, His presence, and His power. Now, in the wine and bread, He gives them His body and blood. He gave Himself unreservedly to all twelve, including Judas.

Traditionally, the Passover is celebrated with one's family. It commemorates the angel of death passing over the children of Israel while slaying the first-born in every Egyptian household. Jesus chose to celebrate with His family, those twelve men who had shared His life and ministry for so long. He says to this special family, *"Behold, the hand of My betrayer is with Me on the table,"* and all twelve begin to question who would do this thing (vv. 21–23). Matthew reports that *each* of them began to say to Him, "Is it I?" Each one was aware that he was potentially a Judas. We are all Judases, actually or potentially. The traitor is the one who has done something to betray the king, who has acted unworthily or dishonestly. What a marvel. The church is a fellowship of forgiven traitors.

In his story, *"The Seed and the Sower"* Laurens Van Der Post describes the scene where Jesus makes His first post-resurrection appearance to the twelve. He asks why they are not all there. They protest that they *are* all there. When He insists someone is missing, they ask if He does not know about Judas, that he hanged himself. Jesus says, "This cannot be true. This life . . . needs Judas as it needs Me. His deed, too, is redeemed."

There's a wonderful story about the cardinal of the Philippines, named, oddly enough, Cardinal Sin. When Cardinal Sin was a bishop, a young woman in his parish claimed that she had visions of Jesus. Bishop Sin was given the task of determining if these visions were authentic. He called her in for an interview, after which he made this request: "Daughter, the next time you see Jesus, would you ask Him what sin your bishop committed as a young priest and then come and tell me His answer." She agreed. The bishop, aware that nobody knew his sin except himself, his confessor, and Jesus, felt this would be a valid test. Months later the young woman returned, reporting she had seen Jesus again. The bishop said, "Good. Did you ask Him about my sin?" She said, "Yes," "What did He say?" "He said, 'I've forgotten.'"

All of us have been, or will be, traitors, in large or small things. Our God not only suffered and died for our sins, He also has promised to remember them no more.

EXPLAINING THE KINGDOM

24 Now there was also a dispute among them, as to which of them should be considered the greatest. 25 And He said to them, "The kings of the Gentiles exercise lordship over them, and those who exercise authority over them are called 'benefactors.' 26 But not so among you; on the contrary, he who is greatest among you, let him be as the younger, and he who governs as he who serves. 27 For who is greater, he who sits at the table, or he who serves? Is it not he who sits at the table? Yet I am among you as the One who serves.

28 "But you are those who have continued with Me in My trials. 29 And I bestow upon you a kingdom, just as My Father bestowed one upon Me, 30 that you may eat and drink at My table in My kingdom, and sit on thrones judging the twelve tribes of Israel."

—Luke 22:24–30

In this final dialogue in the Upper Room, Jesus tells the disciples something of what His kingship is all about. Of the four Gospel writers, only Luke records the disputes among the disciples in the Upper Room. Only Luke tells us that Satan is behind Judas's falling away and the possible defections of others. Luke, the clinician, understands the psychological implications of the disputes and the spiritual implications of the temptations.

Jesus says three things here about the kingdom. He says that His is a different kind of kingdom than they are used to. It's not a temporal kingdom. Napoleon once said, "Alexander and I built two of the greatest empires in the history of the world, and where are they now? Ours were based on fear. Jesus came in love and built a kingdom that grows stronger every year." Jesus speaks of spiritual power and, being primarily of a spiritual nature, you and I know that's a power far beyond nuclear bombs, governments, and armies.

The four paradoxes of Alcoholics Anonymous have tapped into the heart of this kind of spiritual power. They say, "We surrender to win; we give away to keep; we suffer to get well; we die to live." Jesus adds here one further paradox. He says that to lead, one must serve. A leader in His kingdom does not sit at the chief table or demand the biggest office, the highest salary, and the most attention. Jesus says that leadership in His kingdom involves service.

Hermann Hesse's book *Journey to the East* is a beautiful parable demonstrating this principle. Some great princes, nobles, and holy men riding horses and camels are on a sacred quest. One member of the party is called Leo, and at the end of each day he brings out his guitar to sing. He puts up the tent. He builds the first fire, tells stories, and encourages his friends. One morning they awake to find Leo gone. They look everywhere for him, but to no avail. Finally they decide to continue their journey, but in just a few weeks' time, the whole company disbands. Without Leo the journey is too difficult. Much later, one of the travelers sets out to find Leo and discovers that he was actually the head of their spiritual order. He did not ride on the front camel yelling, "Wagons ho," but he made the journey possible for everyone else. Jesus does that for us, and He calls us to serve quietly in the background, affirming, encouraging, and helping.

A PREDICTION

[31] And the Lord said, "Simon, Simon! Indeed, Satan has asked for you, that he may sift *you* as wheat. [32] But I have

prayed for you, that your faith should not fail; and when you have returned to Me, strengthen your brethren."

33 But he said to Him, "Lord, I am ready to go with You, both to prison and to death."

34 Then He said, "I tell you, Peter, the rooster shall not crow this day before you will deny three times that you know Me."

—Luke 22:31–34

In the exchange with Peter, Jesus makes a distinction between real faith and sentimental faith. Sometimes we Christians get caught up in sentimental faith. We say, "Oh, I wish I could have been in Jerusalem in those days and walked with Jesus, been a child in His lap, heard Him speak, seen Him heal." Personally, I don't think that would have changed anything for most of us. That's sentimental nonsense. Twelve disciples were with Him night and day for three years, and yet in this final time before the Crucifixion, they were guilty of jealousy, ambition, denial, and defection. Being with Jesus for three years had not changed them that much.

In the older King James Version, in verse 32b of this passage, Jesus tells Peter, "When thou art converted, strengthen thy brethren," implying he is not yet converted. What does conversion require? Obviously it did not depend on being personally with Jesus during His earthly ministry. Conversion is made possible by the death of Christ, His Resurrection, and the outpouring of His Spirit at Pentecost. That's what enables us to claim forgiveness and new life. You and I have greater power available to us now than the twelve disciples had before Good Friday, Easter, and Pentecost. We have an opportunity for the King Himself to invade us, to make us His domain, and to rebuild us from the inside.

Jesus predicts that when Peter has been converted he will strengthen the brethren. The sixth chapter of Proverbs lists six things the Lord hates and the seventh, which is an abomination to Him, is "a man who sows discord among brethren" (Prov. 6:19). The divisive one, the factious person, is the chief of sinners. Jesus says that the mark of conversion is not simply preaching to the unsaved and performing miracles. The ultimate sign that we are new beings in Christ is that we love and encourage other believers.

Next, Jesus says to Peter (calling him by his old name), "Simon, Satan has asked to have you." Satan wanted not just Peter, but all twelve. Satan did claim Judas, and we don't know how that happened. When Peter came face to face with his own weaknesses and denial, he became Peter the Rock. We need not be ashamed of our weakness, our humanity. It can become a valuable asset. Peter went on to be an unmovable rock in the kingdom, crucified upside down by choice because he felt unworthy to be crucified in the same manner as his Lord. This vacillating, insubstantial man is converted and becomes a new being.

I met a man recently who lost his wife in an automobile accident, and who has been raising their children alone. "I saw a sign in the park that describes me," he told me. "It was posted in an area where new grass had been planted. It said, *'Not ready for use—healing.'"*

I said to him, "No way. That's not you. That's grass. When you are healed, if that ever takes place, you will be less ready for use. While you are still healing, you can reach out to those who are experiencing grief and loss like nobody else." In the kingdom, our own brokenness and humanity become a great resource.

Our society certainly needs technical specialists, but along with that we have a desperate need for life specialists—those who can reach out to others because of their own recent hurts. I counsel many men and women who have been rejected in a marriage and therefore feel worthless. I try to assure them they are still valuable in God's eyes, but I'm not always heard. How much more helpful it would be for them to talk to someone who has gone through that experience, who can empathize with their pain, and assure them they are going to make it. Each of us, because of our painful experiences, is a specialist in how to survive in life to the glory of God.

ADVICE FOR THE FUTURE

35 And He said to them, "When I sent you without money bag, knapsack, and sandals, did you lack anything?"

So they said, "Nothing."

36 Then He said to them, "But now, he who has a money bag, let him take it, and likewise a knapsack; and he who has no sword, let him sell his garment and buy one. 37 For I say to you that this which is written must still be accomplished in Me: 'And He was numbered with the transgressors.' For the things concerning Me have an end."

38 So they said, "Lord, look, here are two swords."

And He said to them, "It is enough.

—Luke 22:35–38

The dialogue in the Upper Room ends with a warning. Jesus had previously told the disciples to go out unprepared and without money or sandals to proclaim the good news of the kingdom. But now, He says, they are to go out ready for anything—that is, pack your suitcase, bring your money, even buy a sword. They missed the point again and produced two swords. Jesus says, *"enough,"* and I do not think He is referring to their two swords. Rather, I think Jesus is saying, "Enough of this. You've missed the point, which is that the strategy must change. A year or two ago I was popular. You went in My name and were received gladly. In a few days' time, I will be killed and you will have no popularity. You are to prepare for those days."

We Christians are stewards of three separate aspects of life in the kingdom. First of all, we're stewards of an event. The event is simply that God became flesh and entered the universe in Jesus. It is an event that needs no explanation. If He has entered our lives, we bear witness to that subsequent event. Beyond the event, we are stewards of the interpretation of the event. What does it mean? We build a theology around the event. Preachers and teachers explain the event, sometimes well, sometimes poorly.

Third, there is application of the event. How do we live because of the event? This is the dimension Jesus is addressing here. We can experience the event and interpret it brilliantly and still be without a strategy for applying it. One of the richest minerally based areas in the world is the Amazon Valley, yet those who live there are among the world's poorest people. They live on land above riches, with no strategy for mining them or using them for their own best interests. There are Christians like that. What do you do with the incredible fact that Jesus came as your King, that there is a kingdom and you are included in it? What does that mean on Monday, Tuesday, and Wednesday? That's where application, or strategy comes in.

One of the great geological, archeological sights in Greece is in Meteora, just north of the Thessalonian plain. Great pedestals of stone rise out of the valley like giant fingers. Hundreds of years ago, Christian monks hauled themselves up there by means of ropes and baskets and built monasteries on the top. In these remote and unapproachable places, they lived lives of pious devotion. That was their strategy for life in the kingdom. At the very same time this was happening in Greece, St. Francis was traveling the known world, spreading the gospel into every area of human life. He was the founder of a whole order of monks who brought the message of the event into slave camps, leper colonies, hospitals—wherever there was need.

The monks of these two different orders undoubtedly agreed about the event—God came into the world in Christ. They agreed on interpretation—the doctrines of Incarnation and Atonement. But their strategies could not have been more opposite. That's what makes these words of Jesus so important. In this, His final dialogue, He wanted the disciples to understand His strategy for them at this point in history. He has a strategy for each of us as well, as we take our places in His kingdom.

CHAPTER FORTY-THREE—DEALING WITH FEELINGS

LUKE 22:39–62

Scripture Outline

Two Kinds of Passion (22:39–53)

Feelings and Actions (22:54–62)

TWO KINDS OF PASSION

³⁹ Coming out, He went to the Mount of Olives, as He was accustomed, and His disciples also followed Him. ⁴⁰ When He came to the place, He said to them, "Pray that you may not enter into temptation."

⁴¹ And He was withdrawn from them about a stone's throw, and He knelt down and prayed, ⁴² saying, "Father, if it is Your will, take this cup away from Me; nevertheless not My will, but Yours, be done." ⁴³ Then an angel appeared to Him from heaven, strengthening Him. ⁴⁴ And being in agony, He prayed more earnestly. Then His sweat became like great drops of blood falling down to the ground.

⁴⁵ When He rose up from prayer, and had come to His disciples, He found them sleeping from sorrow. ⁴⁶ Then He said to them, "Why do you sleep? Rise and pray, lest you enter into temptation."

⁴⁷ And while He was still speaking, behold, a multitude; and he who was called Judas, one of the twelve, went before them and drew near to Jesus to kiss Him. ⁴⁸ But Jesus said to him, "Judas, are you betraying the Son of Man with a kiss?"

⁴⁹ When those around Him saw what was going to happen, they said to Him, "Lord, shall we strike with the sword?" ⁵⁰ And one of them struck the servant of the high priest and cut off his right ear.

⁵¹ But Jesus answered and said, "Permit even this." And He touched his ear and healed him.

52 Then Jesus said to the chief priests, captains of the temple, and the elders who had come to Him, "Have you come out, as against a robber, with swords and clubs? 53 When I was with you daily in the temple, you did not try to seize Me. But this is your hour, and the power of darkness."

—*Luke 22:39–53*

If you have an occasional sleepless night, you're living in the real world. If you never have one, perhaps it's because your life is too safe. It's comforting to know that even Jesus had sleepless nights. We read about one here, one in which He is overwhelmed with all kinds of strong feelings.

You and I are passionate people, full of both constructive and destructive passions, and they sweep over us a good part of the time. Let's examine how we, from the biblical model, can deal with our feelings. Beyond being saved by the mighty act of God in Jesus Christ on the Cross, Paul tells us we are to "work out our salvation with fear and trembling" (Phil. 2:12). For many of us, as we work out our salvation we find we must come to grips with a good many emotions in addition to fear and trembling. How can we do that constructively?

Our Scripture gives us examples of two kinds of passion. There is the passion or suffering here and on the Cross of our Lord, which is the one and only act by which any of us may be saved, now and forever. We read here about His last sleepless night when the forces of good and evil are locked in deadly combat. Jesus is dealing with all kinds of feelings—confusion, anguish, fear, anger, and doubt.

Jesus came to the garden to pray, the night before His final confrontation with Satan. Of the four Gospel writers, only Luke says, *"He went . . . as He was accustomed"* (v. 39). Luke must have researched this point and found this was not an isolated occasion. Jesus went there frequently at night and perhaps often prayed all night. Only Luke tells us that an angel came down from heaven to strengthen Him and that His sweat became like great drops of blood. Matthew and Mark focus on the apathy of the disciples. They tell us Jesus came back to them three times and found them sleeping. Luke reminds us that while the disciples might have failed Him, God was there reassuring Him in the presence of the angel.

The high priests and soldiers finally arrived. Judas is leading the group and attempts to kiss Jesus. Think of the genuine anger that Jesus must have felt as He said, *"Judas, are you betraying the Son of Man with a kiss?"* (v. 48). Our Lord, being totally human, was capable of real anger.

And then there is the passion of Peter, who was there in the garden while Jesus prayed. He was there when they arrested Jesus. We tend to think of Peter in the light of his later betrayal as cowardly or vacillating. John's Gospel indicates that it was he, of all the disciples, who was ready to take on this small army of professional soldiers and temple guards. He is the one who drew his sword and whacked off the ear of one of the high priest's servants. In a passion of anger, he is ready to fight and perhaps even to die to defend his Lord.

FEELINGS AND ACTIONS

54 Having arrested Him, they led Him and brought Him into the high priest's house. But Peter followed at a distance.
55 Now when they had kindled a fire in the midst of the courtyard and sat down together, Peter sat among them. 56 And a certain servant girl, seeing him as he sat by the fire, looked intently at him and said, "This man was also with Him."
57 But he denied Him, saying, "Woman, I do not know Him."
58 And after a little while another saw him and said, "You also are of them."

But Peter said, "Man, I am not!"
59 Then after about an hour had passed, another confidently affirmed, saying, "Surely this fellow also was with Him, for he is a Galilean."
60 But Peter said, "Man, I do not know what you are saying!"

Immediately, while he was still speaking, the rooster crowed. 61 And the Lord turned and looked at Peter. Then Peter remembered the word of the Lord, how He had said to him, "Before the rooster crows, you will deny Me three times."
62 So Peter went out and wept bitterly.

—Luke 22:54–62

In the light of Jesus' arrest, Peter must deal with his fear. First of all, he follows Jesus at a distance to the high priest's house. He settles in the courtyard to watch the proceedings. He is recognized by three different people as one of Jesus' followers, and each time, out of fear for his own life, he denies any connection with Jesus. With the crowing of the rooster, Jesus turns and looks at Peter. We can only imagine what that look might have conveyed—disappointment, love, sadness, forgiveness? Peter leaves immediately and weeps bitter tears of remorse.

All through these scenes, in the garden and in the courtyard, waves of feelings are engulfing not just Jesus and Peter, but all those involved. This brings us to the whole matter of feelings and how we deal with them. Feelings need not be destructive. They are fairly harmless if we understand what they are and where they come from. Take fear, for example. A small child learns a healthy fear for a hot stove, and that's a good thing. But if that same child, as a result of negative experiences, begins to be shy and self-conscious and afraid to relate, his fear is a deadly emotion.

Anger is both destructive and constructive. It can be a kind of neurotic emotion that comes from in-grown eyeballs. Nobody appreciates us, nobody notices us, nobody loves us enough. On the other hand, there is the anger that comes from righteous indignation; the strong abusing the weak, powerful nations indifferent to the plight of the Third World. That's a holy anger, and God help us if we don't experience some of that.

Sexual feelings in themselves are good and healthy, but they get perverted. Lust can be one of the most destructive forces in all of life. On the other hand, I know couples who are right now praying that God will rekindle some passionate, erotic love within their marriage that they may be one in the marvelous mystery of sex.

We tend to think of boredom as a negative feeling, and it is, if we think of it as being disinterested in the people and events around us. "I'm bored with this teacher or this friend I'm having dinner with because their concerns don't affect me." Well, maybe the fighting in Africa, the Orient, or the Middle East doesn't affect us, but God help us if we're bored with war and its consequences.

On the other hand, boredom can be creative. I was in Chicago recently speaking and I met a young man who is an attorney working for reconciliation between Arabs and Jews in Israel. He told me a little about the work going on there, and I asked him how he got into it. He said, "Actually, I started out in seminary, but I dropped out the first year. It was so boring." I confess I was sympathetic. I can't help thinking that if more people dropped out of seminary because they were bored, there'd be some changes in seminaries. If the study of the living God and His Word is boring, something needs to be changed. But this man's boredom catapulted him into an exciting and fulfilling career.

There are totally positive emotions of love, joy, excitement, enthusiasm—all gifts of God. The Greek words for enthusiasm are *en theos* meaning "God in you." The Greeks believed rightly that if you are enthusiastic about life, God is in you. If we turn that around, we would have to say that if you're not enthusiastic, God is *not* in you. The emotion of enthusiasm is a special gift of God for the living of life.

By contrast, there are those feelings that are only negative, among them resentment, jealousy, anxiety. A lot of anxiety is free-floating. We're not sure what we're anxious about. "Something bad is going to happen"—that unfocused feeling of anxiety can be very destructive. Or, perhaps it has a focus. I read about a man who went to see a psychiatrist about his anxiety. Asked to describe his problem, he said, "I am married, with two kids. My wife and I each have a car. We have a home in the city and one in the country." "That all sounds pretty good," responded the doctor. "What's the trouble?" "The trouble is that I earn ninety-five dollars a week." For most of us, anxiety can't be so neatly pinpointed. We feel vaguely worried most of the time for reasons we can't even explain.

From the biblical perspective, feelings are neither good nor bad. Feelings, constructive or destructive, are amoral. We have no control over them. We are not judged for our feelings but by our actions, which is how we behave prompted by our feelings. We can't avoid experiencing lust, jealousy, anxiety, or fear from time to time, any more than we can avoid feeling joy or excitement. The point is, what do we do with these feelings? The new psychiatry takes a different approach to all this from that of the clinical Freudians. Freud's goal was to get patients to feel better about themselves in order that they might perform better. The new thrust is to get you to change your behavior, and, in doing that, you begin to feel better about yourself. When you begin to act responsibly for yourself and be concerned for your neighbor, you are going to feel remarkably better in a short space of time.

Unfortunately, most of us deal in destructive ways with these amoral feelings over which we have no control. There are at least three ways that I can think of. First of all, we can give in to them or be dominated by them. This is the problem of the classic neurotic, who lives in great waves of joy or depression, dramatic ups and downs. When we are up we're productive and when we're down we vegetate. To let our feelings tell us what to do is a very sick way to live. It's the opposite of acting in love. Love makes commitments. Love makes covenants. Love is there whether it feels good or not.

Another destructive way of handling our feelings is to deny them, to refuse to admit we have any bad feelings. My mother taught me long ago that nice people don't have nasty feelings. But nice people *do* have nasty feelings. We all have both nasty feelings and good feelings. I began to understand this while counseling an old saint and prayer warrior in my first pastorate. She asked to see me about a problem. She was so elderly, I thought it might concern her will, or her funeral plans. Here's what she said: "I need to confess to someone. I'm madly in love with a man in our church, and he's not interested in me. I'm full of desire. I feel so guilty." I thought, "Good night, I didn't know elderly people had those feelings." Now that I'm older, I realize that feelings, good and bad, have nothing to do with age. We never graduate from experiencing them.

Somehow we have made a role model of the smiling, unruffled, ever-pleasant person in our midst. We assume that's the way to live life, never losing our cool. Well, that's not the way to live life. On the contrary, the healthy are those who are free to say, "This is a good day or this is a bad day," and to express genuine feeling. Christians hold up the victorious life, implying that if you really know the Lord, you'll never again have any negative feelings. I can't think of any biblical heroes who lived the victorious life. They were capable of anger, jealousy, fear, and lust.

The third way to deal with feelings is to try to control them by an effort of will. Unfortunately, it's been proven that when the imagination and the will are in conflict, the imagination wins every time. The will is not very strong. St. Anthony, one of the great saints of the past, went off in the desert to conquer the problem of lust. He later reported that the devil kept appearing to him in the form of a naked woman.

We have in this passage a biblical model for dealing with feelings. First of all, we can accept our feelings without guilt. When bad feelings come, we can ask God to help us not to act on them. Jesus felt anger at Judas. Jesus teaches us here to express our feelings in the company of others. Jesus brought the disciples with Him to Gethsemane and asked them to watch with Him. They saw His agony and His fear. They saw His anger. They saw His sweat as drops of blood on His forehead. They witnessed His humanity. He did not hide these emotions from them. They were witnesses to His suffering.

Yet it's so hard to let other people into our lives at this level. I was moved by the scene in Henry Kissinger's book on Mr. Nixon's last night in office. Kissinger says:

Nixon was not calm or businesslike, nor was he out of control. He was shattered. [This was his last night.] I found his visible agony more natural than the almost inhuman self-containment that I had known so well. To have striven so hard, to have molded a public personality out of so amorphous an identity, to have sustained that superhuman effort, only to end with every weakness disclosed and error compounding the downfall, that was a fate of biblical proportions.

After about half an hour in the Lincoln Room I returned to my White House office. Soon Nixon called. I must not remember our encounter that evening as a sign of weakness, he said. How strange is the illusion by which men sustain themselves! This evening when he had bared his soul I saw a man of tenacity and resilience. And so I told the stricken president if I ever spoke of the evening, it would be with respect. He had honored me by sharing with me his last free night in the White House. He had conducted himself humanly and worthily.

It's not surprising that Nixon apologized for his finest hour. Most of us have had, from childhood on, injunctions to stifle our emotions. Don't cry and don't laugh, we are told, and above all, don't show weakness.

Our emotions are an integral part of our humanity. Jesus was free to weep and to laugh, to feel good and to feel bad. Somehow, we must deal with our feelings by bringing them out in the open in the family of God. If we're going through a Gethsemane, we must feel free to cry. If we are guests at a wedding, we celebrate. We are to worship God with our total being, and that includes our feelings.

CHAPTER FORTY-FOUR—GOD AND MAN ON TRIAL

LUKE 22:63—23:24

Scripture Outline

> The Trials (22:63–71)
>
> Pilate's Dilemma (23:1–12)
>
> The People's Court (23:13–24)

THE TRIALS

63 Now the men who held Jesus mocked Him and beat Him. 64 And having blindfolded Him, they struck Him on the face and asked Him, saying, "Prophesy! Who is the one who struck You?" 65 And many other things they blasphemously spoke against Him.

66 As soon as it was day, the elders of the people, both chief priests and scribes, came together and led Him into their council, saying, 67 "If You are the Christ, tell us."

But He said to them, "If I tell you, you will by no means believe. 68 And if I also ask you, you will by no means answer Me or let Me go. 69 Hereafter the Son of Man will sit on the right hand of the power of God."

70 Then they all said, "Are You then the Son of God?"

So He said to them, "You rightly say that I am."

71 And they said, "What further testimony do we need? For we have heard it ourselves from His own mouth."

—*Luke 22:63–71*

Many years past the Watergate scandal, we are still trying to figure out what it all proved. We are trying to make sense out of the laws of the land. Is the law a friend or foe? Whimsical definitions of the law come from Charles Dickens's *Oliver Twist*. When Mr. Bumble is accused of mistreating the children in his orphanage, he claims that the fault was all his wife's. Told that the law holds him accountable for the actions of his wife, he is dumbfounded. "If the law does that," he responds, "then the law is an ass and the law is a bachelor."

We read in this passage the account of the most infamous trial in history. God Himself is on trial, not just in one court, but in three. First, Jesus is brought before the court of Jewish religious law, the Sanhedrin. Then He is tried according to Jewish secular law, represented by King Herod. Finally He comes before Pilate, the judge of Roman law.

The Sanhedrin tried Jesus twice, once at night, which was actually illegal, and again just at daybreak. When they ask if He is the Messiah, the Christ, the Son of God, He avoids the question and then says, "You said it." He is guilty by His own confession. He could have saved His life by denying who He was, but He tells them that it is true. Since they don't have the power to kill this man whom they have judged and who is upsetting their religious legalism, they bring Him before Pilate, the Roman ruler of the time.

They do not tell Pilate that He is guilty of blasphemy. A Roman judge would not consider blasphemy a crime. They have three other charges—that He is inciting the people to revolution, that He is urging them not to pay taxes—both outright lies—and, further, that He claims to be King of the Jews—which was true, but taken out of context. These are the charges they press before Pilate. Nevertheless, Pilate finds Him innocent and says so. Isn't it interesting that the secular court is the most just of the three?

Before Jesus ever gets to Pilate's court, He is mocked and beaten by those who are holding Him. We are told He was blindfolded and struck, and then asked to prophesy concerning which one had struck Him. We still try to play blindman's bluff with God, thinking He won't see what's going on. We sneak off and enjoy some secret sin and think God is blind or too busy to notice. Actually, God sees and knows it all and still loves us.

PILATE'S DILEMMA

23:1 Then the whole multitude of them arose and led Him to Pilate. 2 And they began to accuse Him, saying, "We found this fellow perverting the nation, and forbidding to pay taxes to Caesar, saying that He Himself is Christ, a King."

3 Then Pilate asked Him, saying, "Are You the King of the Jews?"

He answered him and said, "It is as you say."

⁴ So Pilate said to the chief priests and the crowd, "I find no fault in this Man."

⁵ But they were the more fierce, saying, "He stirs up the people, teaching throughout all Judea, beginning from Galilee to this place."

⁶ When Pilate heard of Galilee, he asked if the Man were a Galilean. ⁷ And as soon as he knew that He belonged to Herod's jurisdiction, he sent Him to Herod, who was also in Jerusalem at that time.

⁸ Now when Herod saw Jesus, he was exceedingly glad; for he had desired for a long time to see Him, because he had heard many things about Him, and he hoped to see some miracle done by Him. ⁹ Then he questioned Him with many words, but He answered him nothing. ¹⁰ And the chief priests and scribes stood and vehemently accused Him. ¹¹ Then Herod, with his men of war, treated Him with contempt and mocked Him, arrayed Him in a gorgeous robe, and sent Him back to Pilate. ¹² That very day Pilate and Herod became friends with each other, for previously they had been at enmity with each other.

—Luke 23:1–12

In Jesus' trial before Pilate, we find two different kinds of authority confronting each other. Pilate seems to understand something of who this Jesus really is. In an essay about Pilate's relationship with Christ, the famous preacher Francis Speakman describes Pilate reliving the trial and its subsequent results.

> I know that I was there, though it was mid-day and turned as black as the tunnels of hell in that miserable city. While I tried to compose Claudia, my wife, and explain how I'd been trapped, she railed at me with her dream. She has had the dream ever since when she sleeps in the dark. Deeper than the curse is the unfinished business with him.
>
> That, now and then, as I walk by the lake, He's following me. And much as that strikes terror, I wonder if that isn't the only hope. You see, if I could walk up to him and this time salute.

According to Francis Speakman, Pilate was astute enough to know that he was on trial, not Jesus. In some way, Jesus is in control of His own trial and Pilate seems to realize that.

Then, as we often do, he avoided a decision. He says, "Because He is a Galilean, I will pass Him on to King Herod. Let the Jewish ruler deal with Him." This is the same Herod who beheaded John the Baptist. A wanton, a rake, a contemptible man, he was known as "Herod the Fox." Today "fox" is a synonym for "sly." In those days, however, in rabbinical terms, "fox" meant "worthless." Herod was a king of no value. The pleasure-mad Herod is glad to see Jesus. He has heard about His miracles and hopes He can perform some tricks for him. Jesus does not comply, and so He is of no further use. Herod sends Him back to Pilate.

For the second time then Pilate finds Jesus innocent. The Roman law finds Jesus innocent, but the Sanhedrin, the religious group, insist He must be killed. They had their own ideas about serving God and Jesus was undermining their influence with the people. He must be killed. Pilate stalls for time. He suggests a scourging, which meant being beaten with leather thongs that were woven with pieces of bone and iron. Prisoners sometimes died of scourging, and all those who were to be crucified were scourged first. It was illegal to scourge an innocent person, but Pilate is appeasing the Sanhedrin. By meting out a little punishment, they may be satisfied. They are not.

THE PEOPLE'S COURT

13 Then Pilate, when he had called together the chief priests, the rulers, and the people, 14 said to them, "You have brought this Man to me, as one who misleads the people. And indeed, having examined Him in your presence, I have found no fault in this Man concerning those things of which you accuse Him; 15 no, neither did Herod, for I sent you back to him; and indeed nothing deserving of death has been done by Him. 16 I will therefore chastise Him and release Him" 17 (for it was necessary for him to release one to them at the feast).

18 And they all cried out at once, saying, "Away with this Man, and release to us Barabbas"— 19 who had been thrown into prison for a certain rebellion made in the city, and for murder.

20 Pilate, therefore, wishing to release Jesus, again called out to them. 21 But they shouted, saying, "Crucify Him, crucify Him!"

22 Then he said to them the third time, "Why, what evil has He done? I have found no reason for death in Him. I will therefore chastise Him and let Him go."

332

23 But they were insistent, demanding with loud voices that He be crucified. And the voices of these men and of the chief priests prevailed. 24 So Pilate gave sentence that it should be as they requested.

—Luke 23:13–24

By the time these three trials have taken place, the people from whom the Sanhedrin have tried to keep the news of the trial have gathered. Pilate makes a final effort to save Jesus. He pronounces Him not guilty and offers to release Him. The crowd, which just days before had hailed Jesus as king, clamor instead for the release of Barabbas, the murderer and terrorist. From their perspective Jesus had failed them. They had loved Him for a while. They thought He would help them throw off the Roman yoke, but they had become disillusioned. He was of no further value. They still had hope that this man, Barabbas, might do the job—organize an underground army and throw the rascals out.

You might say there were four trials, the last before a people's court. Jesus was condemned by this court as well. Barabbas represented violence and nationalism, while Jesus models humility and love. In Jesus' time and today, the law is a mirror of our own desires. It is not absolute. Our present court system reflects our values. Justice, or the lack of it, depends on how the law is interpreted and administered. The law is not universally fair. (We hear often that there are no rich people on death row and, in fact, very few white people.) The Sanhedrin didn't want justice. They wanted the sanction of the law in disposing of a troublemaker.

It is not hard to identify with any of the principals in these four trials. The Sanhedrin thought they were acting for the good of the nation. Pilate tried to do the right thing, but was pressured by outside circumstances. The soldiers were doing their duty, as every Nazi in the Nuremberg war trials claimed to be. They were merely following orders. We cannot even condemn the crowd. In their concern for their country, they were willing to exchange Jesus for one who might deliver them from their oppressors. We might say they are all innocent. In another sense, they are all guilty. However worthy our motives, there is not an innocent person among us. If we are to be judged by the law, we will be found wanting.

A tourist stood in front of the Mona Lisa at the Louvre in Paris. After examining the painting for a long time, he was heard to remark, "I don't see anything so great about that." The nearby guard was prompted to reply, "Sir, that painting is not on trial. Your taste is." The painting has withstood the test of time. In the same sense, as our lives are held up to the law—the law of that time or this time—God's law or man's law—we find ourselves judged. We begin to see who we are and what we are. The bad news is that in this life there are no innocent people. We are all guilty of sins of omission and commission.

There are two great struggles taking place in this account of Jesus' trials. There is the struggle between Jesus and His accusers—Pilate, the Sanhedrin, Herod, and the people. But the deeper struggle is between principalities and powers. All the primordial forces come together here as God and Satan act out this drama on this puny stage called earth. Ultimately God wins the struggle through the Resurrection. God in His greatness takes Satan's every evil ploy and weaves it into a scenario of His own purpose. The greatness of God is that He can use even evil to accomplish His purposes.

You may have discovered this in your own life. I was really shocked to realize a few years ago that I have been blessed as much by my enemies as I have been by my friends. I have been blessed extravagantly through loyal friends, but some of the best things in my life have happened because of people who did not wish me well and who were, nevertheless, God's instruments. When you and I become part of God's purpose, He can take all of the pain and failure and weave it into His master design for our lives.

This is an awesome account we read here of God Himself on trial, and in reading it we are on trial as well. Jesus is saying here that nothing we can do can make Him stop loving us—not four unfair trials, not scourging, not false witness, not humiliation, not even the Cross. He is the ultimate model for love. In his book *The Problem of Pain*, C. S. Lewis discusses this love God has for us.

> When Christianity says that God loves man it means that God loves man. We are the objects of His love. You asked for a loving God, you have one. The great Spirit you so lightly invoked, the lord of terrible aspect, is present. Not a senile benevolence that drowsily wishes you to be happy in your own way. Not the cold philanthropy of a conscientious magistrate, or the care of a host who feels responsible for the comfort of his guests, but the consuming fire Himself, that love that made the worlds, persistent as the artist's love for his work, and despotic as a man's love for a dog. Provident and venerable as a father's love for a

334

child, jealous, inexorable, exacting as love between the sexes. How this should be I do not know. It passes reason to explain why any creature, not to say creatures such as we, should have a value so prodigious in the Creator's eye.

What then can we say? We are guilty. Law, then and now—any law we choose—reveals our guilt. I was in Texas recently and heard a remarkable story from a companion at lunch. He said, "Two years ago, a neighbor of mine became so upset with the state of the world that he decided to get away from it all, from the threat of nuclear holocaust and World War III. He spent a whole year researching the safest place to live, and one year ago he moved his family to the Falkland Islands." In the spring of 1982, those pastoral islands were the scene of a brief but bloody war between England and Argentina.

The point is, there is no hiding place—not from the law, which finds you guilty, and not from the grace of God. If we demand justice we're done for. What we need is grace. And that is what God is offering to us today and forever—His grace.

CHAPTER FORTY-FIVE—THE CROWD
AROUND THE CROSS

LUKE 23:25–56

Scripture Outline

> The Drafting of Simon (23:25–26)
>
> Saving Our Tears (23:27–31)
>
> Unexpected Responses (23:32–43)
>
> A Symbolic Phenomenon (23:44–49)
>
> An Act of Courage (23:50–56)

THE DRAFTING OF SIMON

25 And he released to them the one they requested, who for rebellion and murder had been thrown into prison; but he delivered Jesus to their will.

26 Now as they led Him away, they laid hold of a certain man, Simon a Cyrenian, who was coming from the country, and on him they laid the cross that he might bear it after Jesus.

—Luke 23:25–26

Jesus' crucifixion was a public event. It is one of the most well-attested facts in all history. Jesus was crucified and everyone was there. Even the sign over the cross was written in the three important languages of the time. Pilate was convinced of Jesus' innocence, but the Sanhedrin insisted on His death. They were outraged chiefly because of His claim to be King of the Jews. As if to spite them, Pilate put up the sign proclaiming to all "King of the Jews." The sign was in Latin, the language of government; in Greek, the language of education; and in Hebrew, the language of religion.

Crucifixion was invented by the Carthaginians and adopted by the Romans. It was the most horrible manner of execution ever devised and it was used only for the lowest type of criminal. Death comes not from loss of blood, but from exhaustion. The victim hangs immobile until all energy is drained. It's amazing to me that not one of the four Gospels report any details of Jesus' sufferings, almost as if they were avoiding any cheap melodrama. They simply say, "They crucified Him."

Luke the physician, my favorite of the four Gospel writers, gives us no theology of the Cross. The other writers interpret what it means. No Gospel writer mentions the Cross more often all through his account than does Luke, but he doesn't tell us what it means. In my own writing, one of the hardest things I have had to learn is not to explain a story or an illustration. My editors, including my wife, tell me that if the story needs explanation, then it's not a good story. Luke describes the Crucifixion for us, and if we can't see what it means, an explanation won't help.

In the crowd around the Cross we find the whole world in microcosm. You and I and our ancestors are all there someplace. But, let's examine some of the people in the crowd whom the Scripture mentions. First of all, there is Simon the Cyrenian, who, through happenstance, is tapped by the soldiers to carry Jesus' cross. Jesus is exhausted from scourging and from being up all night praying in the Garden. So this man from the crowd is drafted. This is not what "taking up your cross" is all about. He did not choose to relieve Jesus.

We don't know any more about Simon the Cyrenian. I like to speculate on what he might have said to his family that night. "Guess what happened? I had the most rotten luck today. I was interrupted as I was going through town on business. The soldiers made me carry a cross for some criminal. I was humiliated." He might have said that. Or, he might have understood that through that interruption, God gave him an opportunity to serve Him and to be remembered by believers for centuries afterward. He might have gone home thrilled. "Guess what? I carried the Cross of the Son of God."

SAVING OUR TEARS

27 And a great multitude of the people followed Him, and women who also mourned and lamented Him. 28 But Jesus, turning to them, said, "Daughters of Jerusalem, do not weep for Me, but weep for yourselves and for your children. 29 For indeed the days are coming in which they will say, 'Blessed are the barren, wombs that never bore, and breasts which never nursed!' 30 Then they will begin 'to say to the mountains, "Fall

on us!" and to the hills, "Cover us!" ' [31]For if they do these things in the green wood, what will be done in the dry?"

—*Luke 23:27–31*

Next, we find the women of Jerusalem, not Jesus' women friends from Galilee who traveled with Him, but the women of the city, who were wailing after Him, saying, "Poor Jesus!" His reply must have shocked them. Remember that to the Jew, children were a sign of blessing. Jesus is saying that the day will come when barren women will be the blessed ones because their children will not suffer the horror that is coming. He seems to be saying, "Ladies, don't give me your sympathy. Save your feelings for yourselves. What I want from you is repentance. Your tears for Me will not save you."

Tolstoy tells a story about prerevolutionary Russia in which a wealthy lady is attending the opera in midwinter while her coachman waits outside. While she is weeping over the death of the heroine on stage, her coachman freezes to death. We can shed sentimental tears over the unreal and remain untouched by the genuine suffering all around us.

UNEXPECTED RESPONSES

[32] There were also two others, criminals, led with Him to be put to death. [33] And when they had come to the place called Calvary, there they crucified Him, and the criminals, one on the right hand and the other on the left. [34] Then Jesus said, "Father, forgive them, for they do not know what they do."

And they divided His garments and cast lots. [35] And the people stood looking on. But even the rulers with them sneered, saying, "He saved others; let Him save Himself if He is the Christ, the chosen of God."

[36] The soldiers also mocked Him, coming and offering Him sour wine, [37] and saying, "If You are the King of the Jews, save Yourself."

[38] And an inscription also was written over Him in letters of Greek, Latin, and Hebrew:

THIS IS THE KING OF THE JEWS.

[39] Then one of the criminals who were hanged blasphemed Him, saying, "If You are the Christ, save Yourself and us."

[40] But the other, answering, rebuked him, saying, "Do you not even fear God, seeing you are under the same condemnation? [41] And we indeed justly, for we receive the due

reward of our deeds; but this Man has done nothing wrong."
42 Then he said to Jesus, "Lord, remember me when You come into Your kingdom."

43 And Jesus said to him, "Assuredly, I say to you, today you will be with Me in Paradise."

—Luke 23:32–43

Next, the narrative moves on to the two thieves. Only Luke tells us about the women and only Luke tells us about the two thieves. Both have sinned and have been rightfully judged. But one repents while the other doesn't. Our sin is not what keeps us from God. Our problem is our inability to respond to the love of God and to repent and change. Only one of the thieves did that.

Then there are the spectators, those in the crowd who are uninvolved and curious. Sometimes people come to church for the first time like that. They may be dragged there by a friend or parent. They come unwilling and curious. It's okay to come that way, but then what? As for the crowd around the Cross, it doesn't matter how they have come. They are now in the presence of the Nazarene on the Cross. If they walk away uninvolved, they are judged.

A SYMBOLIC PHENOMENON

44 Now it was about the sixth hour, and there was darkness over all the earth until the ninth hour. 45 Then the sun was darkened, and the veil of the temple was torn in two.
46 And when Jesus had cried out with a loud voice, He said, "Father, 'into Your hands I commit My spirit.'" Having said this, He breathed His last.

47 So when the centurion saw what had happened, he glorified God, saying, "Certainly this was a righteous Man!"

48 And the whole crowd who came together to that sight, seeing what had been done, beat their breasts and returned.
49 But all His acquaintances, and the women who followed Him from Galilee, stood at a distance, watching these things.

—Luke 23:44–49

The executioners were there, the soldiers who actually carried out the execution of our Lord. Jesus prayed for them. He did not consider them hopeless. How they responded to His forgiveness was their problem. The religious traditionalists were there, those who wanted to keep everything just as it always had been. When

Jesus was crucified, the veil in the temple was torn asunder. The veil was that great curtain that covered the inner holy altar. The Jews considered God so unapproachable that even a priest went in only once a year. A rope was tied around his ankle so that if he had a heart attack he could be pulled out. No one would dare to go in after him. If, standing in God's presence, he dropped dead, he could be pulled out by the rope. The Jews wrote God's name with its four consonants, JHWH, but in their awe of Him they dared not speak it. All of that changed when the veil of the temple was rent. It is symbolic of the availability of God who is our Father. We can say, "Daddy, help." The traditionalists couldn't accept that kind of intimacy with God.

AN ACT OF COURAGE

50 Now behold, there was a man named Joseph, a council member, a good and just man. 51 He had not consented to their decision and deed. He was from Arimathea, a city of the Jews, who himself was also waiting for the kingdom of God. 52 This man went to Pilate and asked for the body of Jesus. 53 Then he took it down, wrapped it in linen, and laid it in a tomb that was hewn out of the rock, where no one had ever lain before. 54 That day was the Preparation, and the Sabbath drew near.

55 And the women who had come with Him from Galilee followed after, and they observed the tomb and how His body was laid.

56 Then they returned and prepared spices and fragrant oils. And they rested on the Sabbath according to the commandment.

—Luke 23:50–56

Finally, Joseph of Arimathea was there. His attitude was one of hopeless hope. That may seem a paradox, but if you have a solid basis for your hope, it isn't really hope. Joseph must have felt he had failed Jesus. The Sanhedrin took a unanimous vote to crucify Jesus, and he belonged to the Sanhedrin. Either he abstained from voting or he wasn't there. Now it was too late. It was a lost cause. In a burst of love and courage, Joseph stood up before his peers and said, "Give me His body." The disciples didn't ask for the body. Neither did the women in His company.

Dante says the hottest places in hell are reserved for those who in a period of moral crisis maintain their neutrality. Robert Kennedy said, "Few men are willing to brave the disapproval of their fellows, the censure of their colleagues, the wrath of their society. Moral courage is a rarer commodity than bravery in battle or great intelligence, yet it is the one essential, vital quality for those who seek to change the world, which yields most painfully to change. I believe that in this generation those with the courage to enter the moral conflict will find themselves with companions in every corner of the world." Joseph of Arimathea demonstrated his moral courage. He took down the body of Jesus and put Him in a virgin hewn-out-of-the-rock tomb which only the wealthy could afford. Jesus was given a glorious burial. It was as though God was indicating that the days of humiliation were over. This was the beginning of the glory of the Lord. Joseph bet on a lost cause, Jesus, and three days later Jesus was alive saying, "Joseph, the kingdom is here."

You and I are in all those people around the Cross. I can find myself in each one. Perhaps most of all, I would like to be like Joseph of Arimathea who bet on a hopeless cause because of his love for Jesus.

CHAPTER FORTY-SIX—THE EASTER EXPERIENCE

LUKE 24:1–12

24:1 Now on the first day of the week, very early in the morning, they, and certain other women with them, came to the tomb bringing the spices which they had prepared. 2 But they found the stone rolled away from the tomb. 3 Then they went in and did not find the body of the Lord Jesus. 4 And it happened, as they were greatly perplexed about this, that behold, two men stood by them in shining garments. 5 Then, as they were afraid and bowed their faces to the earth, they said to them, "Why do you seek the living among the dead? 6 He is not here, but is risen! Remember how He spoke to you when He was still in Galilee, 7 saying, 'The Son of Man must be delivered into the hands of sinful men, and be crucified, and the third day rise again.'"

8 And they remembered His words. 9 Then they returned from the tomb and told all these things to the eleven and to all the rest. 10 It was Mary Magdalene, Joanna, Mary the mother of James, and the other women with them, who told these things to the apostles. 11 And their words seemed to them like idle tales, and they did not believe them. 12 But Peter arose and ran to the tomb; and stooping down, he saw the linen cloths lying by themselves; and he departed, marveling to himself at what had happened.

—Luke 24:1–12

If you have difficulty believing the Easter story, it's understandable. It is so incredible that we ought to have difficulty with it. The Easter story has nothing to do with springtime. We have heard many sermons over the years about putting a bulb in the ground in the fall and then waiting all through the snows of winter until spring's warmth brings that bulb to life. That's a principle of nature, but it's not what Easter is about. We are asked to believe that someone dead and decomposing for three days became alive again. If initially you are a skeptic or a cynic, you have good reason to be. You understand the issues.

Let's examine that first Easter experience. First of all, the women were the first to learn about the Resurrection. How remarkable that in a time when women were less than second-class citizens, the first people to whom Jesus' Resurrection was revealed were faithful and devout women. They came to the cemetery to embalm Him. They came without hope, resigned to His death. The terror of Good Friday was over. The grief of Saturday was still with them and they came mourning, to prepare His body for the long journey into decomposition. They came with no faith that anything would change.

There is a whimsical story about a town suffering a serious drought. It was in farm country and the crops were being ruined. The local preacher decided to hold a prayer meeting to ask God to send rain. He asked all those who believed in God's power to do so to join him at four o'clock in the church. When the hour came, the church was almost filled. But when the preacher got up and looked around, he said, "This meeting is called off. We don't have the faith to pray. I don't see a single umbrella here."

Coming into the cemetery, with no faith and no expectations, the women were met by two angels. They first of all asked the women what they were doing in a cemetery. *"Why do you seek the living among the dead?"* (v. 5). Next, the angels reminded the women of Jesus' own prophecy that on the third day He would be raised from the dead. Hearing this, the women rushed off to tell the apostles. Wonder of wonders, these women, the most faithful and reliable of witnesses, were not believed. The apostles, those who had spent three years intimately with Jesus, who had trusted their lives to Him, simply dismissed the witness of the women. *"Their words seemed to them like idle tales"* (v. 11).

In some ways we can understand their reaction. No words could communicate this most awesome mystery in cosmic history—that one totally dead was now alive. It's not surprising that the apostles did not believe the women's tales. Those of us who are by nature cynical or skeptical have been in that spot. That puts us in the apostolic tradition. The apostles had to experience for themselves Jesus' Resurrection.

The chapter ends with Jesus' appearance in resurrection form to all eleven disciples. Judas had already hanged himself since he could not believe that forgiveness was possible. God is not saying that if we don't believe it's our tough luck. He honors our unbelief. He is saying through these verses that it is all right to test

Him. He wants our faith in Him to be based on an experience of the Resurrection.

I would suggest that we can test that resurrection experience in three important areas of our lives—our past, our present, and our future. If you are having difficulty in believing in the Resurrection, I suggest you ask the Lord to prove Himself in one of these three areas, whichever one represents your own growing edge right now.

Let's begin with the past. We go to the cemetery of our past to look for the Lord of the living. Let's remember Jesus' promise, "If the Son makes you free, you shall be free indeed" (John 8:36). The past can be described as the "if onlys" of our lives. The past is gone and we cannot retrieve it, but much comes out of that past to haunt us. *If only* I had had parents that loved me more. *If only* I had studied harder and made more of my life. *If only* I had chosen a different career. *If only* I had married that other person. *If only* I hadn't married. *If only* my children had not disappointed me. *If only* I had children. *If only* my child had lived. We may want to have a resurrection experience over past addictions—alcohol, drugs, self-pity, fear, destructive attitudes. We can leave those "if onlys" in the cemetery and ask the risen Lord to set us free from those crippling memories.

Or, we can experience the power of the Resurrection in our present. How do we become those people who are extravagant lovers in the world, in our families, with friends? Jesus has given us the commandment to "love one another as I have loved you" (John 13:34). He gave Himself to us. He was vulnerable. He risked with us. He identified with us. He loved us through our failures. We all want to be channels of that kind of love.

A cartoon in *The New Yorker* magazine a while back showed a middle-aged couple in a new car showroom. The husband is examining a car greedily, with a demonic sort of smile. His wife, with arms folded, is saying, "Well, Henry, if buying a front-wheel drive did not make you a better person, what makes you think buying a four-wheel drive will make you a better person?" We're all looking for some way to be a better person. We can test the risen Lord in this area and claim His resurrection power to love those around us right now in the present.

We can claim that power for the future as well. The people of God are those who will dream dreams and see visions. That is the prophecy at Pentecost. God wants to give us His dream for our personal lives and for society. I am on the board of the Union Gospel Mission in Seattle, founded by a young man from Minnesota who was given a dream by God fifty years ago. He came here during the depression years and began a work to feed the hungry, to house the homeless, to help the alcoholic and the lonely. He had no resources except his dreams. His dream is still going on. Every year the Union Gospel Mission provides tens of thousands of meals and beds and caring for needy men and women. God has a dream for you as well. Twenty-five or fifty years from now, other people may be walking around in your dream.

Faith, then, is not believing the unbelievable; faith is risking your life on the unspeakable goodness of God. We can ask Him to give us an experience of the Resurrection for the first time or the one-hundredth time. We need not believe the idle tales of the others who tell us about it. That wasn't good enough for the apostles. We can challenge Jesus to prove who He is in setting us free from the past, teaching us to live and love in the present, and giving us His dream for the future.

CHAPTER FORTY-SEVEN—THE HIDDEN FACTOR

LUKE 24:13–35

Scripture Outline

A Life-Changing Walk (24:13–24)

Recognizing Jesus (24:25–27)

Experiencing Community (24:28–35)

A LIFE-CHANGING WALK

13 Now behold, two of them were traveling that same day to a village called Emmaus, which was seven miles from Jerusalem. 14 And they talked together of all these things which had happened. 15 So it was, while they conversed and reasoned, that Jesus Himself drew near and went with them. 16 But their eyes were restrained, so that they did not know Him.

17 And He said to them, "What kind of conversation *is* this that you have with one another as you walk and are sad?"

18 Then the one whose name was Cleopas answered and said to Him, "Are You the only stranger in Jerusalem, and have You not known the things which happened there in these days?"

19 And He said to them, "What things?"

So they said to Him, "The things concerning Jesus of Nazareth, who was a Prophet mighty in deed and word before God and all the people, 20 and how the chief priests and our rulers delivered Him to be condemned to death, and crucified Him. 21 But we were hoping that it was He who was going to redeem Israel. Indeed, besides all this, today is the third day since these things happened. 22 Yes, and certain women of our company, who arrived at the tomb early, astonished us. 23 When they did not find His body, they came saying that they had also seen a vision of angels who said He was alive. 24 And certain of those *who were* with us went to the tomb and found *it* just as the women had said; but Him they did not see."

—Luke 24:13–24

Most kids are intrigued by the idea of supernatural powers. I think that explains the popularity of such characters as Superman, Wonder Woman, and Spiderman. Children have an innate desire to know secrets and to tap into something beyond the ordinary. Certainly I was that kind of a kid. I was the first in my block to send for Orphan Annie's secret decoder ring. I would decode the secret message and know before anyone else what was going to happen to Joe Corntassel and Annie.

Even as adults, we want to believe there is some hidden factor in life we can tap into and fulfill our destiny. We are fascinated by the idea of extrasensory perception, or ESP, of somehow communicating mysteriously across miles. My father had such an experience a few years before he died. One night he dreamed repeatedly that he was with his favorite sister whom he had not seen in fifty years and who lived in Sweden. All night long he visited with her in his dreams, half awake and half asleep. We learned much later that she had died that very night and called for him. That was enough to convince him of the reality of extrasensory perception.

On the subject of ESP, I heard about a man who asked his wife to balance the checkbook. He came home that night to find she had four neatly typed pages, detailing all the expenses of the past months—the milkman, the cleaners, the grocery store, and many others. One entry read, "ESP $24.21." "What does that mean?" he asked. "Error Some Place," she explained.

I think most of us have this hope that there's somebody out there—a force, a power—trying to get through to us to improve our life. The last place most of us thought of finding that mysterious power was in the Christian faith. Church often seems dull. Christianity may be true, but sometimes it doesn't seem very exciting. That's because we've left out the hidden factor of the Christian faith: that the most powerful force in the universe is present with us.

This is the message of the Emmaus Road story. We are told that five hundred believers saw the risen Christ, but this story is perhaps the most dramatic of all Jesus' post-resurrection appearances. Two believers were walking home to Emmaus after that first Easter Sunday, a trip of about seven miles in a northwesterly direction out of Jerusalem. Since Emmaus is not there now we can only guess at its exact location. The two people might have been a man and a woman. A masculine noun is used in the Greek, but the word could refer to a couple. Since they shared a home, there is speculation that it was Cleophas and his wife. A third person joins them who turns out to be the risen Christ. Again, it is Jesus who takes the initiative; He joins them. When they tell Him the story of Jesus' death and Resurrection, He explains the scriptural basis for all these events and rebukes them for their slowness of heart. Later on in their home, they discover who He is when He takes bread, blesses it, and breaks it.

The events of Easter cannot be reduced to a creed or philosophy. We are not asked to believe the doctrine of the Resurrection. We are asked to meet this person raised from the dead. In faith, we move from belief in a doctrine to knowledge of a person. Ultimate truth is a person. We can say as these two believers did, "We met Him; He is alive."

In His Resurrection, Jesus moves our faith to the present tense, as over against the past tense. The two walking along the road recite the past events. They say, "We *had* hoped." But Jesus Himself is there in the present tense. Many of us have been blessed by reading Charles Sheldon's book *In His Steps*. It is the story of a church transformed when people begin to ask, "What would Jesus do? I want to do what He would do if He were here." It's an interesting question, but it is theologically inaccurate. The question is not "What would Jesus do *if* He were here?" He *is* here. He is the hidden factor in life, the most powerful force in life. The real question is "What are You doing, Jesus? And how can I be part of it?" The King is with us, the constant in the equation of life.

RECOGNIZING JESUS

25 Then He said to them, "O foolish ones, and slow of heart to believe in all that the prophets have spoken! 26 Ought not the Christ to have suffered these things and to enter into His glory?" 27 And beginning at Moses and all the Prophets, He expounded to them in all the Scriptures the things concerning Himself.

—Luke 24:25–27

How do we recognize that ultimate Person as we travel our own Emmaus Road? These verses give us some excellent clues. First, we recognize Him by knowing the Bible. Jesus spoke from the Scriptures to these two travelers. He traced back through the Scriptures all the Old Testament prophecies about the Messiah. He explained that all those recent events were meant to happen in order that God might redeem His world. Psalm 22 is just one example of the cohesive message of the Old and New Testaments.

It describes the Crucifixion in great detail. The Old Testament foreshadows and points to the coming of Jesus and His earthly life.

But it needs to be said that there is a difference between studying Scripture and spending time with the Author. As we study Scripture, we have the privilege of having access to the Author of the Book. God Himself is with us through the Holy Spirit as we read. We can ask Him to give us wisdom and insight about portions that are puzzling. The purpose of Scripture is to point to the Author, who is Father, Son, and Holy Spirit.

John Wesley had his own Emmaus Road experience through the hearing of Scripture. Here's how he describes it. "I went very unwillingly to a society in Aldersgate Street where one was reading Luther's preface to the Epistle to the Romans. About a quarter before nine, while he was describing the change which God works in the heart through faith in Christ, I felt my heart strangely warmed. I felt I did trust in Christ, Christ alone, for salvation, and an assurance was given me that He had taken away my sins—even mine—and saved me from the law of sin and death." The words Wesley heard were three times removed. The speaker was reading Luther's commentary on Paul's Epistle to the Romans. Yet Jesus was there. The Scriptures all point to the One who is our companion on the Emmaus Road.

EXPERIENCING COMMUNITY

28 Then they drew near to the village where they were going, and He indicated that He would have gone farther.
29 But they constrained Him, saying, "Abide with us, for it is toward evening, and the day is far spent." And He went in to stay with them.
30 Now it came to pass, as He sat at the table with them, that He took bread, blessed and broke it, and gave it to them.
31 Then their eyes were opened and they knew Him; and He vanished from their sight.
32 And they said to one another, "Did not our heart burn within us while He talked with us on the road, and while He opened the Scriptures to us?"
33 So they rose up that very hour and returned to Jerusalem, and found the eleven and those who were with them gathered together, 34 saying, "The Lord is risen indeed, and has appeared to Simon!" 35 And they told about the things

that had happened on the road, and how He was known to them in the breaking of bread.

—Luke 24:28–35

Second, as Jesus appeared to these two travelers, fellowship resulted. We have Jesus' promise that where two or three are gathered together in His name, there He is in the midst. So far as I know, none of Jesus' post-resurrection appearances were to just one person. He appeared to twos and threes and twelves. Certainly Jesus is able to manifest Himself to us all alone. But it happens more normally among believers who share their faith and who break bread together. The breaking of bread together is a most intimate act. Believers sitting around the table and sharing food to sustain life, experience an unusual sense of community.

Third, if we are to recognize the ultimate person on our own Emmaus Road we need a heightened awareness. We need to have a sense of expectancy day by day that Jesus will reveal Himself to us. Expect the unexpected. Psychologists are telling us now that we don't believe what we see; we see what we believe. That's how the mind works. We see what we expect to see. As we expect God to reveal Himself to us in Jesus, we'll see Him, for He truly is there. When Jesus rebukes the two travelers, He tells them the trouble is in their hearts, not in their understanding. The Scriptures have prepared them for all that has happened and when their hearts are right they will understand it all.

Things happen when we begin to expect God to show Himself to us. One of my parishioners recently had an experience of this heightened awareness we are speaking of, and she wrote me about it. Incidentally, she is about as unspooky a person as I know. "I had the most extraordinary experience last night. It was an experience of the presence of Jesus that was more real than anything happening around me. I had the TV blaring the news, my dinner bubbling away on the stove, and the dishwasher running, and sat down weary, and in a bit of an anxiety state. I silently raised my thoughts to the Lord in deep need of His peace and the most incredible thing happened. In the midst of all the familiar household noises came this overwhelming awareness of Jesus' presence beside me. He was there, so loving, so comforting, and most of all, so majestic in strength. All I could do was confess my sinfulness and adore Him. I'm still living in the afterglow today and trying to understand why this experience was given to me at this most unexpected time. I wonder if I'm going to need to remember that presence soon for some reason. Then I think nothing that beautiful and peaceful and strong and compelling could be anything but God's good gift."

That Emmaus Road experience did prepare my friend for some very sad experiences over the next few months. I don't question at all why this happened to her. Rather, why aren't these experiences a frequent and normal part of life? Perhaps they would be if our sense of expectancy were heightened.

Finally, the two travelers made time for Jesus. He appeared to be going farther, but *"they constrained Him"* (v. 29). And so He came in and stayed with them. The implication is that had they not made time for Him, He would have gone on. He did not intrude. They had to press Him: "Please come in. It's late. Don't go on. We want you to eat with us." As soon as He broke the bread, their eyes were opened and they knew who it was. They ran back that very night to Jerusalem to tell the eleven. Jesus says in Revelation 3:20: "Behold, I stand at the door and knock. If anyone hears My voice and opens the door, I will come in." We must constrain Him to come in. I suggest taking time every day, five minutes or fifteen minutes, just to say, "Lord, I'm setting this time aside. I constrain You to come in and spend time with me." If we don't, He goes on without bothering us, for He does not intrude.

In every situation in life, remember you have the ultimate source of power and love with you on your Emmaus Road. That is bound to make a difference in every circumstance, wherever you are. We read in Numbers 21:9 that when the Israelites were in danger from poisonous serpents, Moses, by God's command, raised up in their midst a bronze serpent on a pole. If they were bitten, they were to look up at this bronze serpent and remember God's presence with them and they would survive. They were to look up and live, and they did. We have something better than a bronze serpent, though that was a forerunner of Christ: the Healer Himself is among us. He is with us on our journey—our Emmaus Road. He goes before and with us. He says to us, "Look up and live."

CHAPTER FORTY-EIGHT—PROOF POSITIVE
LUKE 24:36–53

Scripture Outline

> The Evidence (24:36–43)
>
> The Commission (24:44–53)

THE EVIDENCE

³⁶ Now as they said these things, Jesus Himself stood in the midst of them, and said to them, "Peace to you." ³⁷ But they were terrified and frightened, and supposed they had seen a spirit. ³⁸ And He said to them, "Why are you troubled? And why do doubts arise in your hearts? ³⁹ Behold My hands and My feet, that it is I Myself. Handle Me and see, for a spirit does not have flesh and bones as you see I have."

⁴⁰ When He had said this, He showed them His hands and His feet. ⁴¹ But while they still did not believe for joy, and marveled, He said to them, "Have you any food here?" ⁴² So they gave Him a piece of a broiled fish and some honeycomb. ⁴³ And He took *it* and ate in their presence.

—Luke 24:36–43

The belief in the Resurrection of Jesus from the dead separates Christianity from all other religions. No other religion claims that its leader and founder was bodily raised from the dead and that his spirit is now present with those who worship and serve him. Belief is harder for some than others. A psychiatrist friend has helped me to understand something about why this might be. He said that we are programmed genetically to believe or to doubt. Some of us have inherited great "faith genes" while others are doubting Thomases. Beyond the genetic, I'd say a psychogenetic factor is involved. If you are surrounded by family members or friends for whom belief is easy, you absorb something of that. If you are exposed primarily to skeptics, you tend to become a skeptic. Most of us bring our genetic and psychogenetic faith, or lack of them, to this fact of the Resurrection.

But beyond believing facts, I believe there is an existential dimension of faith. You may have heard the story about the man who was mountain climbing all alone when he began to fall. Just as he was about to plunge down a thousand-foot ravine, he managed to grab a bush. He was not a believer, but the situation turned him into one. Looking up to heaven, he cried out, "Is there anybody up there who can help me?" By some miracle, a heavenly voice answered. "Yes, I can help you. But first let go of the bush." Hanging on desperately, he called again, "Is there anybody else up there who can help me?" A good many of us turn into believers in the crucible of the existential moment.

I would suggest that there is far more evidence for believing that Jesus was raised from the dead than for not doing so. First of all, there is no logical reason why any of the principals in the Gospel narrative would steal the body. How the Pharisees, faced with this great spiritual awakening that threatened Judaism, would have loved to produce the corpse and give the lie to the Resurrection rumor. They could not. Surely the soldiers were held accountable for the disappearance of the body they were guarding. You can be certain that leaves were canceled, promotions denied. They may have been imprisoned or killed for their negligence. The soldiers would be extremely eager to produce the body.

It's inconceivable that the disciples might have stolen the body. They were a broken, defeated, demoralized group after the Crucifixion. With the appearance of the risen Christ they were filled with a holy boldness which endured for the rest of their lives. If the Resurrection was a myth, there is no way to explain psychologically the actions of the early Christians—some of whom were crucified or fed to lions as a result of their faith. The evidence is overwhelming that something supernatural occurred.

Luke insists on a bodily resurrection. He describes with great accuracy the scene where Jesus stands in the midst of the eleven and says, "*Handle Me and see, for a spirit does not have flesh and bones as you see I have*" (v. 39). The risen Christ was alive in another dimension with a body of flesh and bones.

It's a startling concept, especially coming through Luke, a Greek familiar with the Greek philosophy that the body and its appetites were evil. The soul and mind were good. The Greeks believed that in death the mind and spirit were freed from their bondage to the body. The Jews were more realistic. They believed our total being was capable of sin and God must redeem us totally—body, mind, and spirit. All that is corruptible is raised incorruptible. In his narration, Luke, in spite of his Greek background, underscores the Hebrew theology and philosophy in terms of the unity of body, mind, and soul.

We read here that Jesus in His resurrection form could walk through walls and eat a fish. We can explain even that by means of the new physics. We all look so solid—some of us more solid than others—but we are simply particles of energy—atoms and molecules. We are more space than substance. They tell us that if the space between the particles of energy in your body were removed, the matter left would fit on the head of a pin. The chair you sit in is just atoms held together by a force field. In terms of the new physics, it is not unthinkable that Jesus in a new form could pass through a force field or eat some fish.

In verse 39 Jesus offered the disciples proof positive. He wants us to have that same proof. Beyond that, He wants to prove that He is our friend. God is on our side. The basic sin of Adam and Eve, our forebears, was doubting God's love and friendship. Satan persuaded them that God was not their friend and that the fruit of the tree of knowledge was forbidden because in eating it they would become as wise as God. He convinced them that God was not trustworthy. The Old and New Testaments are the records of God's attempts ever since to convince us that He is our friend and that we can trust Him.

In my middle years, I was taught to sail by a neighbor of mine in Florida, a kind and good man, but a determined atheist. Just before his death at age eighty-two, I visited him in the hospital. I tried to tell him at that time that God was his friend. I said, "Larry, what happens if when you die you discover that there is a God in Jesus Christ who loves you?" He said, "Bruce, even if I find that I've been wrong all these years, I will go into eternity with my unbelief. I'm too honorable to plead with God to take me in." I tried to convince him that God was not playing some game, daring us to believe in Him and smashing us if we don't. Even at the very last, God wants to give us proof positive that we may believe and trust Him.

Faith is not belief in spite of evidence. It's a life lived in scorn of consequences. If we choose not to believe, it is not for lack of evidence. There is abundant evidence of the truth of the Resurrection. The fact of the Resurrection has relevance for all the difficult experiences of our lives as well. We can have proof positive of His presence in the death of someone we love, in the difficult times of our marriage. Jesus Christ wants to stand with us through job uncertainty, illness, loneliness, and estrangement.

THE COMMISSION

44 Then He said to them, "These are the words which I spoke to you while I was still with you, that all things must be fulfilled which were written in the Law of Moses and the Prophets and the Psalms concerning Me." 45 And He opened their understanding, that they might comprehend the Scriptures.

46 Then He said to them, "Thus it is written, and thus it was necessary for the Christ to suffer and to rise from the dead the third day, 47 and that repentance and remission of sins should be preached in His name to all nations, beginning at Jerusalem. 48 And you are witnesses of these things.

49 Behold, I send the Promise of My Father upon you; but tarry in the city of Jerusalem until you are endued with power from on high."

50 And He led them out as far as Bethany, and He lifted up His hands and blessed them. 51 Now it came to pass, while He blessed them, that He was parted from them and carried up into heaven. 52 And they worshiped Him, and returned to Jerusalem with great joy, 53 and were continually in the temple praising and blessing God. Amen.

—Luke 24:44–53

So much is crammed into these verses. Verses 44–46 outline the bare bones of biblical theology. Verse 47 describes a program of worldwide evangelism. Verse 48 touches on apostolic succession. The apostles are the first witnesses, but through the power of the Holy Spirit, all believers are the custodians of apostolic truth down through the years. God poured out His Spirit upon us at Pentecost. That Spirit is a present power in our lives. We are being healed, transformed, liberated, and sent on missions because of the supernatural God living in and among us by His Spirit. If we needed further proof positive, we would have it in the hosts of creative, bold, caring people throughout history whose only motivating force was the risen Christ in their midst.

Jesus' Ascension remains a great mystery. Obviously there is no "up" in the universe. But His dramatic physical leave-taking means we shall see Him no more in His resurrection presence until that day when the whole world will see His return. In the meantime, all the generations of the Lord's people join with those early disciples in living with great joy, *"continually in the temple praising and blessing God. Amen."*

BIBLIOGRAPHY

Arndt, William. *Bible Commentary: The Gospel According to St. Luke.* St. Louis: Concordia Publishing House, 1956.

_____, and Gingrich, F. Wilbur. *A Greek-English Lexicon of the New Testament and Other Early Christian Literature.* Chicago: University of Chicago Press, 1957; 2nd rev. and aug. ed., 1979.

Balmforth, Henry. *The Gospel According to Saint Luke.* Oxford: The Clarendon Press, 1930.

Barclay, William. *The Gospel of Luke,* in Daily Study Bible, vol. 2. Philadelphia: Westminster Press, 1966.

Blaiklock, E. M. *Saint Luke.* Scripture Union Bible Study Books. Grand Rapids: Eerdmans, 1967.

Browning, Wilfrid R. F. *The Gospel According to Saint Luke.* Torch Bible Commentary. New York: Macmillan, 1960.

Buttrick, George A. *The Parables of Jesus.* New York: 1928.

_____, ed. *Luke; John.* The Interpreter's Bible, vol. 8. Nashville: Abingdon Press, 1952.

Chapman, J. *Matthew, Mark and Luke.* New York: Longmans, 1937.

Cleverley, F. D. *A Reading of Saint Luke's Gospel.* New York: J. B. Lippincott Co., 1967.

Creed, John Martin. *The Gospel According to St. Luke.* London: Macmillan, 1942.

Dodd, C. H. *The Parables of the Kingdom.* New York: Charles Scribner's Sons, 1956.

Easton, Burton Scott. *The Gospel According to St. Luke.* Edinburgh: T. and T. Clark, 1926.

Ellis, E. Earle. *The Gospel of Luke.* Century Bible, New Series, 1966.

Erdman, Charles R. *The Gospel of Luke: An Exposition.* Philadelphia: Westminster Press, 1942.

Findlay, James Alexander. *The Gospel According to St. Luke.* London: SCM Press, 1937.

Geldenhuis, Norval. *The Gospel of Luke.* New International Commentary on the New Testament. Grand Rapids: Wm. B. Eerdmans, 1979.

Harnack, Adolf von. *Luke the Physician.* New York: C. P. Putnam's Sons, English translation, 1907.

Harrington, Wilfrid J. *The Gospel According to St. Luke.* London: G. Chapman, 1968.

Manson, T. W. *The Sayings of Jesus.* London: SCM Press, 1964.

_____.*The Gospel of Luke.* The Moffatt New Testament Commentary. London: Hodder and Stoughton, 1930.

Morgan, G. Campbell. *The Gospel According to St. Luke.* New York: Revell, 1931.

Morris, Leon. *The Gospel According to St. Luke.* Tyndale New Testament Commentaries. Grand Rapids: Wm. B. Eerdmans, 1974.

Otto, Rudolf. *The Kingdom of God and the Son of Man.* London: The Lutterworth Press, The United Society for Christian Literature, English translation, 1943.

Plummer, A. *The Gospel According to St. Luke,* 5th ed. The International Critical Commentary. New York: Charles Scribner's Sons, 1953.

Ramsay, William M. *Luke the Physician.* London: Hodder and Stoughton, 1908.

Rawlinson, Alfred E. J. *The New Testament Doctrine of Christ.* Toronto: Longmans, Green, 1929.

Richardson, Alan. *The Miracle Stories of the Gospels.* London: SCM Press, 1942.

Schweitzer, Albert. *The Quest of the Historical Jesus.* London: A. & C. Black, Ltd., 1911.

Streeter, B. H. *The Four Gospels.* New York: Macmillan, 1925.

Taylor, Vincent. *Behind the Third Gospel.* Oxford: Clarendon Press, 1926.

Trench, Richard C. *Notes on the Parables of Our Lord,* 14th ed., 1882. London: George Routledge & Sons, 1907.

Wilcock, Michael. *Savior of the World: The Message of Luke's Gospel.* Downers Grove, Ill.: InterVarsity Press, 1979.

Wright, Arthur. *The Gospel According to St. Luke in Greek.* New York: Macmillan, 1900.